DANCING IN THE STREETS

DANCING

IN THE

STREETS

A HISTORY OF COLLECTIVE JOY

BARBARA EHRENREICH

METROPOLITAN BOOKS
Henry Holt and Company   New York

Metropolitan Books
Henry Holt and Company, LLC
Publishers since 1866
175 Fifth Avenue
New York, New York 10010
www.henryholt.com

Metropolitan Books® and ® are registered
trademarks of Henry Holt and Company, LLC.

Library of Congress Cataloging-in-Publication Data

Ehrenreich, Barbara.
   Dancing in the streets: a history of collective joy / Barbara Ehrenreich.—1st ed.
      p. cm.
   Includes bibliographical references and index.
   ISBN-13: 978-0-8050-5723-2
   ISBN-10: 0-8050-5723-4
      1. Festivals—History.   2. Fasts and feasts—History.   3. Spectacular, The—History.
4. Collective behavior—History.   5. Happiness—History.   I. Title.

GT3940.E47 2007
394.26—dc22   2006046673

Henry Holt books are available for special promotions and
premiums. For details contact: Director, Special Markets.

First Edition 2007

Designed by Kelly S. Too

Printed in the United States of America

1   3   5   7   9   10   8   6   4   2

To Anna and Clara—you know how to do it.

CONTENTS

DANCING IN THE STREETS

Introduction:
Invitation to the Dance

When Europeans undertook their campaigns of conquest and exploration in what seemed to them "new" worlds, they found the natives engaged in many strange and lurid activities. Cannibalism was reported, though seldom convincingly documented, along with human sacrifice, bodily mutilation, body and face painting, and flagrantly open sexual practices. Equally jarring to European sensibilities was the almost ubiquitous practice of ecstatic ritual, in which the natives would gather to dance, sing, or chant to a state of exhaustion and, beyond that, sometimes trance. Everywhere they went—among the hunter-gatherers of Australia, the horticulturists of Polynesia, the village peoples of India—white men and occasionally women witnessed these electrifying rites so frequently that there seemed to them to be, among "the present societies of savage men . . . an extraordinary uniformity, in spite of much local variation, in ritual and mythology."[1] The European idea of the "savage" came to focus on the image of painted and bizarrely costumed bodies, drumming and dancing with wild abandon by the light of a fire.

What did they actually see? A single ritual could look very different to different observers. When he arrived in Tahiti in the late

1700s, Captain Cook watched groups of girls performing "a very indecent dance which they call Timorodee, singing the most indecent songs and using most indecent actions . . . In doing this they keep time to a great nicety."[2] About sixty years later, Herman Melville found the same ritual, by then called "Lory-Lory" and perhaps modified in other ways, full of sensual charm.

> Presently, raising a strange chant, they softly sway themselves, gradually quickening the movement, until at length, for a few passionate moments with throbbing bosoms, and glowing cheeks, they abandon themselves to all the spirit of the dance, apparently lost to everything around. But soon subsiding again into the same languid measure as before, the eyes swimming in their heads, join in one wild chorus, and sink into each other's arms.[3]

Like Captain Cook, Charles Darwin was repelled by the corroborree rite of western Australians, reporting that

> the dancing consisted in their running either sideways or in Indian file into an open space, and stamping the ground with great force as they marched together. Their heavy footsteps were accompanied with a kind of grunt, by beating their clubs and spears together, and by various other gesticulations, such as extending their arms and wriggling their bodies. It was a most rude, barbarous scene, and, to our ideas, without any sort of meaning.[4]

But to the anthropologists Baldwin Spencer and Frank Gillen, a similar Aboriginal rite was far more compelling, perhaps even enticing: "The smoke, the blazing torches, the showers of sparks falling in all directions and the masses of dancing, yelling men formed a genuinely wild and savage scene of which it is impossible to convey any adequate idea in words."[5] It was this description that fed into the great French sociologist Emile Durkheim's notion of *collective effervescence:* the ritually induced passion or ecstasy that cements social bonds and, he proposed, forms the ultimate basis of religion.

Through the institution of slavery, European Americans had the opportunity to observe their own captive "natives" at close range, and they too reported varying and contradictory responses to the ecstatic rituals of the transplanted Africans. Many whites of the slave-owning class saw such practices as "noisy, crude, impious, and, simply, dissolute,"[6] and took strong measures to suppress them. The nineteenth-century absentee owner of a Jamaican plantation found his slaves doing a *myal* dance, probably derived from an initiation rite of the Azande people of Africa, and described them as engaged in "a great variety of grotesque actions, and chanting all the while something between a song and a howl."[7] Similarly, an English visitor to Trinidad in 1845 reported disgustedly that

> on Christmas Eve, it seemed as if, under the guise of religion, all Pandemonium had been let loose . . . Drunkenness bursting forth in yells and bacchanalian orgies, was universal amongst the blacks . . . Sleep was out of the question, in the midst of such a disgusting and fiendish saturnalia . . . The musicians were attended by a multitude of drunken people of both sexes, the women being of the lowest class; and all dancing, screaming and clapping their hands, like so many demons. All this was the effect of the "midnight mass," ending, as all such masses do, in every species of depravity.[8]

Other white observers, though, were sometimes surprised to find themselves drawn in by the peculiar power of such African-derived rituals and festivities. Traveling in the mid-nineteenth century, Frederick Law Olmsted observed a black Christian service in New Orleans and was swept up by the "shouts, and groans, terrific shrieks, and indescribable expressions of ecstasy—of pleasure or agony," to the point where he found his own face "glowing" and feet stamping, as if he had been "infected unconsciously."[9] Clinton

Furness, a traveler to South Carolina in the 1920s, reported a similar experience while watching an African American *ring-shout*, or danced form of religious worship.

> Several men moved their feet alternately, in strange syncopation. A rhythm was born, almost without reference to the words of the preacher. It seemed to take place almost visibly, and grow. I was gripped with the feeling of a mass-intelligence, a self-conscious entity, gradually informing the crowd and taking possession of every mind there, including my own . . . I felt as if some conscious plan or purpose were carrying us along, call it mob-mind, communal composition, or what you will.[10]

On the whole, though, white observers regarded the ecstatic rituals of darker-skinned peoples with horror and revulsion. *Grotesque* is one word that appears again and again in European accounts of such events; *hideous* is another. Henri Junod, a nineteenth-century Swiss missionary among the Ba-Ronga people of southern Mozambique, complained of the drums' "frightful din" and "infernal racket."[11] Other Catholic missionaries, upon hearing the African drumbeat announcing a ritual event, felt it was their duty to disrupt "the hellish practice."[12] Well into the twentieth century, the sound of drumming was enough to spook the white traveler, suggestive as it was of a world beyond human ken. "I have never heard an eerier sound," a young English visitor to South Africa reports in the 1910 novel *Prester John*. "Neither human nor animal it seemed, but the voice of that world between which is hid from man's sight and hearing."[13] In the introduction to his 1926 book on tribal dancing, the writer W. D. Hambly pleaded with his readers for a little "sympathy" for his subject.

> The student of primitive music and dancing will have to cultivate a habit of broad-minded consideration for the actions of backward races . . . Music and dancing performed wildly by firelight in a

tropical forest have not seldom provoked the censure and disgust of European visitors, who have seen only what is grotesque or sensual.[14]

Or, in many cases, may have elected not to see at all: When the intrepid entomologist Evelyn Cheeseman tramped through New Guinea in search of new insect species in the early 1930s, she showed not the slightest curiosity about the many native "dancing grounds" she passed through. At one village she and her bearers were asked to leave because there was to be a feast and dance that evening, which were *tambu*, or forbidden, for outsiders to witness. Cheeseman was miffed by this glitch in her plans but comforted herself with the thought that "it is of course well known that it is not particularly desirable to stop in a strange village when the natives are being worked up to their usual frenzy of devil worship."[15]

Particularly disturbing to white observers was the occasional climax of ecstatic ritual, in which some or all of the participants would, after prolonged dancing and singing or chanting, enter what we might now call an "altered state of consciousness," or trance. People caught up in trance might speak in a strange voice or language, display a marked indifference to pain, contort their bodies in ways seemingly impossible in normal life, foam at the mouth, see visions, believe themselves to be possessed by a spirit or deity, and ultimately collapse.*

A missionary among the Fiji Islanders described such a trance state as "a horrible sight,"[16] but it was sight that was not always possible for the traveler to avoid. In her 1963 survey of the ethnographic literature, the anthropologist Erika Bourguignon found that 92 percent of small-scale societies surveyed encouraged some sort of religious trances, in most cases through ecstatic group ritual.[17] In

---

*The anthropologist Vincent Crapanzano defines *trance* as "a complete or partial dissociation, characterized by changes in such functions as identity, memory, the sensory modalities, and thought. It may involve the loss of voluntary control over movement, and may be accompanied by hallucinations and visions." (*The Hamadsha*, fn, p. 195.)

one of the many accounts of trance behavior among "primitive" peoples, the early-twentieth-century German scholar T. K. Oesterreich offers this, from a white visitor to Polynesia.

> As soon as the god was supposed to have entered the priest, the latter became violently agitated, and worked himself up to the highest pitch of apparent frenzy, the muscles of the limbs seemed convulsed, the body swelled, the countenance became terrific, the features distorted, the eyes wild and strained. In this state he often rolled on the earth, foaming at the mouth.[18]

Promiscuous sex was at least comprehensible to the European mind; even human sacrifice and cannibalism have echoes in Christian rite. But as the anthropologist Michael Taussig writes, "It's the ability to become *possessed* . . . that signifies to Europeans awesome Otherness if not downright savagery."[19] Trance was what many of those wild rituals seemed to lead up to, and for Europeans, it represented the very heart of darkness—a place beyond the human self.

Or, what was worse—a place *within* the human self. In *Heart of Darkness*, Joseph Conrad's narrator observes an African ritual and reflects that

> it was unearthly, and the men were—No, they were not inhuman. Well, you know, that was the worst of it—this suspicion of their not being inhuman. It would come slowly to one. They howled and leaped, and spun, and made horrid faces; but what thrilled you was just the thought of their humanity—like yours—the thought of your remote kinship with this wild and passionate uproar. Ugly. Yes, it was ugly enough; but if you were man enough you would admit to yourself that there was in you just the faintest trace of a response to the terrible frankness of that noise, a dim suspicion of their being a meaning in it which you—so remote from the night of first ages—could comprehend. And why not? The mind of man is capable of anything.[20]

To Europeans, there was an obvious explanation for the ecstatic practices of native peoples around the world. Since these strange behaviors could be found in "primitive" cultures almost everywhere, and since they were never indulged in by the "civilized," it followed that they must result from some fundamental defect of the "savage mind." It was less stable than the civilized mind, more childlike, "plastic," and vulnerable to irrational influence or "auto-suggestion."[21] In some instances, the savage mind was described as "out of control" and lacking the discipline and restraint that Europeans of the seventeenth century and beyond came to see as their own defining characteristics. In other accounts, the savage was perhaps too much *under* control—of his or her "witch doctor," that is—or as a victim of "mob psychology."[22] The American political scientist Frederick Morgan Davenport even proposed an anatomical explanation for the bizarre behavior of primitives: They had only a "single spinal ganglion" to process incoming sensory signals and convert them into muscular responses, while the civilized mind had, of course, an entire brain with which to assess the incoming data and weigh the body's responses.[23] Hence the susceptibility of the savage to the compelling music and visual imagery of his or her culture's religious rituals—which was regrettable, since "the last thing the superstitious and impulsive negro race needs is a stirring of the emotions."[24]

But if they thought about it, many Europeans must have realized that the group ecstasy so common among "natives" had certain parallels within Europe itself. For example, Catholic missionaries setting out from France after the 1730s would have heard about the heretical Parisian "convulsionary" cult, whose customary style of worship featured scenes as wild as anything that could be found among the "savages."

While the assembled company redoubled their prayers and collectively reached extreme heights of religious enthusiasm, at least one of their number would suddenly lapse into uncontrolled motor activity

. . . They thrashed about on the floor in a state of frenzy, screaming, roaring, trembling, and twitching . . . The excitement and the disordered movements, which might last for several hours, usually proved highly contagious, with certain convulsionaries apparently serving as a catalyst for the onset of various bodily agitations in others.[25]

Later catalogers of "primitive" ecstatic behavior, like T. K. Oesterreich, recognized a more mundane European analogue to the bewildering rites of "savages" in the familiar tradition of carnival, where otherwise sober people costumed themselves, drank to excess, danced through the night, and otherwise inverted the normal staid and Christian order. "It must . . . be admitted," he wrote, "that civilized people show a high degree of autosuggestibility in certain circumstances. By way of example we may quote the peculiar psychic intoxication to which in certain places (e.g., Munich and Cologne) a large part of the population falls victim on a given day of the year (Carnival)."[26] Critics of the traditional European festivities sometimes drove home their point by imagining the colonial encounter in reverse, with a "savage" registering shock at the behavior of European carnival-goers. In 1805, for example, a founder of the Basle Bible Society published a brochure entitled *Conversation of a Converted Hottentot with a European Christian During Carnival Time*, in which the "Hottentot" concludes that Basle is partially inhabited by "barbarous non-converted heathens." At the end of the nineteenth century, a similar pamphlet featured a visiting "converted Hindu," who confides that the wild doings at Basle's *Fastnacht* festivities put him in mind of "the idolatrous feasts and dances of my fellow-countrymen who are still heathens."[27]

It was among their social inferiors, however, that Europeans found a more immediate analogue to the foreign "savage." By the eighteenth century, the anthropologist Ann Stoler writes, "strong parallels were made between the immoral lives of the British underclass, Irish peasants, and 'primitive' Africans."[28] The English saw parallels between their own lower classes and Native Americans: "Savage slaves be in great Britaine here, as any you can show me there."[29] Similarly, a mid-nineteenth-century visitor to rural Burgundy, in France, offered the caustic observation that "you don't have to go to America to see savages."[30] And who were those people whose revels disrupted whole cities during carnivals in Germany, France, England, and Spain? By the eighteenth and nineteenth centuries, they were likely to be peasants and the urban poor, with respectable folk doing their best to stay indoors during these dangerously licentious times.

So when the phenomenon of collective ecstasy entered the colonialist European mind, it was stained with feelings of hostility, contempt, and fear. Group ecstasy was something "others" experienced—savages or lower-class Europeans. In fact, the capacity for abandonment, for self-loss in the rhythms and emotions of the group, was a defining feature of "savagery" or otherness generally, signaling some fatal weakness of mind. As horrified witnesses of ecstatic ritual, Europeans may have learned very little about the peoples they visited (and often destroyed in the process)—their deities and traditions, their cultures and worldview. But they did learn, or imaginatively construct, something centrally important about themselves: that the essence of the Western mind, and particularly the Western male, upper-class mind, was its ability to resist the contagious rhythm of the drums, to wall itself up in a fortress of ego and rationality against the seductive wildness of the world.

Science Confronts the Ecstatic

With the rise of the social sciences, and especially the anthropology of the 1930s and thereafter, Westerners began to view the ecstatic practices of non-Westerners in an ostensibly more open-minded way. Words like *savage* and *primitive* dropped from the ethnographic vocabulary, along with the notion that the people who had once borne these labels represented a biologically less evolved form of *Homo sapiens*. Medical science could find no differences in the brains of the former primitives to account for their different behavior; colonialists necessarily observed that yesterday's "savage" might be today's shopkeeper, soldier, or servant. As humanity began to look more like a family of potential equals, Westerners had to concede that the ecstatic behavior found in traditional cultures was not the hallmark of savage "otherness" but the expression of a capacity that may exist, for better or for worse, in all of us.

By the 1930s, anthropologists had begun to think of the rituals of small-scale societies as *functional*, meaning in some sense rational. Humans are social animals, and rituals, ecstatic or otherwise, could be an expression of this sociality, a way of renewing the bonds that held a community together. In the functionalist anthropology that reached full bloom in the 1940s and '50s, many of the formerly bizarre-seeming activities of native peoples were explained in this way: as mechanisms for achieving cohesiveness and generating feelings of unity. Americans tried to achieve the same thing through patriotic and religious rituals; the "natives" simply had a different approach.

But right up to our own time, even the most scientific and sympathetic observers have tended to view the *ecstatic* rituals of non-Western cultures with deep misgivings, when they choose to view them at all. A certain distaste for the proceedings infects the anthropologist Vincent Crapanzano's 1973 description of ecstatic rites conducted by the Hamadsha brotherhoods of Morocco. "The drumming, by this time, was beginning to have a dulling effect on me," he reported, "and the music of the ghita an irritating one . . . The smell of all the hot, close, sweating bodies was stifling."[31]

Or consider a curious silence in the anthropologist Victor Turner's famous study of "the ritual process." Perhaps more than any other anthropologist of the mid-twentieth century, he recognized collective ecstasy as a universal capacity and saw it as an expression of what he called *communitas*, meaning, roughly, the spontaneous love and solidarity that can arise within a community of equals. In *The Ritual Process*, Turner admitted to an initial "prejudice against ritual" and tendency to discount "the thudding of ritual drums."[32] Setting out to correct this oversight, he launched a detailed study of the Isoma cult ritual of the Ndembu people, which he introduces to the reader as consisting of three parts. The first two parts, which involve the manipulation of symbolic objects, are described in great detail and subjected to a thorough structuralist analysis. But the third and final phase, the Ku-tumbuka, or "festive dance," which one might imagine was the climax of the entire business, is never mentioned again. Apparently Turner decided to skip that part.*

Turner's theories have been widely credited with giving ecstatic—as well as merely spontaneous and unruly—group behavior a legitimate place in anthropology. In fact, it was a marginal and second-rate place he offered it. To Turner, the central thing about a culture was its *structure*, meaning, essentially, its hierarchies and rules. The function of ecstatic ritual, he proposed, was to keep the structure from becoming overly rigid and unstable by providing occasional relief in the form of collective excitement and festivity. But only very *occasional* relief. The thrills of *communitas* had to be "liminal," or marginal, in Turner's scheme; otherwise social breakdown might ensue, "speedily followed by despotism."[33] Hence his irritation with the hippies of his own mid-1960s American culture, who, in his description, employed " 'mind-expanding' drugs, 'rock' music, and flashing lights . . . to establish a 'total' communion with one another," and who imagined that "the ecstasy of spontaneous communitas" could be prolonged into a routine condition.[34] This "Edenic fantasy" seemed utterly irresponsible to Turner, who— apparently not noticing that many of these hippies were involved in

---

*At a conference on ritual and festivities at Bowling Green State University in 2003, the Ghanaian anthropologist Klevor Abo presented a fascinating account of the Hogbetsotso festival of the Anlo-Ewe people, focusing on how elements of the ritual re-created historical events. When I asked, in the discussion that followed his presentation, whether there was any music and dancing involved, his face brightened and he said that that was in fact his favorite part. Then he proceeded to briefly demonstrate the dance that accompanied the ritual—which somehow had not seemed important enough to mention in his formal presentation.

subsistence agriculture and other productive ventures—reminded his reader that we do have to worry about "the supplying of humble needs, such as food, drink, clothing." Echoing the conventional Western cultural bias toward individualism, he added that it's a good idea to keep a certain "mystery of mutual distance" between individuals.[35]

Other anthropologists turned to psychology to explain the extravagant rituals of non-Western peoples. Where European and American travelers had once seen savagery, they now saw mental illness, perhaps even nutritional in origin; Crapanzano wondered whether the Hamadsha ecstatics might be suffering from a calcium deficiency.[36] The most frequent diagnosis was *hysteria*, a term invented to describe the neurotic symptoms of upper-middle-class Viennese women near the turn of the century, but now blithely applied to Haitian villagers, Sri Lankan peasants, and anyone else whose behavior defied rational analysis. Alfred Métraux, the renowned ethnographer of the ecstatic Haitian tradition of Vodou, or voodoo, thought that "the symptoms of the opening phase of trance are clearly psychopathological. They conform exactly, in their main features, to the stock clinical description of hysteria."[37] And in a 1981 book on female ecstatics in Sri Lanka, another anthropologist judged that "many of these women are, in a purely clinical sense, hysterical."[38]

In very basic ways, psychology was ill-prepared to shoulder the burden anthropologists tried to throw its way. The new science aimed at a universal theory of human emotion and personality, but its theories were derived entirely from studies of the various compulsions, phobias, tics, and "neuraesthenias" afflicting affluent, urban Westerners—disorders that seemed to have no counterpart among "primitives" in their native lands.[39] Not only was the science of psychology narrowly culture-bound; its emphasis on pathology largely precluded any careful study of the more pleasurable emotions, including the kind of joy—growing into ecstasy—that was the hallmark of so many "native" rituals and celebrations. In the psychological language of *needs* and *drives*, people do not freely and affirmatively search for pleasure; rather, they are "driven" by cravings that resemble pain. To this day, and no doubt for good reasons, suffering remains the almost exclusive preoccupation of professional psychology. Journals in the field have published forty-five thousand articles in the last thirty years on depression, but only four hundred on joy.[40]

There was one form of pleasure that deeply interested psychologists, from Sigmund Freud on, and that was sexual pleasure. If the festivities and ecstatic rituals of "primitives" had routinely culminated in sexual acts, either public or private, psychology might have been more comfortable with them. The music, the excitement, the close-packed bodies could then all be understood as aphrodisiacs, allowing people to throw off their normal restraints. This is in fact how many Westerners chose to interpret the rituals they observed anyway—as indecent, wanton, and surely sexual in aim.

Some ecstatic rituals did indeed include sexual acts—most commonly pantomimed—or at least ended with couples drifting off together in the night. The Australian corroborree, for example, sometimes featured sexual intercourse of a deliberately "incestuous" kind; that is, involving men and women of the same tribal subunit, which is normally taboo. But even in that case, sex was only part of the proceedings, and by no means the grand climax, so to speak. More commonly, ecstatic rituals were rather chaste undertakings, involving women and men of all ages, following careful scripts, and serving a function that is perhaps best described as "religious." The self-loss that participants sought in ecstatic ritual was not through physical merger with another person but through a kind of spiritual merger with the group.

Sexual ecstasy usually arises among dyads, or groups of two, but the ritual ecstasy of "primitives" emerged within groups generally composed of thirty or more participants. Thanks to psychology and the psychological concerns of Western culture generally, we have a rich language for describing the emotions drawing one person to another—from the most fleeting sexual attraction, to ego-dissolving love, all the way to the destructive force of obsession. What we lack is any way of describing and understanding the "love" that may exist among dozens of people at a time; and it is this kind of love that is expressed in ecstatic ritual. Durkheim's notion of *collective efferves-cence* and Turner's idea of *communitas* each reach, in their own ways, toward some conception of love that serves to knit people together in groups larger than two. But if homosexual attraction is the love "that dares not speak its name," the love that binds people to the collective has no name at all to speak. *Communitas* and *collective efferves-cence* describe aspects or moments of communal excitement; there is no word for the love—or force or need—that leads individuals to seek ecstatic merger with the group.

Freud, the patriarch of Western psychology, was unprepared or unwilling to shed any light on the subject. It is doubtful that he ever witnessed, much less experienced, anything in the way of collective ecstasy. He was aware of the European tradition of carnival, for example, but saw it through the usual prejudices of his class. In a letter to his fiancée, Martha Bernays, he agreed with her that the behavior of the lower-class revelers at the town fair in Wandsbeck was "neither pleasant nor edifying," especially when compared to the more acceptable and bourgeois pleasures of "an hour's chat nestling close to one's love" or "the reading of a book."[41] In his theoretical work too, he could see nothing very edifying about the emotions linking people in groups or, as he put it, crowds. As the anthropologist Charles Lindholm writes, Freud was much taken with the "expansive and intoxicating self-loss" accompanying the love between two individuals, while "in his discourse on the group the emphasis remains on guilt, anxiety and repressed aggression."[42] What people found in the crowd, Freud opined, was a chance to submit to a leader playing the Oedipal role of "primal father"—a "witch doctor," presumably, or demagogue.

In Freud's scheme of human affinities, there was only one kind of love: the dyadic, erotic love of one individual for another. This is the problem he set forth in *Civilization and Its Discontents:* "The antithesis between civilization and sexuality [derives] from the circumstance that sexual love is a relationship between individuals in which a third can only be superfluous or disturbing, whereas civilization is founded on relations between a considerable number of individuals."[43] Unfortunately for civilization, Freud could not imagine a kind of love binding such larger groups of persons. Eros, he said, could unite people two by two, but "he is not willing to go further." Hence the excitement of groups could only be derivative of the individuals' dyadic love for the group leader; never mind that ecstatic groups, of the kind observed in "primitive" ritual, often had no leader or central figure at all.

But Western psychology was disabled from comprehending the phenomenon of collective ecstasy in a more philosophically profound way as well. Psychology, almost by definition, focuses on the individual self; its therapies are aimed at bolstering that self against the force of irrational or repressed emotion. But the *self* is itself a parochial concept, far more meaningful in early-twentieth-century Cambridge or Vienna than in the distant outposts of nineteenth-century European colonialism. As Luh Ketut Suryani and Gordon Jensen, ethnographers of Balinese ecstatic ritual, observe: "The sense of being in control of one's self is prominent and highly valued in Western personality and thought. This trait is not characteristic of the Balinese, whose lives have in the main been controlled by their families, their ancestors, and the supernatural."[44]

To the "self"-admiring Western mind, any form of self-loss—other than the kind associated with romantic love—could only be pathological. And that is how modern psychology has tended to categorize it. The *Diagnostic and Statistical Manual of Mental Disorders* (fourth edition), or *DSM-IV*, the standard psychiatric guide to mental disorders, lists something called *depersonalization disorder,* which involves a feeling of being "detached from, and as if one is an outside observer of, one's mental processes or body."[45] As Lindholm comments, the psychological model for understanding collective ecstasy "is strongly value loaded. It assumes that the desire for self-loss *must* be a result of antisocial and regressive id drives."[46] Those dancing, exulting practitioners of ecstatic ritual may have thought they were communing with the deities, building community solidarity, or even performing acts of healing. But in the eyes of Western psychology, they were only manifesting the symptoms of their illness.

One might expect that sociology, which ordinarily deals with groups larger than two, would have some insights to offer into the phenomenon of collective ecstasy. But where psychology found only illness and irrationality, sociology has tended, in recent decades anyway, to go too far in the other direction, interpreting group behavior as an entirely rational and self-interested undertaking on the part of each participant. The scores of sociological articles on crowd behavior published since the 1960s display an almost exclusive focus on such relatively dry matters as "the structure of the group . . . its pattern of recruitment, its ideology and its contradictions, the mechanisms used to gain commitment, and the maintenance and evolution of the group within a given social context."[47] As a result, according to Lindholm, we get no sense of "the excitement of participation in an ecstatic group." Another dissenter from the conventional view, the sociologist John Lofland, demanded of his fellow scholars in the early 1980s: "Who now seriously speaks of 'ecstatic crowds,' 'social epidemics,' 'fevers,' 'religious hysterias,' 'passionate enthusiasms,' 'frantic and disheveled dances'?"[48]

Techniques of Ecstasy

That is my mission in this book: to speak seriously of the largely ignored and perhaps incommunicable thrill of the group deliberately united in joy and exaltation. Not every form of "irrational" group behavior will be considered here; panics, crazes, fads, and spontaneous "mob" activities do not fall within our purview. Lynchings—or, for that matter, riots—may generate intense excitement and pleasure in their participants, but the focus here is on the kinds of events witnessed by Europeans in "primitive" societies and recalled in the European carnival tradition. These were not spontaneous outbreaks of "hysteria," as some Europeans tended to imagine; nor were they occasions for the suspension of all inhibitions and a general "letting go." The behavior that seemed so "savage" and wild to Western observers was in fact deliberately planned, organized, and at all times subject to cultural rules and expectations.

When later Westerners studied indigenous rituals in a relatively nonjudgmental way, they learned that such rituals and festivities were far from spontaneous in their timing, for example. The occasion might be a seasonal change, a calendrical event, the initiation of young people, a wedding, funeral, or coronation—in other words, something that could be anticipated for weeks or months and carefully prepared for. Appropriate foods had to be gathered and prepared in advance; costumes and masks designed; songs and dances rehearsed. These were group efforts, the result of careful and sober planning.

Furthermore, even at the height of the supposed frenzy, cultural expectations guided behavior, determining the special roles of the sexes and age groups, and going so far as to regulate that "wildest" of experiences—trance. In some festive settings—meaning those that can be construed as relatively secular or recreational—trance does not occur and is not expected to. In others, such as certain West African–derived religious rites or !Kung healing rituals, the achievement of trance is welcomed as a mark of spiritual status and is sought with great discipline and concentration. Each ecstatic ritual, as the ethnographers who followed the colonialists learned, was specific to its own culture, endowed with different meanings to its participants, and shaped by human creativity and intellect.

Yet for all the local variations, there are certain commonalities, or at least common ingredients, that can be found in ecstatic rituals and festivities worldwide and throughout the ages. As Turner observed, "Each kind of ritual, ceremony, or festival comes to be coupled with special types of attire, music, dance, food and drink . . . and, often, masks, body-painting, headgear, furniture and shrines."[49] These ingredients of ecstatic rituals and festivities—music, dancing, eating, drinking or indulging in other mind-altering drugs, costuming and/or various forms of self-decoration, such as face and body painting—seem to be universal.* Other common, but not universal, ingredients, especially of longer and more elaborate events, include processions, religious rituals involving the manipulation of sacred objects, athletic and other contests, dramatic performances, and comedy, generally of a mocking or satirical nature.[50] But the core elements are, again and again, the dancing, the feasting, the artistic decoration of faces and bodies.

Darwin could find no "meaning" in the Aboriginal rites he witnessed, and meaning is indeed a hard thing for cultural outsiders to ascribe. People have employed the same constellation of activities—dancing, feasting, costuming, et cetera—in pursuit of very different ends. Some of these rites are recognizably religious, in the sense that they aim to evoke the presence of a deity or deities. Others, like the !Kung rituals, are understood by their participants to serve an almost medical function, whether or not a deity is enlisted. Still others seem to be "merely" recreational, if we are safe in assuming that the distinctions between religion, healing, and recreation carry over from Western culture to others. Anthropologists have tended to believe that they do, and draw a line between *ritual* and *festivity*, with the former being seen as having religious or healing functions, whereas "festival designates occasions considered to

---

*Another anthropologist asserts: "The vocabulary of festival is the language of extreme experiences through contrasts . . . The body is made into an object of dressing up, costuming, and masking . . . And, of course, singing and dancing and other kinds of play are part and parcel of festive celebrations, again with the idea of overextending the self. All of these motives underscore the spirit of increase, of stretching life to the fullest, that lies at the heart of festive celebrations." (Roger D. Abraham, in Turner [ed.], 1982, pp. 167–68.) Or, as Richard Schechner, a historian of theater, put it: "Dancing, singing, wearing masks and costumes, impersonating other people, animals or supernaturals (or being possessed by these others); acting stories, retelling the hunt . . . rehearsing and preparing special places and times for these presentations—all are coexistent with the human condition." (Quoted in Garfinkel, p. 40.)

be pagan, recreational, or for children."[51] But it is not clear that this distinction between ritual and festivity, religion and recreation, is always meaningful to the participants. A Georgia slave recalled that other slaves used to say of their church services or "meetings"—and please forgive the patronizing rendition of dialect in my source here—"I like meetin' jus' as good as I like a party."[52]

In this book, I will observe the anthropological distinction between rituals and festivities as much as possible, but the emphasis will be on the phenomenon itself—the group activities of dancing, feasting, and so on—and the feelings they seem to inspire. Whatever the stated meaning of the ritual—to contact the deities, celebrate a wedding, or gear up for war—this same constellation of activities has been used again and again to achieve communal pleasure, even ecstasy or bliss. Why these activities and not others? We will return to this question in the next chapter, but for now, the simplest answer is that these are the activities that *work*. That through millennia of experimentation, humankind discovered what the historian Mircea Eliade, in his analysis of shamanistic rites, termed *techniques of ecstasy*.

The question that motivates this book originates in a sense of loss: If ecstatic rituals and festivities were once so widespread, why is so little left of them today? If the "techniques" of ecstasy represent an important part of the human cultural heritage, why have we forgotten them, if indeed we have? I will approach these questions historically, following the long, drawn-out struggle over ecstatic rituals from ancient times to the present. Everyone is vaguely aware of the decline of community human societies have endured in the last few centuries, a development many social scientists have analyzed in depth. Here we are looking at a much sharper, more intense form of pleasure than anything implied by the word *community*, with its evocations of coziness and small-town sociability. The loss of *ecstatic* pleasure, of the kind once routinely generated by rituals involving dancing, music, and so on, deserves the same attention accorded to *community*, and to be equally mourned.

This sense of loss has, in my case, a personal dimension. Intellectually, the roots of this book lie in a prior book, *Blood Rites: Origins and History of the Passions of War.* In that book I explored the dark side of human collective excitement, as expressed in rites of human sacrifice and war. As I ventured into the less destructive kinds of festivities that concern us here, I recognized emotional themes I had encountered decades ago, at rock concerts, informal parties, and organized "happenings." I suspect that many readers will have similar points of reference—whether religious or "recreational"—for the material in this book, and will be willing to ask with me: If we possess this capacity for collective ecstasy, why do we so seldom put it to use?

1

The Archaic Roots of Ecstasy

Go back ten thousand years and you will find humans toiling away at the many mundane activities required for survival: hunting, food gathering, making weapons and garments, beginning to experiment with agriculture. But if you land on the right moonlit night or seasonal turning point, you might also find them engaged in what seems, by comparison, to be a gratuitous waste of energy: dancing in lines or circles, sometimes wearing masks or what appear to be costumes, often waving branches or sticks. Most likely, both sexes would be dancing, each in its separate line or circle. Their faces and bodies might be painted with red ochre, or so archaeologists guess from the widespread presence of that colored ore in the sites of human settlements. The scene, in other words, might not be too different from the "savage" rituals encountered by nineteenth-century Westerners among native peoples of the world.

We can infer these scenes from prehistoric rock art depicting dancing figures, which has been discovered at sites in Africa, India, Australia, Italy, Turkey, Israel, Iran, and Egypt, among other places. Whatever else they did, our distant ancestors seemed to find plenty of time for the kinds of activities the anthropologist Victor Turner described as liminal, or peripheral to the main business of life.

Festive dancing was not a rare or incidental subject for prehistoric artists. The Israeli archaeologist Yosef Garfinkel asserts that dancing scenes "were a most popular, indeed almost the only, subject used to describe interaction between people in the Neolithic and Chalcolithic periods."[1] When such danced rituals originated is not known, but there is evidence that they may go back well into the Paleolithic era, or Stone Age. At one recently discovered site in England, drawings on the ceiling of a cave show "conga lines" of female dancers, along with drawings of animals like bison and ibex, which are known to have become extinct in England ten thousand years ago.[2] So well before people had a written language, and possibly before they took up a settled lifestyle, they danced and understood dancing as an activity important enough to record on stone.

It is not easy to read the excitement of a danced ritual into prehistoric drawings. The figures are highly stylized; many of those cataloged by Garfinkel are little more than stick figures or silhouettes; few possess facial features or anything like a facial expression. Even the identification of them as *dancers* takes some interpretive work; the figures have to be using their limbs in ways not associated with normal activities: holding their arms up, holding hands in a circle, raising their legs, or leaping, for example. Yet even in these crude, two-dimensional depictions, some of the recognizable ingredients of more recent festive traditions shine through—masking and costuming, for example. Some of the male figures wear masks in the form of animal heads or abstract designs; other dancers wear what archaeologists interpret as "costumes," such as leopard skins. In the clearest sign of motion, and possibly excitement, some of the figures have long, flowing hair standing out from their heads, as if they are moving rapidly and tossing their heads to some long-silenced drumbeat.

Clearly, danced rituals did not seem like a waste of energy to prehistoric peoples. They took the time to fashion masks and costumes; they wantonly expended calories in the execution of the dance; they preferred to record these scenes over any other group activity. Thus anthropologist Victor Turner's consignment of danced ritual to an occasional, marginal, or liminal status seems especially unwarranted in the prehistoric case—and more representative of the production-oriented mentality of our own industrial age than of prehistoric priorities. Surely these people knew hardship and were often threatened by food shortages, disease, and wild animals. But ritual, of a danced and possibly ecstatic nature, was central to their lives. Perhaps only because our own lives, so much easier in many ways, are also so constrained by the imperative to work, we have to wonder *why*.

Anthropologists tend to agree that the evolutionary function of dance was to enable—or encourage—humans to live in groups larger than small bands of closely related individuals. The advantage of larger group size is presumed to be the same as it is for those primates who still live in the wild: Larger groups are better able to defend themselves against predators. Unlike most animals—antelopes, for example—primates are capable of mounting a group defense: mobbing the intruding predator, threatening it with branches, or at least attempting to scare it off by making an infernal racket. In the case of early humans, the danger may have come not only from predatory animals like the big cats but from other now-extinct hominids or even from fellow *Homo sapiens* bent on raiding. And of course, in the human case, the forms of defense would have included fire, rocks, and sharpened sticks. But the first line of defense was to come together as a group.

In his justly popular book *Grooming, Gossip, and the Evolution of Language*, the British anthropologist Robin Dunbar argues for an optimal Paleolithic group size of about 150. He speculates that speech—the *gossip* in his title—may have helped bind humans into groups of that size, much as mutual grooming—picking insects and bits of dirt out of each other's hair—appears to do in the case of other primates. But although it does not appear in his title, it is in fact *dance* that he invokes to hold these early human groups together. The problem with speech, according to Dunbar, is "its complete inadequacy at the emotional level":

Just as we were acquiring the ability to argue and rationalize, we needed a more primitive emotional mechanism to bond our large groups . . . Something deeper and more emotional was needed to overpower the cold logic of verbal arguments. It seems that we needed music and physical touch to do that.[3]

In fact, he sees language as subservient to danced rituals—"a way to formalize their spontaneity" and provide them with a "metaphysical or religious significance." And it should be noted that while hundreds of prehistoric images of dancing figures have been found, there are no rock drawings of stick figures apparently engaged in conversation.

Dunbar is not the only one to see group dancing—especially in lines and circles—as the great leveler and binder of human communities, uniting all who participate in the kind of *communitas* that Turner found in twentieth-century native rituals. Interestingly, the Greek word *nomos*, meaning "law," also has the musical meaning of "melody." To submit, bodily, to the music through dance is to be incorporated into the community in a way far deeper than shared myth or common custom can achieve. In synchronous movement to music or chanting voices, the petty rivalries and factional differences that might divide a group could be transmuted into harmless competition over one's prowess as a dancer, or forgotten. "Dance," as a neuroscientist put it, is "the biotechnology of group formation."*

Thus groups—and the individuals within them—capable of holding themselves together through dance would have had an evolutionary advantage over more weakly bonded groups and individuals: the advantage of being better able to mount a collective defense against any animals or hostile humans who encroached on their territory or otherwise threatened them. No other species ever figured out how to do this. Birds have their signature songs; fireflies can synchronize their light displays; chimpanzees sometimes stamp around together and wave their arms in what ethologists describe as

---

*It would be interesting to know the minimal group size for an effective danced ritual, but I have found no published work on this topic.

a "carnival." But if any other animals create music and move in synchrony to it, they have kept this talent well hidden from humans. We alone are gifted with the kind of love that Freud was unable to imagine: a love, or at least affinity, holding people together in groups much larger than two.

Of course dance cannot work to bind people unless (1) it is intrinsically pleasurable, and (2) it provides a kind of pleasure not achievable by smaller groups.[4] Whatever the ritual dancers of prehistoric times thought they were doing—healing divisions in the group or preparing for the next encounter with their foes—they were also doing something that they liked to do and liked enough to invest considerable energy in. Practitioners of ecstatic danced rituals in "native" societies attested to the pleasures of their rituals; so can any modern Westerners who have participated in the dances and other rhythmic activities associated with rock concerts, raves, or the current club scene. As the historian William H. McNeill pointed out in his book *Keeping Together in Time,* there is a deep satisfaction—even a thrill—to the simplest synchronous group activities, like marching or chanting together. He writes of his experience as a young soldier drilling during basic training for World War II.

> Words are inadequate to describe the emotion aroused by the prolonged movement in unison that drilling involved. A sense of pervasive well-being is what I recall; more specifically, a strange sense of personal enlargement; a sort of swelling out, becoming bigger than life, thanks to participation in collective ritual.[5]

In fact, we tend to enjoy rhythmic music and may be so aroused by watching others dance that we have a hard time keeping ourselves from jumping in. As some Western observers of native or enslaved people's rituals observed, dancing is contagious; humans experience strong desires to synchronize their own bodies' motions with those of others. The stimuli, which can be auditory or visual or derived from an internal sense of one's own muscular response to the rhythm, can, in one psychiatrist's summary of the research, "drive cortical rhythms and eventually produce an intensely pleasurable, ineffable experience in humans."[6]

Why should humans be rewarded so generously for moving their bodies together in time? We are also pleasurably rewarded for sexual activity, and it is easy to figure out why: Individuals who fail to engage in sex, or heterosexual intercourse anyway, leave no genetic trace. When nature requires us to do something—like eating or having sex—it kindly wires our brains to make that activity enjoyable. If synchronous rhythmic activity was, in fact, important to human collective defense, natural selection might have favored those individuals who found such activity pleasurable. In other words, evolution would have led to stronger neural connections between the motor centers that control motion, the visual centers that report on the motions of others, and the sites of pleasure in the limbic system of the brain. The joy of the rhythmic activity would have helped overcome the fear of confronting predators and other threats, just as marching music has pumped up soldiers in historical times.

We do not yet understand the neuronal basis of this pleasure, but an interesting line of speculation has opened up only recently. Humans are highly imitative creatures, more so even than monkeys and others of our primate cousins. As all parents learn, to their amazement, an infant can respond to a smile with a smile, or stick out its tongue when a parent does. How does an infant transform the visual image of a protruding tongue into the muscular actions required to make its own tongue stick out? The answer may lie in the discovery of *mirror neurons*, nerve cells that fire both when an action is perceived—when the parent sticks out his tongue, for example—and when it is performed by the perceiver.[7] In other words, the perception of an action is closely tied to the execution of the same action by the beholder. We cannot see a dancer, for example, without unconsciously starting up the neural processes that are the basis of our own participation in the dance. As the neuroscientist Marcel Kinsbourne writes:

Perceived behavior gives a leg up to more of the same in the observer, who becomes a participant . . . The rhythm of the drum drowns out independent judgment and induces a reversion to the primordial state. To cite [Walter J.] Freeman . . . "to dance is to engage in rhythmic movements that invite corresponding movements from others." Dancers synchronize, reciprocate, or alternate—all of which are forms of entrainment open to the infant. Entraining with others into a shared rhythm—marching, chanting, dancing—may trigger a primitive sense of irrational and beguiling belonging, and a shared mindset.[8]

It is important to point out, though, that dance does not simply merge the individual into the group in the regressive way that Kinsbourne seems to imply. This is a common Western prejudice, but as I pointed out in the introduction, dancers in existing "traditional" societies often devote great effort to composing music for the dance, perfecting their dance steps or other moves, and preparing their costumes or other body decorations. They may experience self-loss in the dance, or a kind of merger with the group, but they also seek a chance to shine, as individuals, for their skills and talents. There may even have been what evolutionary biologists call sexual selection for the ability to dance well, or at least make a good appearance at the dance—just as there appears to have been sexual selection for males with deep voices and females with hourglass figures. The ability to dance or make music is not confined to a single sex, but we are often attracted to individuals who excel at these activities, and this could have given them a definite reproductive advantage.

In fact, the seasonal rituals and festivities of larger groups—several hundred people from different bands or subgroups gathering at an astronomically determined time—probably also served a reproductive function, providing an opportunity to find a mate outside of one's close circle of kin. In this endeavor, talent at music and dance might well have been an asset. At least such a possibility is suggested by a study of young, unmarried Samburu men in Kenya in recent times.

> These "odd men out," suspended between boyhood and adulthood in an uncomfortably prolonged adolescence, regularly go into trance, shaking with extreme bodily agitation, in frustrating situations. Typical precipitating circumstances are those where one group of [such young men] is outdanced by a rival group in front of girls.[9]

To be "outdanced" is to risk reproductive failure, probably for the deeper evolutionary reason that the "girls" will, at some unconscious level, judge you less capable of participating in group defense.

I cannot leave the subject of evolution, though, without throwing in my own speculation about the adaptive value of music and dance. Dunbar and others emphasize their role in keeping people together in sizable groups, but they may once have served the function of group defense in a far more direct way. Like primates in the wild today, early humans probably faced off predatory animals collectively—banding together in a tight group, stamping their feet, shouting, and waving sticks or branches. In our own time, for example, hikers are often advised to try to repel bears they encounter in the wild with the same sorts of behavior, with the arm and stick waving being recommended as a way of exaggerating the humans' height. At some point, early humans or hominids may have learned to synchronize their stampings and stick-wavings in the face of a predator, and the core of my speculation is that the predator might be tricked by this synchronous behavior into thinking that it faced—not a group of individually weak and defenseless humans— but a single, very large animal. When sticks are being brandished and feet stamped in unison, probably accompanied by synchronized chanting or shouting, it would be easy for an animal observer to conclude that only a single mind, or at least a single nervous system, is at work. Better, from the predator's point of view, to wait to catch a human alone than to tangle with what appears to be a twenty-foot-long, noisy, multilegged beast.*

This form of confrontation might well have carried over into communal forms of hunting, in which game animals are driven by the human group into nets or cul de sacs or over cliffs. Many of the game animals hunted by prehistoric humans—like bison and aurochs—were themselves dangerous, and to confront them required courage. In communal hunting, the entire group—men, women, and children—advances against a herd of game animals, shouting, stamping, and waving sticks or torches. The archaeological evidence suggests that this form of hunting goes back to the Paleolithic era and possibly predates the practice of stalking individual animals by small groups of men.[10] As in collective defense against predatory animals, synchronous movement could have augmented the human group's effectiveness—making it appear to be a single, oversized antagonist.

Various features of the prehistoric dancing revealed in rock art are consistent with this hypothesis. The prehistoric dancing figures often sport high headgear or head-expanding masks, often in the form of animal faces; they wave branches above their heads. One can imagine danced rituals originating as reenactments of successful animal encounters, serving both to build group cohesion for the next encounter and to instruct the young in how the human group had learned to prevail and survive.

Over time, as communal hunting waned and the threat of animal predators declined, the thrill of the human triumph over animals could still be reinvoked as ritual. Through rhythm, people had learned to weld themselves into a single unit of motion meant to

---

*This is an experimentally testable proposition. Hungry predatory animals, such as lions and leopards, could be confronted with different human groups—some standing still, some moving in place but in a nonsynchronous way, and some moving synchronously. For safety's sake, invisible electric fences could be used to protect the human subjects from the predator animal. I look forward to learning the results, should anyone be courageous enough to undertake the experiment.

project their collective strength and terrify the animals they hunted or that hunted them. Taken individually, humans are fragile, vulnerable, clawless creatures. But banded together through rhythm and enlarged through the artifice of masks and sticks, the group can feel—and perhaps appear—to be as formidable as any nonhuman beast. When we speak of transcendent experience in terms of "feeling part of something larger than ourselves," it may be this ancient many-headed pseudocreature that we unconsciously invoke.

The God of Ecstasy

Once we leave the realm of speculation that is prehistory and enter the historical period, beginning roughly five thousand years ago, written records and abundant works of art provide a firmer basis for understanding human cultures. We know from these writings and artifacts that danced rituals persisted into the early phases of civilization—a condition marked by the rise of agriculture, cities, social hierarchies, and, eventually, writing. Vase and wall paintings depicting lines and circles of dancers have been found in ancient Mesopotamian, Greek, Indian, and Palestinian archaeological sites. Rural people in ancient China danced in separate lines of men and women, and observed ecstatic rituals well into historical times. As the French scholar of Chinese history Marcel Granet reported:

> The festivals of the winter season had a dramatic character. Extreme excitement was general. Even in the day of Confucius, those who took part were all "like madmen" (meaning that they felt themselves filled with a divine spirit) . . . Dances, to the sound of clay timbrels, induced a state of ecstasy. Drunkenness brought it to perfection. The exorcists [a kind of shaman] wore the skins of animals. Animal dances were performed.[11]

In the ancient Near East, the Old Testament makes it clear that the ancient Hebrews enjoyed a robust tradition of festive dancing, usually associated with feasting and wine-drinking. In Exodus, for example, Miriam the prophetess takes "a timbrel [tambourine] in her hand; and all the women went out after her with timbrels and with dances." When the Israelite forces returned from their victory over the Philistines, "the women came out of all cities of Israel, singing and dancing, to meet king Saul, with tabrets, with joy, and with instruments of musick" (1 Samuel 18:6). It is not clear whether the officially approved rites and dances achieved an intensity that could be called ecstatic. One historian has concluded that "orgiastic, vigorous ecstasy is alien to the Israelite prophets," who instead experience "a calm, sometimes paralytically calm, seeing and hearing of the word of YHWH."[12] But as Garfinkel observes, the Hebrew word *hag* means both "festival" and to "go in a circle"—suggesting that the primordial form of many traditional Jewish festivals was the circle dance.[13]

There was, without question, a tradition of collective ecstasy among the Hebrews, but it was hardly officially approved. In fact, we know of it only through its opponents, the worshippers of Yahweh who wrote the Old Testament. This was the old polytheistic religion associated with Israel's indigenous Canaanites, centered on Mesopotamian deities like Baal and the goddesses Anat and Asherah, and featuring what seem to have been mass ecstatic rites, the nature of which we can only guess at. Idolatry, drunkenness, and sexual orgies are described or hinted at, and possibly human sacrifice; at least that seems to have been the crime committed by King Asa's goddess-worshipping grandmother, who lost "the honor of being a great lady because she had committed a horror for Asherah."[14] How much of these charges was slanderous there is no way of knowing, but something was going on, generation after generation, that horrified Yahweh's faithful. Centuries after Moses delivered the commandment to worship only the one God, Yahweh, the prophets were still railing against the old religious ways. The Hebrews couldn't keep themselves from backsliding and were apparently performing the forbidden goddess-centered rites as late as the fifth century BCE.[15]

But it was the Greeks, the supposedly most rational and "Western" of ancient peoples, who left us the clearest evidence of ecstatic ritual behavior, verging on the dangerously disruptive. Dance, whether of the ecstatic or more stately variety, was a central and defining activity of the ancient Greek community: line and circle dances, dances of young men or young women or both together, dances at regularly scheduled festivities or what appear to have been spontaneous outbreaks, dances for victory, for the gods, or for the sheer fun of it.[16] In myth, Theseus leads the young men and women he has freed from the Minotaur in a circle dance performed with "crane steps," imitating the high-stepping wading bird.[17] In Homer's account of the heroic age, we learn that young Greeks danced "at marriages, at vintage, or simply to give vent to their youthful exuberance—*choreia* [dance], the Greeks think, must come from *chara*, 'joy.' "[18] Achilles' shield bore the image, not of some terrifying predator, but of a scene that must have seemed, to his homesick comrades in arms, quintessentially Greek.

> There were youths dancing, and maidens of costly wooing, their hands upon one another's wrists . . . And now would they run round with deft feet exceeding lightly . . . and now anon they would run in lines to meet each other. And a great company stood round the lovely dance in joy; and among them a divine minstrel was making music on his lyre, and through the midst of them, leading the measure, two tumblers whirled.[19]

Dance was a ubiquitous theme of ancient Greek art. Dancing figures commonly graced their vases, and the great dramas of classical times were musical performances in which the chorus danced as well as sang. In fact the word *tragedy* is derived from words meaning goat and song, and the chorus was originally composed of men dressed in goatskins to resemble the satyrs—half men and half goat—who danced attendance on their master, the god Dionysus.

To an extent we can only guess at today, the religion of the ancient

Greeks was a "danced religion," much like those of the "savages" European travelers were later to discover around the world. As Aldous Huxley once observed, "Ritual dances provide a religious experience that seems more satisfying and convincing than any other . . . It is with their muscles that humans most easily obtain knowledge of the divine."[20]

Lillian Lawler, writing in the 1960s, leaves no doubt that ecstatic dancing was indigenous to the mainstream Greek tradition, in, for example, the worship of Artemis, goddess of childbirth and the hunt. *Tympana*, or kettle drums, have been found at the shrine of Artemis Limnatis in southern Greece, and this instrument, Lawler claims, was "helpful in inducing frenzy." Dances to Artemis were known to be especially wild in Sparta—though whether in a religious or sexual sense we do not know, only that women and girls danced wearing "only one chiton," or the equivalent of a slip.[21]

Within the ancient Western world, many deities served as the objects of ecstatic worship: in Greece, Artemis and Demeter; in Rome, the imported deities Isis (from Egypt), Cybele, the Great Mother, or Magna Mater (from Asia Minor), and Mithras (from Persia). But there was one Greek god for whom ecstatic worship was not simply an option; it was a requirement. To ignore his call was to risk a fate far worse than death or even physical torture; those who resisted him would be driven mad and forced to destroy their own children. This god, source of both ecstasy and terror, was Dionysus, or, as he was known to the Romans, Bacchus. His mundane jurisdiction covered vineyards and wine, but his more spiritual responsibility was to preside over the *orgeia* (literally, rites performed in the forest at night, from which we derive the word *orgy*), where his devotees danced themselves into a state of trance. The fact that the Greeks felt the need for such a deity tells us something about the importance of ecstatic experience in their world; just as their pantheon included gods for love, for war, for agriculture, metalworking, and hunting, they needed a god to give the experience of ecstasy a human form and face.

Far more so than most of his fellow deities, Dionysus was an accessible and democratic god, whose *thiasos*, or sacred band, stood open to the humble as well as the mighty.[22] As Nietzsche envisioned his rites: "Now the slave emerges as a freeman; all the rigid, hostile walls which either necessity or despotism has erected between men are shattered."[23] It was Nietzsche, of all the European classical scholars, who emphasized the Dionysian roots of ancient Greek drama, who saw the mad, ecstatic inspiration behind the Greeks' stately art—who, metaphorically speaking, dared consider not just the deathless symmetry of the vase but the wild dancing figures painted on its surface. What the god demanded, according to Nietzsche, was nothing less than the human soul, released by ecstatic ritual from the "horror of individual existence" into the "mystical Oneness" of rhythmic unity in the dance.[24]

Women, above all, responded to Dionysus's call. In fact, the association between the god and his band of female devotees is so strong that it's worth underscoring the fact that men also worshipped him, whether at village festivals to celebrate the new wine or by piously getting drunk together in honor of the god. But Dionysus had a special appeal to the women of the Greek city-state, who were ordinarily excluded from much of public life. While men plotted wars or devised philosophies, women's activities were largely confined to the domestic sphere, and boys still young enough to be kept in the women's quarters were said to live "in darkness," barred from the pleasures and challenges of public life. In many Greek cities, women were not even allowed to drink wine.[25]

The most notorious feminine form of Dionysian worship, the *oreibaia*, or winter dance, looks to modern eyes like a crude pantomime of feminist revolt. In mythical accounts, women "called" by the god to participate drop their spinning and abandon their children to run outdoors and into the mountains, where they dress in fawn skins and engage in a "frenzied dance." These maenads, as Dionysus's female cult members were called, run through the woods calling out the name of the god, or uttering the characteristic bacchic cry *"euoi,"* they toss their hair and brandish their *thyrsos*—sticks to which pinecones have been attached. Finally, they achieve a state of mind the Greeks called *enthousiasmos*—literally, having the god within oneself—or what many cultures in our own time would call a "possession trance." These were not solely mythical events; in some times and places, the *oreibasia* was officially condoned and scheduled for every other year, in the dead of winter. Pausanias, who wrote in the second century CE, tells of a party of maenads who reached the eight-thousand-foot summit of Mt. Parnassus—an impressive athletic achievement, especially if performed in the winter—and Plutarch wrote of an occasion when a group of female worshippers were cut off by a snowstorm and had to be rescued.[26]

Dionysus was no respecter of ethnic boundaries. According to the archaeologist Sir Arthur Evans, the worship of gods resembling Dionysus ranged over five thousand miles, from Portugal through North Africa to India, with the god appearing under various names, including "Bakkhos, Pan, Eleuthereus, Minotaur, Sabazios, Inuus, Faunus, Priapus, Liber, Ammon, Osiris, Shiva, Cerenunnus," and, we might add, the delightfully named Etruscan analog of Dionysus: Fufluns.[27] In his brilliant rendition of the Indian epics, for example, Roberto Calasso describes the Hindu god Shiva as "this stranger, this woman-stealer, this enemy of our rules and ties, this wanderer who loves the ashes of the dead, who speaks of things divine to the lowest of the low, this man who sometimes seems crazy, who has something obscene about him, who grows his hair long as a girl's."[28] Like Dionysus, Shiva bore an association with wine, his cult being "particularly widespread in the mountains where the vine is cultivated," according to a Greek who lived in India in the fourth century BCE.[29]

In India, Krishna, too, exerted a Dionysian effect on women—especially those who worked as *gopis*, or cowherders, "charm[ing] them beyond caring by the sound of his flute in the forest, so that they left their homes, husbands, and families and fled to him in the night."[30] Inspired by Krishna's example, the sixteenth-century religious teacher Caitanya built up a following of "women of . . . casteless groups, washerwomen or women of low castes."[31] "They danced ecstatically and sang; they were as if mad," Victor Turner reported, going on to comment that "it is hard to think that there is nothing in common between the ecstatic communitas of Dionysus and that of Krishna. Indeed, Ovid's *puer aeternus* [eternal boy, referring to Dionysus] came from . . . 'Dark India girdled by the farthest Ganges.'"[32] Other scholars, though, locate Dionysus's origins in the prehistoric cultures—Cretan and Mycenaean—of Greece itself. The fact that he was often depicted as a horned god, or part animal, suggests that he may have been one of the older Greek gods, rather than a relatively recent import from India.

Maenadism, as the Greek women's frenzied worship of Dionysus is called, seems not to have been inspired by the common feminine concern with fertility. This can be ruled out as an aim, the classicist E. R. Dodds argued, by the fact that the rite was observed biennially, rather than once a year, and that it was conducted in winter, on "barren mountain-tops," rather than in the burgeoning fields of the spring that were the usual site for fertility rituals.[33] Nor was there apparently anything sexual about the rites. In ancient vase paintings, the female worshippers are often depicted in the company of lascivious male satyrs, but the women fight them off with such weapons as a staff, a *thyrsos*, or even a "writhing snake."[34] The most famous literary account of maenadism, Euripides' play *The Bacchae*, clearly refutes the notion that sex or even drunkenness was involved. Instead, an eyewitness reports to King Pentheus, who is obsessed with prurient curiosity about the maenads' secret rites, that he came across the women sleeping: "They lay just as they had thrown themselves down on the ground—but with modesty in their posture; they were not drunk with wine, as you told us, or with music of flutes; nor was there any love-making in the loveliness of the woods."[35]

No, the single most shocking feature of maenadism—to Euripides no less than to his readers today—was its reputed violence. At the height of their frenzy, the women worshippers were said to catch wild animals in the woods, tear them apart while still alive, and eat them raw. There are even words in Greek to describe these actions: *sparagmos*, for the rending of a living creature, and *omophagia*, for the eating of the raw meat, torn from the bones by hand. The victims included small creatures like snakes, but also deer and bear and wolves, and, in myth or fiction anyway, sometimes even humans; the plot of *The Bacchae* hinges on the revelers' mistaking their own king for a lion and tearing him limb from limb.

Such treatment of animals may have been less repulsive to the Greeks, who practiced routine animal sacrifice, than it seems to us. The potentially shocking feature of the maenads' behavior is that they, of course, are female. Usually they are said to kill their prey by hand, but in at least one depiction (on a *pyxis*, a container for salves), according to Lillian Joyce, two maenads, their hair flying out behind them, "suspend a deer belly up with its head hanging limply. This is the moment before the victim will be torn into pieces. The violence of the scene is revved up to a degree by the presence of the sword, a traditionally male implement."[36]

Clearly, the maenads' animal victims did not offer themselves up willingly for capture; the women who ran off into the mountains to worship Dionysus were also *hunting*. Lillian Portefaix has suggested that maenadism may have been a reenactment of archaic communal hunting—before metal weapons and the male monopolization of hunting skills—when a group of people or women alone would chase and surround their prey, killing it with whatever implements lay at hand and perhaps eating it on the spot.[37] If I am right about the origins of danced rituals in communal hunting and other confrontations with animals—and the violence of the maenads is certainly consistent with this hypothesis—then maenadism would seem to be a very primordial form of festival: one in which dancing, revelry, feasting, and costuming still bore traces of the collective human encounter with animals.

It may be relevant here that, in myth, Dionysus occasionally takes the form of Zagreus, the great hunter. In their reenactment of prehistoric communal hunting, his worshippers were boldly subverting the division of labor between the sexes that prevailed in historic times. The maenad was beautiful and feminine, portrayed in vase paintings with long flowing hair and sometimes an exposed breast, which a fawn might suckle at. But she was also a hunter, who had acquired male strength and usurped the male monopoly over violence. In this way, the Dionysian rites offered the kind of "ritual of inversion" that could be found in the Roman festival of Saturnalia, European carnival, and the festivities of so many other cultures, in which members of subordinate groups—in this case, women—temporarily take the roles of their social superiors. During Saturnalia, masters had to wait on their slaves; carnival allowed peasants to impersonate kings; and Dionysian worship gave women license to hunt.

Who was this god who could intoxicate the mighty as well as the poor, who dared to challenge the power of men over women? Modern scholars have often looked at Dionysus with the same bafflement and dismay that European travelers brought to the "savage" rites they witnessed in distant lands. In his introduction to *The Bacchae*, written in 1954, Philip Vellacott opined that this is not a god whom "decent people will be prepared to worship."[38] Walter Otto, in his book on Dionysus, exclaimed: "A god who is mad! A god, part of whose nature it is to be insane! What did they experience or see—these men on whom the horror of this concept must have forced itself?"[39]

The facts, such as they are, about the god are first that he was beautiful, in an androgynous way, to both men and women. Euripides describes him with "long curls . . . cascading close over [his] cheeks, most seductively."[40] Cross-dressing was a part of Dionysian worship in some locales.[41] Although he had occasional liaisons with women, like the Cretan princess Ariadne, he is usually portrayed as "detached and unconcerned with sex."[42] In vase paintings he is never shown "involved in the satyrs' sexual shenanigans. He may dance, he may drink, but he is never shown paired with . . . any of the female companions."[43]

As one of the few Greek gods with a specific following, he had a special relationship to humans. They could evoke him by their dancing, and it was he who "possessed" them in their frenzy. He is, in other words, difficult to separate from the form that his worship took, and this may explain his rage at those who refused to join in his revels, for Dionysus cannot fully exist without his rites. Other gods demanded animal sacrifice, but the sacrifice was an act of obeisance or propitiation, not the hallmark of the god himself. Dionysus, in contrast, was not worshipped for ulterior reasons (to increase the crops or win the war) but for the sheer joy of his rite itself. Not only does he demand and instigate; he *is* the ecstatic experience that, according to Durkheim, defines the sacred and sets it apart from daily life.[44]

So it may make more sense to explain the anthropomorphized persona of the god in terms of his rituals, rather than the other way around. The fact that he is asexual may embody the Greeks' understanding that collective ecstasy is not fundamentally sexual in nature, in contrast to the imaginings of later Europeans. Besides, men would hardly have stood by while their wives ran off to orgies of a sexual nature; the god's well-known indifference guarantees their chastity on the mountaintops. The fact that he is sometimes violent may reflect Greek ambivalence toward his rites: On the one hand, from an elite male perspective, the communal ecstasy of underlings (women in this case) is threatening to the entire social order. On the other hand, the god's potential cruelty serves to help justify each woman's participation, since the most terrible madness and violence are always inflicted on those who abstain from his worship. The god may have been invented, then, to explain and justify preexisting rites.

If so, the Dionysian rites may have originated in some "nonreligious" practice, assuming that it is even possible to distinguish the "religious" from other aspects of a distant culture. E. R. Dodds conjectured that the rites originally arose as "spontaneous attacks of mass hysteria,"[45] and indeed, there are mythic accounts of manic dancing in ancient Greece unrelated to Dionysus or any other god. Lawler suggests that waves of "dance mania" may have swept through the Myceneaen culture of prehistoric Greece and relates the myth of the three princesses of Tiryns, who, when the time came for them to marry, conveniently went mad: "They rushed out of doors, and in a frenzied dance ranged over the countryside, singing weird songs, and tearing their garments, unable to stop dancing."[46] Now possibly there were such spontaneous outbreaks of "madness" predating Dionysian ritual, but something must have set them off and given them their form. One person can go "mad" spontaneously, but what was the signal that called scores or hundreds of women from their homes at the same time? Who provided the music, for example, or remembered to bring the wine?*

There is a possible historical basis for the Dionysian rite and indeed for the god himself. The classicist Walter Burkert mentions the existence, in ancient and—earlier than that—archaic Greece, of itinerant charismatics, men who traveled from place to place, serving as healers, priests, and seers.[47] As early as the fifth century BCE, men called *orpheotelestae* traveled through Greece offering to cure illnesses, including mental ones, by dancing around the sick person, "not infrequently in the form of a ring-dance."[48] Dionysus arrives in the city of Thebes in the form of such a traveler, and when Dionysian worship comes to Rome about two centuries after Euripides' time, it is brought by a wandering magician-priest. As a healer, the itinerant charismatic cured by drawing the afflicted into ecstatic dances[49]—which may well have been effective in the case of psychosomatic and mental illnesses—suggesting that he was a musician and dancer as well as a priest. It was probably his arrival, announced by the beating of the *tympana*, that drew the women out

---

*If, indeed, they drank wine. In Euripides' account, they did not, and the scholarly consensus seems to be that while male worshippers of Dionysus drank freely, female worshippers required no chemical assistance in their rites. (Roth, pp. 41–42.)

from their houses and into the "madness" that was also a *cure* for madness.

These itinerant musicians and masters of ecstatic ritual may well have been the prototype for the god Dionysus. As one scholar writes, the god in many ways resembles a certain kind of wandering musician in our own time, one who is also capable of inspiring "hysteria" in his devotees: the "male leader of the pop group, who for all the violence of music, gestures, and words is neither traditionally masculine nor yet effeminate. To the established order he may be a threat but not to the adoring young, especially the young women."[50] With his long hair, his hints of violence, and his promise of ecstasy, Dionysus was the first rock star.

2

Civilization and Backlash

Almost as soon as ecstatic rituals appear in the historical—that is, written—record, a note of ambivalence enters into the story, a suggestion of social tensions surrounding these rituals, and even violent hostility toward their participants. Euripides' play *The Bacchae*, for example, both records these tensions and expresses what seems to be a tormented ambivalence on the part of the playwright. In the play, Pentheus, the king of Thebes, greets the god with derision and determines to suppress him by force. "Go at once to the Electran gate," he commands his officers. "Tell all my men who bear shields, heavy or light, all who ride fast horses or twang the bowstring, to meet me there in readiness for an assault on the Bacchae [maenads]. This is past all bearing, if we are to let women so defy us."[1] At first the play seems to take the god's side—mocking the uptight Pentheus and showing the community elders piously joining the maenads in their revelry. After all, if the beautiful young stranger is indeed a god, it is incumbent on good citizens to observe his rites. But things end badly for both sides: Pentheus is killed and dismembered by his own mother, who—in her god-given ecstasy—mistakes him for a lion.

The ambivalence and hostility found in ancient written records may tell us more about the conditions under which writing was invented than about any long-standing prior conflict over ecstatic rituals themselves. Writing arises with "civilization," in particular, with the emergence of social stratification and the rise of elites. In fact, writing was probably invented, along with arithmetic, as a means of keeping track of the elite's possessions: herds, stored grain, and slaves. From an elite perspective, there is one inherent problem with traditional festivities and ecstatic rituals, and that is their leveling effect, the way in which they dissolve rank and other forms of social difference. It's difficult, if not impossible, to retain one's regal dignity in the mad excitement of the dance. Masks and other forms of costuming may render participants equally anonymous or equally "special." The deity may choose to possess—and speak through—a lowly shepherdess as readily as a queen.

We have some evidence—from a very different part of the ancient world—of the dampening effect of civilization and social hierarchy on traditional rituals. Recent carbon-14 dating of an archaeological site in Oaxaca suggests that the earliest residents, who were hunter-gatherers living about nine thousand years ago, met on a cleared "dance ground" for rituals that included the entire community. Later, with the rise of agriculture, rituals appear to have been enacted solely by initiates who were "social achievers," or members of an elite, and most likely men. Finally, with the emergence of organized and militarized states two thousand years ago, the archaeologists deduce that "many important rituals were performed only by trained full-time priests using religious calendars and occupying temples built by corvée labor." In the Oaxacan case, only a few thousand years appear to have elapsed between the archaic danced rituals of Paleolithic bands and their refinement into the formal rituals of the civilized state.[2]

The rise of social hierarchy, anthropologists agree, goes hand in hand with the rise of militarism and war, which are in their own way also usually hostile to the danced rituals of the archaic past.

Possibly the first social elite consisted of men who specialized in fighting the men of other tribes or villages and who could thus impose a kind of "protection racket" on their fellow citizens: Feed us, or else we will leave you to the mercies of the thugs from neighboring settlements; do the planting and herding for us, or we will turn our weapons on you, our own clanspeople. Through raiding and more prolonged forms of warfare, this early elite would have further enriched itself, until we have the kind of state Dionysus threatened in *The Bacchae*—one ruled by a warrior-king.[3]

In ancient Israel, both militarism and concerns about the maintenance of hierarchy seem to have worked against the old ecstatic rituals. After Michal, King Saul's daughter and the wife of King David, sees her husband perform his near-naked victory dance through the streets of Jerusalem, she "despises him in her heart" and greets him with sarcasm: "How glorious was the king of Israel today, who uncovered himself! . . . today in the eyes of the handmaids of his servants, as one of the vain fellows shamelessly uncovereth himself." To dance—especially ecstatically—in the company or even the presence of one's inferiors was to upset the increasingly rigid hierarchy of wealth and status.

But the most common explanation for the ancient Israelis' hostility to group ecstatic rites is a military one. Harassed by the Philistines from the west, Egyptians from the south, and Hittites and others from the north, the Hebrews could ill afford to lose themselves in collective rapture—or so the reasoning goes. As Robert Graves put it:

> It became clear that if Judaea, a small buffer state between Egypt and Assyria, was to keep its political independence, a stronger religious discipline must be inculcated, and the people trained to arms. Hitherto most Israelites had clung to the orgiastic Canaanite cult in which goddesses played the leading role, with demigods as their consorts. This, though admirably suited to peaceful times, could not steel the Jews to resist the invading armies of Egypt and Assyria.[4]

Their god Yahweh was the perfect disciplinarian—a war god known as Yahweh Sabaoth, Lord God of Hosts, with *hosts* referring to armies. The religious scholar Karen Armstrong also explains the Hebrews' religious vacillations in terms of military pressures: "They remembered [their covenant with Yahweh] in times of war, when they needed Yahweh's skilled military protection, but when times were easy they worshipped Baal, Anat and Asherah in the old way."[5]

A concern for military preparedness seems also to have soured the Greek view of ecstatic rituals. In *The Bacchae*, Euripides posed a basic incompatibility between the warrior-king Pentheus and Diony- sus, who is descibed as a "lover of peace." Arthur Evans, in his book on Dionysus, argues that he is the antiwar god, citing among other things the fourth-century BCE Greek philosopher Diodorus's praise of Dionysus for founding festivals "everywhere" and "in general resolv[ing] the conflicts of nations and states, and in place of domestic strife and war . . . la[ying] the grounds for concord and great peace."[6] Dionysus could be violent, but not in a war- rior's way. At their first encounter, Pentheus taunts Dionysus for his effeminacy: "Those long curls of yours show that you're no wrestler."

But the ancient Greek elite did not abandon the old ecstatic rit- uals; instead, they simply took them underground, where they could be indulged in out of sight of the hoi polloi. As early as the sixth century BCE, there emerges a strange new form of religious grouping in Greece: *mystery cults*, drawing on social elites, whose members gathered periodically for secret rites apparently aimed, above all, at engendering collective ecstasy. The secrets were well kept, leaving scholars to guess at what exactly went on at the cults' gatherings. Surely there was dancing, since the ancients admitted this much, as well as wine drinking and possibly the ingestion of hallucinatory drugs, along with striking sound and light effects. "We hear of frenzied nocturnal dances, with crazed outcries, to the stirring accompaniment of shrill flutes, tympana, metal cymbals, castanets . . . 'bull-roarers,' and rattles," Lawler reports. "We hear of snake-handling, of trances, of prophesying, even of self-mutilation."[7]

In his book *Ancient Mystery Cults*, Walter Burkert infers a sequence of activities not unlike that which anthropologists have observed in many "primitive" societies, in which new initiates to the cult are first isolated and deliberately terrified, then finally embraced by the whole group in dance.

> The initiands, seated, are . . . smeared with a mixture of clay and chaff; from the dark the priestess appears like a frightening demon; clean again and rising to their feet, the initiates exclaim "I escaped from evil, I found the better," and the bystanders yell in a high, shrieking voice (*ololyge*) as though in the presence of some divine agent. In the daytime there follows the integration of the initiates into the group of celebrants . . . people are crowned with fennel and white poplar; they dance and utter rhythmic cries . . . some brandishing live snakes.[8]

Because the participants were members of a literate elite, some subjective reports of the rituals' effects have survived. Initiates described the experience as purifying, healing, and deeply reassuring; certainly it was transformative. "I came out of the mystery hall feeling like a stranger to myself," said one participant of the mystery rites held at Eleusis in honor of the goddess Demeter.[9] In fact, it is to this kind of experience that we owe the very word *ecstasy*, derived from Greek words meaning "to stand outside of oneself."

Repression in Rome

Where the Greek elite had dithered—looking askance at the disorderly maenads while celebrating their own secret ecstatic rites—the Romans took a firm stand. In Roman culture, militarism triumphs over the old traditions of communal ecstasy; the god of war—here called Mars—finally vanquishes Dionysus, who, in his Roman form, has already been diminished to Bacchus, the fun-loving god of wine. It is in Rome that the Greek word *orgeia*, for ecstatic religious rites, takes on its modern connotations of grossness and excess, of too much food, drink, and sex promiscuously indulged in all at once, while the Greek word *ekstasis* itself often gets translated into Latin as *superstitio*.[10]

Even those elementary ingredients of ecstatic traditions—music and dance—were "alien," as one historian of dance put it, to the "sober, realistically minded Roman, certainly by the time of the empire."[11] True, the Romans had their annual Saturnalia, which involved drinking, feasting, and a so-called ritual of inversion in which masters and slaves briefly exchanged roles. But apparently even more so than among the ancient Hebrews and Greeks, social inequality served both to inhibit the powerful and to make them distrustful of exuberant outbursts from below. Max Weber observed that "the nobles, who constituted a rational nobility of office of increasing range, and who possessed whole cities and provinces as client holdings of single families, completely rejected ecstasy, like the dance, as utterly unseemly and unworthy of a nobleman's sense of honor."[12] So thorough was the official Roman condemnation of the dance that the Roman scholar Cornelius Nepos, writing in the time of Augustus, had to explain to his readers why a prominent Greek might indulge in such an unseemly activity: "Readers should not judge foreign customs by their own . . . We do not need to be told that, by Roman convention, music is unbecoming to a person of prominence, and dancing is thought to be positively vicious. In Greece, on the other hand, these are held to be agreeable and laudable diversions."[13] Just as Roman architecture and statuary projected the implacable calm of absolute power, the individual Roman patrician sought, in his everyday demeanor, to impress observers with his personal authority. Public ecstasy of any kind was not a temptation, because it "involves the loss of that dignity that was so carefully projected by the honorific statues which enshrine so much of the civil elite's behavioural ideal."[14]

Certainly dancing occurred, at least indoors, within the wealthy Roman household, but it was regarded with ambivalence and usually relegated to professionals of dubious reputation. In 150 BCE we find the consul Scipio Aemilianus Africanus ordering that dancing schools for Roman children be closed.[15] A couple of hundred years later there are references to women dancing for guests within their homes, though these women were likely to incur criticism if their dancing was thought to be too "professional," meaning overly skillful or perhaps indecent.[16] The satirist Juvenal, for example, saw in the dancing of highborn Roman women only a display of sexual lust, calculated to "warm the age-chilled balls" of elderly men.

> Ah, what a vast mounting passion fills their spirits
> To get themselves mounted! Such lustful yelps, such a copious
> Downflow of vintage liquor splashing their thighs!
> Off goes Saufeia's wreath, she challenges the call-girls
> To a contest of bumps and grinds, emerges victorious,
> Herself admires the shimmy of Medullina's buttocks.[17]

Official Roman religion was, not surprisingly, a "cold and prosaic" affair,[18] designed to reinforce the social hierarchy rather than to offer the worshipper an experience of communion with the deities. Instead of a specialized priesthood, men of noble rank were appointed to perform the rites; and once the emperor had achieved divinity, starting when Augustus declared himself a god, the connection between religious and secular authority was indissoluble. As for the rites themselves, no one expected them to transform, excite, or in any way appeal to the emotions. Rather, the emphasis was on exact and perfect performance, down to the smallest detail. In animal sacrifice—the most common form of religious observance—the animal had to be physically perfect and, ideally, willing to die, which it demonstrated by obligingly stretching forth its neck for the knife. If the sacrificial rite was marred in any detail, it had to be repeated until the presiding officials got it right. One man acting as priest was forced to quit because his hat fell off while he was sacrificing.[19] The gods, and not the humans present, were the true connoisseurs of the Roman rites, and they were known to be sensitive to the least liturgical lapse.

But there was a risk inherent in the aristocratic formality of Roman religion. Maybe the tedious official rites did serve to reinforce hierarchy and obedience, but they also left the Roman gods vulnerable to repeated challenges from more emotionally accessible foreign deities. And with an empire embracing so many subjugated peoples—from the tribal Gauls and Britons to the urbane Greeks and Egyptians—there was no way to insulate Rome from the ecstatic rites of alien gods. Historians until recently referred to these ecstatic alternatives somewhat pejoratively, as "oriental religions," in the usual attempt to locate the sources of the "irrational" somewhere far outside the West, and blamed them in part for the empire's eventual decadence and decline. Geographically, though, the term *oriental* applies only to the cult of Cybele, the Great Mother, which was introduced to Rome from Anatolia in 204 BCE. The goddess Isis, whose worship was widespread in Rome at the start of the Christian era, hailed from Egypt; and Dionysus/Bacchus was hardly foreign at all.

On the whole, the Romans were remarkably tolerant toward the gods of their subject peoples, to the point of adopting particularly attractive or efficacious ones. But insofar as these imported deities drew their adherents from marginalized groups within Roman society—women and slaves—the "oriental" cults of Isis, Cybele, and Dionysus carried a hint of political menace. The public worship of Cybele was particularly outrageous, as the historian Mary Beard reports: "With their flowing hair, extravagant jewelry, and long yellow silken robes, they [the devotees of Cybele] offered an image of mad religious frenzy involving not only ecstatic dancing but frenetic self-flagellation and . . . [in the case of male worshippers] the act of self-castration performed in a divine trance."[20] This was the ultimate challenge to Roman masculine propriety: Not only did Cybele call forth bands of female worshippers on her holy days;

she demanded that her male priests, or *galli*, lop off their testicles in public. Since a man could perform that act of obeisance only once, he was expected, on future occasions of worship, to slash his skin with a knife and proceed through the streets bleeding as he danced in what must have looked, to the status-conscious Romans, like an inexplicable display of self-abasement. Modern historians agree that the worship of Cybele constituted a form of "resistance to dominant elite goals."[21] As Beard puts it:

> On the one hand was the routinized, formal approach of the traditional priesthood, embedded in the political and social hierarchies of the city. On the other hand were the claims of the galli that they enjoyed direct inspiration from the gods—an inspiration that came with frenzy and trance, open to anyone, without consideration of political or social status . . . By challenging the position of the Roman elite as the sole guardians of access to the gods, the eunuch priests were effectively challenging the wider authority of that elite and the social and cultural norms they have long guaranteed.[22]

But, on account of her alleged assistance to the Romans during the Punic Wars, there wasn't much the authorities could do about Cybele and her followers—except to mock them, as Juvenal did with glee.

> . . . Now here come the devotees
> of frenzied Bellona, and Cybele, Mother of Gods,
> with a huge eunuch, a face for lesser obscenities
> to revere. Long ago, with a sherd, he lopped off his soft genitals:
> now neither the howling rabble nor all the kettledrums can outshriek
>   him.
> A Phrygian mitre [or bonnet, a kind of headgear associated with
>   Dionysian worship in Greece] tops his plebeian cheeks.[23]

Dionysus, or Bacchus, however, did not enjoy the official protection accorded Cybele. He had not helped Rome militarily or offered any other service to the state. As a result, his devotees could be forcibly suppressed and were in fact eradicated with a viciousness comparable to the repression of Christians a few centuries later. One thing that bothered the authorities was the simple fact that people were gathering without official authorization. To quote the consul who convened the assembly where the Dionysian rites were first denounced: "Your ancestors did not wish that even the citizens should assemble fortuitously, without good reason: they did not wish you to assemble except when the standard was set up on the citadel, or when the army was called out for an election, or when the tribunes had proclaimed a council of the plebs."[24] "Freedom of assembly" was not yet even a distant aspiration; Romans were to express their desire for social contact only at the level of the family or that of the entire mass, and then only when that mass was duly convened by the state. Anything in between was politically suspect. Thus when Pliny the Younger became governor of Bithynia, in Asia Minor, he hesitated to permit the formation of a volunteer fire department. "Will you consider whether you think a company of firemen might be formed, limited to 150 members?" he wrote to the emperor Trajan. "It will not be difficult to keep such small numbers under observation." Even so, Trajan refused to grant permission, responding that "if people assemble for a common purpose, whatever name we give them and for whatever purpose, they soon turn into a political club."[25]

At the time of the crackdown on Bacchic rites, the worship of Dionysus/Bacchus had been widespread and deeply rooted in Italy for decades.[26] According to the Roman historian Livy, the trouble begins with the arrival of a charismatic stranger, just as in Euripides' play *The Bacchae*. In the Roman case, the stranger is an itinerant, no-account Greek who "dealt in sacrifices and soothsaying."[27] At first he recruits only women, who observe the rites by day; only when men are included do the rites move to nighttime.

> When the license offered by darkness had been added, no sort of crime, no kind of immorality, was left unattempted. There were

more obscenities practised between men than between men and women. Anyone refusing to submit to outrage or reluctant to commit crimes was slaughtered as a sacrificial victim . . . Men, apparently out of their wits, would utter prophecies with frenzied bodily convulsions: matrons, attired as Bacchantes, with their hair dishevelled and carrying blazing torches, would run down to the Tiber, plunge their torches into the water and bring them out still alight.[28]

The allegations of male homosexual activity were alarming enough to the Romans, who shared none of the Greeks' enthusiasm for same-sex love. But perhaps equally alarming, from a pragmatic Roman point of view, the cult was allegedly "a source of supply of false witnesses, forged documents and wills, and perjured evidence."[29]

It was the latter kind of chicanery that provided the excuse for forcible suppression. In 186 BCE—just eight years after the unsettling introduction of the cult of Cybele—the widow of an elite cavalryman plotted to somehow defraud her grown son Publius Aebutius of his inheritance by having him initiated in the Bacchic rite. According to Livy, Publius agreed to prepare for his initiation and confided as much to his girlfriend, Hispala, a former slave who had become a wealthy prostitute. Having been initiated herself years ago as a slave, she knew the horrible violations that awaited Publius and pleaded with him to ignore his mother's wishes and forgo the initiation. When his mother insisted, Hispala broke her vow of secrecy to the cult and, despite the "trembling [that] seized every part of her body," revealed the cult's activities to the Roman authorities.

Their response was little short of hysterical; an assembly was called to denounce the "conspiracy" represented by Bacchic forms of worship and order its complete uprooting. Informers were to be rewarded; no one was to leave the city until the investigations were complete. Apparently Rome was crawling with secret Bacchists, since the announcement of the purge plunged the city into "extreme terror," with thousands attempting to escape before the authorities could get to them. In the ensuing crackdown, about seven thousand men and women were detained, and the majority of them executed—males by the state, women handed over to their families to be killed in private.

We cannot of course know how much of Livy's story, and the lurid allegations contained within it, are true. Did the Roman worshippers of Dionysus really engage in homosexual orgies in addition to the standard Greek practice of dancing to ecstasy? And how did they manage to carry on the painstaking work of forging wills, brewing poisons, etcetera, in the midst of their frenzied rites?

At most, we can deduce from Livy's story some of the anxieties that afflicted the Roman elite—if not in 186 BCE, then at least near the time of Christ's birth, when Livy was writing. Clearly, concern over the integrity of Roman manhood was chief among them: A young man, a warrior's son, was to be cheated of his inheritance by a woman, his mother, and women in general "are the source of this evil thing," meaning the entire Bacchic "conspiracy." Homosexual rape was among the crimes attributed to the male cult members, who were, in Livy's words, "scarcely distinguishable from females."[30] There is no question, though, that whatever went on in the secret rites rendered men unfit for the Romans' militaristic idea of manhood. "Citizens of Rome," demands the consul who led the attack on the Bacchic "conspiracy":

> Do you feel that young men, initiated by this oath of allegiance, should be made soldiers? That arms should be entrusted to men called up from this obscene shrine? These men are steeped in their own debauchery and the debauchery of others; will they take up the sword to the end in defence of the chastity of your wives and your children?[31]

Scholars still debate whether the Bacchic cult suppressed in 186 BCE constituted a protest movement of some kind or an actual conspiracy with political intentions. No doubt the Roman male elite had reason to worry about unsupervised ecstatic gatherings: Their wealth had been gained at sword point, their comforts were provided by slaves, their households managed by women who chafed—much more noisily than their sisters in Greece—against the restrictions imposed by a perpetually male political leadership. Two centuries after the repression of Dionysian worship in Italy, in 19 CE, the Roman authorities cracked down on another "oriental" religion featuring ecstatic rites: the cult of Isis. Again there was a scandal involving the use of a cult for nefarious purposes, though this time the victim was a woman, reportedly tricked, by a rejected lover, into having sex with him in the goddess's temple. In another seeming overreaction, the emperor Tiberius had the priests of Isis crucified and the goddess's followers exiled to Sardinia along with four thousand other "brigands."[32] There would be no secrets in Rome, and no communal thrills other than those sponsored and staged by the powerful—at their circuses and gladiatorial games, for example.

So it is tempting to divide the ancient temperament into a realm of Dionysus and a realm of Yahweh—hedonism and egalitarianism versus hierarchy and war. On the one hand, a willingness to seek delight in the here and now; on the other, a determination to prepare for future danger. A feminine, or androgynous, spirit of playfulness versus the cold principle of patriarchal authority. This is in fact how Robert Graves, Joseph Campbell, and many since them have understood the emergence of a distinctly Western culture: As the triumph of masculinism and militarism over the anarchic traditions of a simpler agrarian age, of the patriarchal "sky-gods" like Yahweh and Zeus over the great goddess and her consorts. The old deities were accessible to all through ritually induced ecstasy. The new gods spoke only through their priests or prophets, and then in terrifying tones of warning and command.

But this entire dichotomy breaks down with the arrival of Jesus, whose followers claimed him as the son of Yahweh. Jesus gave the implacable Yahweh a human face, making him more accessible and forgiving. At the same time, though—and less often noted—Jesus was, or was portrayed by his followers as, a continuation of the quintessentially pagan Dionysus.

3

Jesus and Dionysus

In what has been called "one of the most haunting passages in Western literature," the Greek historian Plutarch tells the story of how passengers on a Greek merchant ship, sometime during the reign of Tiberius (14–37 BCE), heard a loud cry coming from the island of Paxos. The voice instructed the ship's pilot to call out, when he sailed past Palodes, "The Great God Pan is dead." As soon as he did so, the passengers heard, floating back to them from across the water, "a great cry of lamentation, not of one person, but of many."[1]

It's a strange story: one disembodied voice after another issuing from over the water. Early Christian writers seemed only to hear the first voice, which signaled to them the collapse of paganism in the face of a nascent Christianity. Pan, the horned god who overlapped Dionysus as a deity of dance and ecstatic states, had to die to make room for the stately and sober Jesus. Only centuries later did Plutarch's readers fully attend to the answering voices of lamentation and begin to grasp what was lost with the rise of monotheism. In a world without Dionysus/Pan/Bacchus/Sabazios, nature would be dead, joy would be postponed to an afterlife, and the forests would no longer ring with the sound of pipes and flutes.

The absolute incompatibility of Jesus and Dionysus—or, more generally, Christianity and the old ecstatic religions—was a tenet of later Christian theology, if not of "Western" thought more generally. But to a Roman living in the first or second century, when Christianity emerged, the new religion would not have seemed so hostile to Dionysus or his half-animal version, Pan. From a Roman perspective, Christianity was at first just another "oriental" religion coming out of the east, and, like others of similar provenance, attractive to women and the poor. It offered direct communion with the deity, with the promise of eternal life, but so did many of the other imported religions that so vexed the Roman authorities. In fact, there is reason to think that early Christianity was itself an ecstatic religion, overlapping the cult of Dionysus.

To begin with the deities themselves: The general parallels between Jesus and various pagan gods were laid out long ago by James Frazer in *The Golden Bough*. Like the Egyptian god Osiris and Attis, who derived from Asia Minor, Jesus was a "dying god," or victim god, whose death redounded to the benefit of humankind. Dionysus, too, had endured a kind of martyrdom. His divine persecutor was Hera, the matronly consort of Zeus, whose anger stemmed from the fact that it was Zeus who fathered Dionysus with a mortal woman, Semele. Hera ordered the baby Dionysus torn to shreds, but he was reassembled by his grandmother. Later Hera tracked down the grown Dionysus and afflicted him with the divine madness that caused him to roam the world, spreading viniculture and revelry. In this story, we can discern a theme found in the mythologies of many apparently unrelated cultures: that of the primordial god whose suffering, and often dismemberment, comprise, or are necessary elements of, his gifts to humankind.

The obvious parallel between the Christ story and that of pagan victim gods was a source of great chagrin to second-century Church fathers. Surely their own precious savior god could not have been copied, or plagiarized, from disreputable pagan cults. So they ingeniously explained the parallel as a result of "diabolical mimicry": Anticipating the arrival of Jesus Christ many centuries later, the pagans had cleverly designed their gods to resemble him.[2] Never mind that this explanation attributed supernatural, almost godlike powers of prophecy to the pagan inventors of Osiris, Attis, and Dionysus.

Leaving aside Christ as the generic pagan victim god, we find far more intriguing parallels between Jesus the historical figure and the *specific* pagan god Dionysus. Both were wandering charismatics who attracted devoted followings, or cults; both had a special appeal to women and the poor. Strikingly, both are associated with wine: Dionysus first brought it to humankind; Jesus could make it out of water. Each was purported to be the son of a great father-god— Zeus or the Hebrew god Yahweh—and a mortal mother. Neither was an ascetic—Jesus loved his wine and meat—but both were apparently asexual or at least lacking a regular female consort. Both were healers—Jesus directly, Dionysus through participation in his rites— and both were miracle workers, and possibly, in Jesus' case, a magician.[3] Each faced persecution by secular authorities, represented by Pentheus, among others, in the case of Dionysus, and Pontius Pilate in the case of Jesus. For what it's worth, they even had similar symbolic creatures: the fish for Jesus, the dolphin for Dionysus.

In at least one significant respect, Jesus far more resembles Dionysus than Attis. Attis was a fertility god who died and was reborn again each year along with the earth's vegetation, while Jesus, like Dionysus, was markedly indifferent to the entire business of reproduction. For example, we know that Jewish women in the Old Testament were devastated by infertility. But although Jesus could cure just about anything, to the point of reviving the dead, he is never said to have "cured" a childless woman—a surprising omission if he were somehow derived from a pagan god of fertility.

Furthermore, to the extent to which Dionysus can be said to have a philosophy or ethical stance, it bears a certain resemblance to that of Jesus. Dionysus was a lover of peace, as we have seen; and, like Jesus, he upheld the poor and rejected the prevailing social hierarchy. According to Euripides, who was certainly not an unambivalent admirer of the wine god, the Dionysian man is:

> Watchful to keep aloof both mind and heart
> From men whose pride claims more than mortals may.
> The life that wins the poor man's common voice,
> His creed, his practice—this shall be my choice.[4]

Rounding out their shared bohemian perspective, both were scornful of the toil and striving that take up so much human energy. Dionysus was always pulling women away from their housework to join his manic rites. Jesus advised his followers to quit worrying about where their next meal would come from and emulate the lilies of the field and the fowls of the air: "for they sow not, neither do they reap, nor gather into barns." Both, in fancier words, upheld what has been called a *hedonic* vision of community, based on egalitarianism and the joyous immediacy of human experience—as against the *agonic* reality of the cruelly unequal and warlike societies they briefly favored with their presence.[5]

There is one more parallel between Jesus and Dionysus. Long before Jesus' arrival, Dionysus had himself become a god of personal salvation, holding out the promise of life beyond the grave. The official patriarchal gods—Zeus (Jupiter to the Romans) and Yahweh—had little to offer by way of an afterlife, but the various ecstatic cults available in the Greco-Roman world—those centered on Demeter, Isis, Cybele, and Mithra, for example—all held out their mysteries as portals to eternal life. According to Burkert, "The same is true for the Dionysiac mysteries from at least the fifth century B.C. onward [although] scholars have been reluctant to acknowledge this dimension of Dionysiac worship."[6] The widespread use of Dionysian imagery on gravestones testifies, most likely, to the wine god's promise of salvation.[7] This was not simply a verbal promise, as it was for Christians; pagans could apprehend their immortality directly, through participation in the god's ecstatic rites. To "lose oneself" in ecstasy—to let go of one's physical and temporal boundaries—is to glimpse, however briefly, the prospect of eternity.

Dionysus and the Jews

How to explain the resemblance between the son of Zeus and the son of Yahweh? It could be argued that each is a manifestation of some underlying archetype, existing within the human imagination, of a divine or semidivine rebel and savior figure. But there is another possibility: that the historical figure of Jesus was subtly altered and shaped by his early followers and chroniclers *in order* to make him more closely resemble Dionysus. As hellenized Jews, who spoke and wrote in Greek, these early chroniclers were familiar with Dionysus and the entire extended family of pagan deities. In fact, more so than other Jews, the early Christians were intellectually engaged with the ideas and philosophies of classical pagan culture.[8] But why should they want to style their own god-man after a pagan deity, and an apparently disreputable one at that?

The answer must be connected to the strange fact that, in apparent defiance of the First Commandment, the Jews of Roman Israel were *already* worshipping Dionysus at the time of Jesus and identifying him with their "one" god Yahweh. The historian Morton Smith pointed out that the god Dionysus was worshipped throughout the Hebrew world in Roman times: "Accordingly, it is not surprising that Yahweh was often identified by gentiles with Dionysus . . . The surprising fact is that this identification first appears among the Jews themselves." On a Hebrew coin, for example, Yahweh is portrayed (and the mere fact of his portrayal is a startling break from Jewish tradition) with Dionysian attributes—wearing a satyr's mask and driving the chariot of Triptolemus, which Dionysus had used for his travels around the world.[9]

In addition, there are reports of Jewish worship of Dionysus in Rome, while in Jerusalem the Jews may have been ecumenical enough to worship Yahweh in the form of both Zeus and Dionysus.

Considering the "popularity of the cult of Dionysus in Palestine" as well as the material evidence from coins, funerary objects, and building ornaments showing that Yahweh and Dionysus were often elided or confused, Smith concluded that "these factors taken together make it incredible that these symbols were meaningless to the Jews who used them. The history of their use shows a persistent association with Yahweh of attributes of the wine god."[10] As the theologian Robert M. Price writes:

> There surely was such a thing as Jews taking attractive features of Gentile faiths and mixing them with their own . . . Maccabees 6:7 tells us that Antiochus converted large numbers of Jews to the worship of Dionysus. One suspects it was no arduous task, given that some Greek writers already considered Jehovah simply another local variant of Dionysus anyway. The Sabazius religion of Phrygia is plainly an example of worshipping Jehovah as Dionysus.[11]

Thus Jesus was born into a Jewish culture that had embraced, to a certain extent, the pagan gods, especially Zeus and Dionysus. According to the classicist Carl Kerényi, Jesus' early followers, and probably Jesus himself, were aware of "the existence of a massive non-Greek religion of Dionysus between the lake of Genesareth and the Phoenician coast." Jesus traveled in this region and took many of his metaphors from viniculture. In particular his odd insistence that he is "the true vine" makes little sense unless there is also a false vine, and has been interpreted as a direct challenge to Dionysus.[12] As for Jesus' Dionysus-like trick of turning water into wine, this was, Smith argues, derived from "a myth about Dionysus told in a Dionysiac festival celebrated at Sidon." A first- or second-century CE report of the festival "shows striking similarities, even in wording, to the gospel material."[13]

There are several features of Dionysus that would have made him an attractive prototype for the deified Jesus. First, of course, were the ecstatic elements of Dionysian worship; the Maccabees had introduced elements of Dionysian ritual into Jewish festivities two centuries before Jesus' birth, and Smith says these were very popular. In a broader sense, the early Jewish followers of Jesus may have been impressed, as were the Greeks and Romans before them, by the wine god's accessibility to the individual worshipper. Yahweh—at least before his own apparent merger with Dionysus—had been a stern and impersonal deity, while Dionysus always held out the possibility of a direct and personal relationship through participation in his rites. Furthermore, unlike so many deities, Yahweh included, Dionysus was not a local or parochial god; his cult was universal and potentially open to anyone, anywhere.

When the historical Jesus was executed by the Roman authorities, his followers coped with this tragedy by turning him into a god—but not just any god. They seem to have chosen as their model a particular god who was already at large in their community, a god who held out the promise of immortal life and divine communion, and who welcomed even the lowliest of individuals. I am not suggesting that this was a conscious choice, made by certain followers of Jesus who secretly fancied the god Dionysus. But Dionysiac themes were ever present in the pagan/Jewish culture in which Jesus' followers sought to interpret their leader's brief life and tortured death. There were forty years between Jesus' death and the first written account of his life—time enough for his followers to assemble a myth of his divine lineage and mission out of the cultural bricolage available to them, which already included the notion of a wine-bringing, life-giving, populist, victim god. Christ crucified was, perhaps in a more than merely symbolic way, Dionysus risen.

Could there have been any actual overlap between the cults of Jesus and Dionysus, or fraternal mixing of the two? In support of that possibility, Timothy Freke and Peter Gandy, in their somewhat sensationalist book *The Jesus Mysteries*, offer a number of cases, from the second and third centuries, in which Dionysus—who is identified by name—is depicted hanging from a cross.[14] Then there is what the archaeologist Franz Cumont called "a strange fact for which no satis-factory explanation has as yet been furnished": the burial of a priest of Sabazios, along with another follower of this god, who was a vari-ant of Dionysus common to Asia Minor, in the Christian catacomb in Rome.[15] Accompanying the burial site are frescoes depicting "how Vibia [the follower of Sabazios] was carried away by Death, as Kore had been carried away by Hades, how she was judged and acquitted, and how she was introduced by a 'good angel' to the sacred meal of the blessed."[16] The presence of Dionysus/Sabazios in a Christian burial site decorated with a very Christian story of death and the af-terlife would seem to suggest that the deified Jesus and the old wine god were, however briefly, once on excellent terms with each other.

Ecstatic Christianity

More to the point, for our purposes, is the evidence—frustratingly scattered and inconclusive, I admit—that the early Christians en-gaged in ecstatic practices resembling those of the mystery cults in Greece and the "oriental" religions in Rome. Certainly the Romans suspected that they did. The first-century Roman writer Celsus compared Christians to practitioners of the "Bacchic mysteries" and to the "begging priests of Cybele and soothsayers, and to wor-shippers of Mithras and Sabazius."[17] Beyond that, Romans imag-ined Christians performing all the lewd acts attributed to the cult of Bacchus, with even more diabolical variations such as human sacri-fice, infanticide, and cannibalism thrown in. As Fronto, the tutor of the emperor Marcus Aurelius, understood the Christian sacrament of communion: "It is the blood of this [sacrificed] infant—I shud-der to mention it—it is this blood that they lick with thirsty lips; these are the limbs they distribute eagerly; this is the victim by which they seal their covenant."[18]

The attractiveness of Christianity to women, and the conse-quent mingling of the sexes, was another source of prurient Roman speculation.

On a special day they gather in a feast with all their children, sisters, mothers—all sexes and all ages. There, flushed with the banquet after such feasting and drinking, they begin to burn with incestuous passions . . . with unspeakable lust they copulate in random unions, all equally being guilty of incest, some by deed, but everyone by complicity.[19]

Most of what Christians of the first and second centuries actually did together—whether they even possessed a standardized form of worship, for example—is unknown to us today, but the general scholarly view is that "church services were noisy, charismatic affairs, quite different from a tasteful evensong today at the parish church."[20] They met in people's homes, where their central ritual was a shared meal that was no doubt washed down with Jesus' favorite beverage, wine.[21] There is reason to think they sang too, and that the songs were sometimes accompanied by instrumental music.[22] Justin Martyr, a gentile convert who died at the hands of the Romans in 165 CE, once wrote that children should sing together, "just as in the same way one enjoys songs and similar music in church."[23] Very likely, Christians also danced; at least this is how the historian Louis Backman interpreted various statements of the second-century Church fathers. Clement of Alexandria (150–216 CE), for example, instructed the faithful to "dance in a ring, together with the angels, around Him who is without beginning or end," suggesting that the Christian initiation rite included a ring-dance around the altar. At another point Clement wrote that in order to invoke the "zest and delight of the spirit," Christians "raise our heads and our hands to heaven and move our feet just at the end of the prayer—*pedes excitamus*," where, according to Backman, *pedes excitamus* is "a technical term for *dancing*."[24]

So Christians sang and possibly danced, but did they dance *ecstatically*, as did members of the old Dionysian cults? The evidence for ecstatic dancing, such as it is, hinges on Paul's instruction, in his letter to the Corinthian congregation, that women should keep their heads covered in church (1 Cor. 11:5). This may represent nothing more than a concern that Christianity remain within the normal pagan and Jewish bounds of gender decorum. After all, Paul did not want women prophesying or even speaking in church, despite the fact that he worked with women as fellow proselytizers and had at one point proclaimed that "male and female are one in Christ." An alternative explanation for the head-covering rule, proposed by the theologian E. S. Fiorenza, is that the women of Corinth were becoming a little too exuberant for Paul's tastes.

> It seems that during their ecstatic-pneumatic worship celebrations some of the Corinthian women prophets and liturgists unbound their hair, letting it flow freely rather than keeping it in its fashionable coiffure, which often was quite elaborate and enhanced with jewelry, ribbons and veils. Such a sight of disheveled hair would have been quite common in the ecstatic worship of oriental deities.[25]

Roman women spent hours on their tight coiffures, leaving the long, unbound look to the worshippers of Dionysus, Cybele, and Isis. If we know one thing about Paul, it is that he was greatly concerned about making Christianity respectable to the Romans, and hence as little like the other "oriental" religions—with their disorderly dancing women—as possible.

This may seem like a rather tenuous inference, but the association between hair-tossing and ecstatic practice is widespread and was well established in the ancient world. Recall the prehistoric depictions of dancing women whose flowing hair suggests head-tossing or at least rapid motion. In the second-century Roman Empire, the Syrian writer Lucian reported that the *galli*, or male worshippers of Cybele, "shook off their caps and rolled their heads downward from the neck," while Apuleius described them as "hanging down their heads a long while, moving their necks around with supple motions, and whirling their loose hair round and round."[26] E. R. Dodds, in his famous work *The Greeks and the Irrational*, suggested that hair-tossing might be a universal hallmark of religious ecstasy. A nineteenth-century missionary, for example, who witnessed a "cannibal dance" in British Columbia, thought that "the continual jerking [of] their heads back, causing their long black hair to twist about, added much to their savage appearance." Similarly, a notable feature of certain Moroccan dancers was that "their long hair was tossed about by the rapid to-and-fro movements of the head."[27] An observer of the eighteenth-century American Great Revival reported of people overcome by "the spirit":

> Their heads would jerk back suddenly, frequently causing them to yelp, or make some other involuntary noise . . . Sometimes the head would fly every way so quickly that their features could not be recognized. I have seen their heads fly back and forth so quickly that the hair of females would be made to crack like a carriage whip, but not very loud.[28]

The hypothesis that Paul was concerned with controlling ecstatic activity, and not just women, is at least consistent with the fact that, a few verses after the hair-covering line in his letter to the Corinthians, he warns Christian men to keep *their* hair cut short (1 Cor. 11:14). Furthermore, there is archaeological evidence for the continuing worship of Dionysus in Corinth during Paul's lifetime, prompting one twentieth-century evangelical Christian scholar to conclude that "the Dionysian religion would probably have had some influence" on the overly exuberant Corinthian Christians.[29]

Without question, the early Christians indulged in one very odd form of behavior, but whether it was truly ecstatic, or even communal, is not so clear. This was speaking in tongues, technically called *glossolalia* and colloquially, in our own time, *tongue-speaking*. It first occurs among the biblical Christians in the Book of Acts, when hundreds of the faithful have gathered to observe the Jewish Pentecost.

> And suddenly there came a sound from heaven as of a rushing mighty wind . . .
>
> And there appeared unto them cloven tongues like as of fire, and it sat upon each of them.
>
> And they were all filled with the Holy Ghost, and began to speak with other tongues, as the spirit gave them utterance. (Acts 2:2–4)

Passersby assume they are drunk, but what has happened is that, miraculously, the assembled Christians of all nationalities— Parthians, Medes, Elamites, Cretans, Arabians, Egyptians, Romans, and Jews are among those mentioned—can at last understand one another. The mutual unintelligibility of human languages, which had frustrated the Hebrews since the Tower of Babel story in the Old Testament, was finally overcome.

Later we encounter tongue-speaking among the Corinthians, who are again being rebuked by Paul for excessively enthusiastic behavior. He does not denounce the practice, describing it as a legitimate "gift of the spirit," but unfortunately this god-given form of speech has by now become unintelligible. Concerned as usual with public relations, Paul worries about how this practice might appear to the unconverted: "If therefore the whole church be come together in one place, and all speak with tongues, and there come in those that are unlearned, or unbelievers, will they not say that ye are mad?" (1 Cor. 14:23).

But is tongue-speaking really a sign, or symptom, of communal ecstasy or some trancelike state induced by it? William Samarin, a sociolinguist and the author of a 1972 book on glossolalia, insists that it has nothing to do with ecstasy, either now or among the ancients. "Anyone can do it," he told me. "All you have to do is believe you can speak another language."[30] True enough, unlike some of the physical symptoms of trance—convulsions, for example, or unusual bodily contortions—glossolalia is easily faked or at least consciously indulged in, and there might well have been a motive to do so: The "gift" of glossolalia seems to have been a source of prestige within the early Christian community; Paul himself boasts to the Corinthians that he can do it "more than all of you." Similarly in our own time, charismatic television preachers will sometimes demonstrate their spiritual authority by breaking into short bursts of tongue-speaking, after which they return to English without the slightest change of demeanor or tone of voice. And unlike the extraordinary mental states sometimes brought on by music and dance, tongue-speaking does not always take place in the context of an emotionally charged group. There are many reports of its occurrence during solitary prayer, although these are of course impossible to verify.[31]

On the other hand, in many of the cultures in which it occurs, glossolalia is associated with what appear to be "altered states of consciousness"—among shamans, for example, or members of certain African charismatic Christian cults that also practice ecstatic dance. An ethnographic account of a Caddo harvest ritual in North America describes an old man delivering "a harangue of pure jargon in a hasty, high-pitched voice without saying an intelligible word."[32] In the 1970s, the linguist and anthropologist Felicitas Goodman surveyed glossolalic utterances in a number of different cultures and found what she thought was a universal intonational pattern within them, suggesting some common underlying mental state. In our own time, Christian tongue-speakers sometimes report feelings of bliss, as in the case of the Reverend Darlene Miller of Knoxville, Tennessee: "It's a beautiful, peaceful, comforting feeling. You know the presence of God, the power of God. It is sweet, beautiful, a rushing sensation, a power of God throughout the body. It has to come forth in the audible voice of tongues. The body cannot control it."[33] Or to quote a modern Catholic charismatic, who first experienced glossolalia when praying alone: "And then it happened. Very quietly, very softly, I began to praise God in ecstatic language. And in that instant I understood that in giving myself to God, I was not consumed but fulfilled, complete. The Spirit was singing for me the inexpressible love I felt."[34]

In the ancient Mediterranean world, glossolalia was well known before the Christians and clearly associated with ecstatic experience, in particular with ecstatic prophecy. The Pythia, the priestess who delivered oracles at the Greek shrine at Delphi, ingested what were said to be laurel leaves—by chewing them or inhaling the smoke—before delivering predictions, which usually came out in unintelligible form, requiring detailed interpretation by priests. Apollo was supposed to be the source of her insights, except in the winter months, when Dionysus took over this responsibility. It is probably from the Delphic oracle that the early Christians got the idea of glossolalia as an appropriate way of expressing the feeling of being "possessed" by a deity or overcome by religious emotion.

This is not to diminish the experience of early Christians or to say that they simply copied the Pythia and other Greek ecstatic adepts. But along with so many other bits of Greek culture, the early Christians may have absorbed the idea that glossolalia was a good way to communicate the fact that one has entered an extraordinary mental state, presumably granted by the deity. Some may indeed have "faked" it, that is, learned to make glossolalic utterances while in a normal, nonecstatic state of consciousness. And almost everyone could control its onset and duration—otherwise Paul's injunction against excessive tongue-speaking would have been meaningless. Wayne A. Meeks argues that glossolalia was a more or less controlled and ritual element of early Christian worship, occurring "at predictable times, accompanied by distinctive bodily movements," perhaps triggered by other ritual events, and serving to both increase the prestige of the gifted and heighten the solidarity of the group.[35]

Without question, the early Christians themselves understood glossolalia as a sign of god-given ecstasy. To the second- and third-century church leader Tertullian, for example, it was even a criterion of God's favor, and he challenged the Gnostic heretic Marcion to match him if he could: "Let him produce a psalm, a vision, a prayer—only let it be by the Spirit, in an ecstasy, that is, in a rapture, whenever an interpretation of tongues has occurred to him."[36] Very likely, early Christians expected their meetings to be productive of extraordinary feelings—of communion, rapture, or bliss. Meeks suggests that the experience of baptism was another occasion for the experience of at least "mild dissociation," because when the baptizands—naked and dripping—cried out *"Abba!"* (the Aramaic word for "father"), they signaled that "the Spirit" had entered and possessed them.[37]

So it is fair to say that first- and second-century Christianity offered an experience in some ways similar to that provided by the Greek mystery cults and the "oriental" religions in Rome—one of great emotional intensity, sometimes culminating in ecstatic states. Unlike worshippers of Cybele, Christians did not slash themselves with knives (though a few, like Origen, did castrate themselves); and unlike Dionysus's followers, they did not dash into the mountains and devour small animals. But they sang and chanted, leaped up to prophesy either in tongues or in normal speech, drank wine, and probably danced and tossed their hair about.

Generalization is unwise here, since there may have been as many forms of Christian worship as there were Christian cells or congregations. It seems likely that Paul's home congregation was unusually staid, with the tongue-speaking restricted to leaders like himself and the speaking in general left to male members of the group. At the other extreme of early Christian worship, there were the Montanists in Phrygia, led by Montanus and two female prophets, Priscilla and Maximilla, who prophesied in a state of trance and were said to indulge in ecstatic practices resembling those of the "oriental" religions. Montanus himself may have been a former priest of Cybele. It is worth mentioning, given the persistent tendency to confuse communal ecstasy and sexual abandon, that the Montanists were far more sexually puritanical than other Christians.[38] Perhaps made more appealing by its ecstatic practices, the Montanist movement spread rapidly throughout Asia Minor in the second century and boasted Tertullian as its most prominent recruit.

Of the "oriental" cults that swept through the ancient Greek and Roman worlds, Christianity is the only one to have survived in any form. The reason for its success, at least in the first two centuries, probably lies in a quality that the other cults never attained and, as far as we know, never even tried to attain: namely, a sense of community that could outlast the emotional charge of the ceremonies and rituals themselves. Burkert points out that the pagan mystery cults led "to integration into a 'blessed chorus' for celebrations . . . Yet festive togetherness of this kind does not outlast the festival; the chorus dances for a day or a night and is disbanded thereafter."[39] No doubt these cults had some sort of administrative structure to provide continuity—Isis and Cybele even had temples and priests—but the concept of a lasting community of the faithful takes hold only with Christianity. While the poor might find a few hours of ecstatic release in the cult of Dionysus or the Great Mother, they found concrete material support among the Christians, or at least a free meal, sponsored by their more affluent brethren, at every worship session. Single women and widows might achieve a temporary feeling of liberation in the pagan cults, but Christianity offered them an ongoing network of support, material as well as social.[40] A Roman commentator observed, perhaps a little enviously, that Christians "recognize each other by secret marks and signs . . . everywhere they introduce a kind of religious lust, a promiscuous 'brotherhood' and 'sisterhood.' "[41]

Christian solidarity stemmed in part from Jesus' sweet and spontaneous form of socialism, but it had a dark, apocalyptic side too. He had preached that the existing social order was soon to give way to the kingdom of heaven, hence the irrelevance of the old social ties of family and tribe. Since the final days were imminent, it was no longer necessary to have children or to even cleave to one's (unbelieving) spouse or kin—a feature of their religion that "pro-family" Christians in our own time conveniently ignore. Christians had only one another, clinging together in a community forged in part on eschatology. And through much of the first two centuries of the Common Era, their sense of doom was justified. The Romans hated the Christians for their clannishness, which exceeded that of the non-Christian Jews, and Roman persecution, in turn, pulled Christians ever more tightly together.

But as Christianity evolved from suppressed cult to official Church, it shed both the loving solidarity and the communal ecstasies that enriched its early years. In Paul's time, Christianity possessed no formal "structure of ministry and governance"—no hierarchy, in other words, and no gradient of prestige other than that derived from individual charisma.[42] By the end of the first century, however, formal officers—bishops and deacons—make their appearance, and in the early fourth century, the emperor himself was converted, making Christianity the Roman Empire's official religion. Little is heard of glossolalia after Paul's time, and, starting in the middle of the fourth century, the Church began to crack down on religious dancing, especially by women. Basileios, the bishop of Caesarea, railed against the unseemly behavior of Christian women at the celebration of the Resurrection, and in terms suggesting that the Pauline insistence on head coverings had indeed been aimed at the suppression of ecstatic dancing in church.

> Casting aside the yoke of service under Christ and the veil of virtue from their heads, despising God and His Angels, they [the women] shamelessly attract the attention of every man. With unkempt hair, clothed in bodices and hopping about, they dance with lustful eyes and loud laughter; as if seized by a kind of frenzy they excite the lust of the youths. They execute ring-dances in the churches of the Martyrs and at their graves . . . With harlots' songs they pollute the air and sully the degraded earth with their feet in shameful postures.[43]

Whether the women's dances were really lewd or only appeared so to Baseleios, we have no way of judging, but there was a clear effort in the fourth century to "spiritualize" church dancing and eliminate what the Church authorities saw as its grosser, sensual aspects. In the fourth century, Gregory of Nazianzus strained to distinguish an acceptably solemn form of dancing from the boisterous and suggestive alternatives.

> Let us sing hymns instead of striking drums, have psalms instead of frivolous music and song . . . modesty instead of laughter, wise contemplation instead of intoxication, seriousness instead of delirium. But even if you wish to dance in devotion at this happy ceremony and festival, then dance, but not the shameless dance of the daughter of Herod.[44]

By the end of the fourth century, the fiery and intolerant John Chrysostom, the archbishop of Constantinople, virtually ended the discussion with his pronouncement: "For where there is a dance, there also is the Devil."[45] Very likely, some Christians merely continued pagan religious practices outside the purview of the Christian Church, because as late as 691 CE, we find the Council of Constantinople inveighing against the worship of Dionysus with the decree that "no man shall put on a woman's dress nor a woman, clothes that belong to men, nor shall any disguise themselves with colic, satyr, or tragic masks, nor call out the name of disgusting Dionysos while pressing grapes in the press or pouring wine in vats."[46]

Social scientists of the twentieth century have tended to portray the early Church's assault on ecstatic, or even festive, forms of worship as part of an inevitable process of maturation. In his classic 1971 book *Ecstatic Religion*, I. M. Lewis observed that "new faiths may announce their advent with a flourish of ecstatic revelations, but once they become securely established they have little time or tolerance for enthusiasm. For the religious enthusiast, with his direct claim to divine knowledge, is always a threat to the established order."[47] When a religion becomes established, possession experiences are discouraged and may even be seen as a form of "satanic heresy." Lewis goes on: "This certainly is the pattern which is clearly and deeply inscribed in the long history of Christianity."[48] Max Weber, in *The Sociology of Religion*, approved of this process of settling down, if only from the "viewpoint of hygiene," since "hysterical suffusion with religious emotionalism leads to psychic collapse."[49] For him, the great developmental task facing each new religion was the substitution of a "rational system of ethics" for the earlier wildness of ecstatic inspiration. China had achieved this in the first century BCE, he observed, replacing its charismatic and festive indigenous religion with the cool rationality of Confucianism; and Christianity had done the same.[50] The only major difference between the Chinese and the Roman Christian cases was, in Weber's view, that Christianity had always upheld a "rational ethic"—"even in the earliest period, when all sorts of irrational charismatic gifts of the spirit were regarded as the decisive hallmark of sanctity."[51]

But how "rational" was the ethic that Christianity began with? There is nothing rational or calculated about Jesus' command to turn the other cheek to the man who smites you, or to sell all that you have and give to the poor. As Jesus commands: "And if any man will sue thee at the law, and take away thy coat, let him have thy cloak also. And whosoever shall compel thee to go a mile, go with him twain" (Matthew 5:40–41). Christians in our own time wriggle mightily to evade these teachings,* which, from a cold, capitalistic perspective, look like sheer madness. But Jesus' instructions may have made perfect sense to the early acolytes, who spoke in tongues and drank and

---

*The popular American Life Application Study Bible struggles, in a footnote, to explain the socialistic nature of the early Church as follows: "The early church was able to share possessions and property as a result of the unity brought by the Holy Spirit working in and through the believers' lives. This way of living is different from communism because (1) the sharing was voluntary; (2) it didn't involve all private property, but only as much as was needed; (3) it was not a membership requirement in order to be a part of the church." (Life Application Study Bible, New American Standard Bible, updated edition [Grand Rapids, MI: Zondervan, 2000], p. 1895.)

danced together with their hair streaming. What are possessions, what is individual pride, to people who can routinely achieve ecstatic merger through their communal rites? The early Christian patriarchs may not have realized that, in attempting to suppress ecstatic practices, they were throwing out much of Jesus too.

Weber was wrong, too, to suggest that Christians just tired of their strenuous and "hysterical" forms of worship; over time, these practices were increasingly forbidden to them. As the early Christian community became the institution of the Church, all forms of *enthusiasm*—in the original sense of being filled with or possessed by a deity—came under fire. And when the community of believers could no longer access the deity on their own, through ecstatic forms of worship, the community itself was reduced to a state of dependency on central ecclesiastic authorities. "Prophesying" became the business of the priest; singing was relegated to a specialized choir; and that characteristic feature of early Christian worship— the communal meal or feast—shriveled into a morsel that could only tantalize the hungry. But it was to take many centuries before large numbers of Christians came to accept this diminished form of Christianity.

4

From the Churches to the Streets: The Creation of Carnival

Almost a thousand years after the early Church fathers issued their first condemnations of dancing in churches, we find the leaders of Catholicism still railing against ecstatic and "lascivious" behavior at Christian services. Judging from the volume of condemnations from on high, the custom of dancing in churches was thoroughly entrenched in the late Middle Ages and apparently tolerated—if not actually enjoyed—even by many parish priests. Priests danced; women danced; whole congregations joined in.* Despite the efforts of the Church hierarchy, Christianity remained, to a certain extent, a danced religion.

In the twelfth and thirteenth centuries, Catholic leaders finally purged the churches of unruly and ecstatic behavior. They must have known that they could not prohibit such behavior in the society at large. If the people were so determined to frolic, condemnations and bans would not suffice; some kind of compromise had to

---

*According to the historian William H. McNeill, European churches did not have pews until sometime in the eighteenth century. People stood or milled around, creating a very different dynamic than we find in today's churches, where people are expected to spend most of their time sitting. (Personal communication with the author, June 1, 2006.)

be worked out—some kind of balance between obedience and piety on the one hand, and riotous good times on the other.

The form that this compromise took helped shape European culture for centuries: Simply put, the laity could dance on Church holidays and otherwise amuse themselves more or less to their hearts' content; they just could not do so in churches. Extruded from the physical realm of the church, the dancing, drinking, and other forms of play that so irritated the ecclesiastic authorities became the festivities that filled up the late medieval and early modern Church calendar: on saints' days, just before Lent, and on a host of other occasions throughout the year. In its battle with the ecstatic strain within Christianity, the Church, no doubt inadvertently, invented carnival.*

Elements of carnival had of course existed for centuries. "In the early and central Middle Ages," observes the French historian Aron Gurevich, "carnival had not yet crystallized in time and space; its elements were diffused everywhere, and hence there was no carnival as such."[1] In his study of festive traditions in England, Ronald Hutton found that, at the beginning of the fifteenth century, many of the elements of festivity—such as dances around maypoles and the mockery associated with a "lord of misrule," the English version of a "king of fools"—were themselves relatively recent; in fact "many had been either introduced or embellished only a few generations before or even within living memory." Gurevich offers no clue as to the reasons for the burst of festive creativity in the thirteenth and fourteenth centuries, and Hutton, too, comes up empty from his review of the English scene: "It must be concluded, very lamely, that there is no clear and obvious reason for the apparent greater investment in English seasonal ceremony during the later Middle Ages."[2]

But the dots can be connected. The reason for the expansion of festivities may be simply that festive behavior was increasingly

---

*Technically, *carnival* refers to the specific holiday preceding Lent, but the term is also used in a generic way to denote similar festivities occurring throughout the year.

prohibited within the churches. Once, people could rely on official church services as occasions for dancing and perhaps drinking and other forms of carrying on. As the services became more disciplined and orderly, people had to create their own festive occasions outside of church property and official times of worship, usually on holy days. "One thing is certain," the historian Jean Delumeau writes. "People danced in both churches and cemeteries in the Middle Ages, especially on holidays such as the Feast of Fools, the Day of the Innocents, and so on, [until] the Council of Basel . . . ruled against this practice."[3] There may have been no burst of festive creativity in the late Middle Ages—only a change of venue.

Church leaders tolerated, though with considerable uneasiness, the festive behavior they drove from churches. Complete repression was probably impossible and certainly unwise, since suppressed ecstatic desires could always find alternative sites for expression in the heretical, millenarian movements that sprang up again and again to bedevil the Church. In the thirteenth century, when carnival-like activities so decisively expand, the Church was facing its gravest challenges since the time of the Roman Empire. Heretical movements swept Germany, southern France, and northern Spain, threatening to splinter the Church into rival sects. So great was the danger that in 1233 Pope Gregory IX established a permanent institution for the suppression of heresy—the papal Inquisition—which was made all the more effective when, twenty-nine years later, it adopted torture as one of its tools of interrogation.

At roughly the same time as the institution of the Inquisition, though in a less centralized fashion, Church authorities applied themselves to making Catholicism more emotionally and sensually engaging, as if to compete with the festive alternatives. Church buildings were beautified or at least physically embellished; there was a proliferation of special prayers, relics (typically, the alleged bones and other remains of saints), and indulgences. Along with the improved production values, there were new special effects, like the addition of incense to the mass. As the ecclesiastical rites grew more complex, they, in turn, encouraged the development of ecclesiastical dramas in which liturgy was expanded into narrative. New holidays were added, like the feast of Corpus Christi, adopted in the mid-thirteenth century at the urging of the order of laywomen known as Beguines. All in all, Christianity became busier, more demanding, and, especially in the larger towns, gaudier.

The solution represented by externalizing festivities suited both the repressive impulses of the Church and its desire to be more accessible to laypeople who might otherwise be tempted by competing religious sects. Purged of disorderly behavior, church property could be devoted to rites whose solemnity was in keeping with the vast and intricate hierarchy the Church had become. At the same time, the people could have their fun—though only at times designated by the Church calendar, outside of church and churchyard, for limited periods, under of the aegis of the Church, and surrounded by the trappings and symbols of the Christian religion.

The War on Dance

In the centuries leading up to this compromise, the activity that most vexed Church leaders, or at least the more puritanical among them, was dancing. Just as in ancient times, the perpetrators were often female—at least it was women's dancing that brought down some of the angriest condemnations. In the ninth century, bishops meeting at the Council of Rome complained that women were coming to church only to "sing shameless songs and perform choir dances." According to the medieval historian E. K. Chambers: "Upon great feasts and wake-days, choruses of women invaded with wanton *cantica* and *ballationes* the precincts of the churches and even the sacred buildings themselves, a desecration against which generation after generation of ecclesiastical authorities was fain to protest."[4]

One clerical tactic was to warn of dire supernatural punishments. There was a legend—or, perhaps, as we might now say, an

urban myth—of how the people of Kolbigk had persisted in dancing while the priest said mass on Christmas day and, as a result,
were condemned to dance year-round without a break, causing
most of them to die of exhaustion. In other minatory tales, dancers
are carried away by the devil, struck by lightning, or surprised to
discover that the musician to whose music they have been dancing is
none other than the devil himself. Traditional "death watches," in
which the mourners danced the night away in the church's grave-
yard, presented another opportunity for the devil to snatch up an
errant soul.

In fact, Satan, the purported leader of the illicit dance, resembles no one so much as Dionysus, who, like his manifestation as
Pan, was sometimes portrayed with horns and tail, and his companion satyrs. As Steven Lonsdale writes:

> Like the satyr, the Devil is a rakishly handsome man with at least
> one cloven hoof, a long tail, horns or goat's ears. Both are master
> musicians—the satyr plays the lyre or pipes, the Devil the violin.
> Both scamper in dance-like movements of the goat, performing
> caprioles. In theatrical embodiment Satan and the satyr again coin-
> cide. The Devil, dressed in a furry skin, not unlike the satyrs, per-
> formed wild antics, pantomimes and dances akin to those enacted
> by the chorus in the Greek satyr play. The dramatic effect was one
> and the same.[5]

By the thirteenth century, the condemnations of dancing had
grown in volume and intensity. The Lateran Council of 1215 instituted a new means of social control—the requirement of an annual
confession of one's sins to a priest—and one of the sins was dancing, and certainly dancing of the "lascivious" sort. "Immoderate" or
"lascivious" dancing was again listed as a confessable sin in an important *summa*, or directory of sins, promulgated in 1317. For the
most part, though, the Church aimed its condemnations not at
dancing in general but at dancing *within churches* or their immediate

physical environs. E. Louis Backman, a historian of dance in the Christian Church, reports:

> Shortly before 1208 the Bishop of Paris forbade dancing in churches, churchyards, and processions . . . In 1206 the Synod of Cahors threatened with excommunication those who danced inside or in front of churches . . . The Council of Trier in 1227 forbade three-step and ring-dances and other worldly games in churchyards and churches . . . A council of Buda, in Hungary, in 1279 exhorted the priests to prevent dancing in churchyards and churches . . . In Liège it was only dances in churches, porches and churchyards that were forbidden . . . The Council of Würzburg in 1298 attacked these dances expressly, threatening heavy punishment and describing them as grievous sin.[6]

In their condemnations, Church officials sometimes described dancing—meaning especially dancing in churches or their vicinities—as a pagan custom, and this is how many medievalists have interpreted it too: Christian churches were often intentionally erected on the sites of preexisting pagan temples, so it was within them that people naturally sought to reenact their ancient rites. Thus the war on dance could be interpreted as a continuation of the Church's war on pre-Christian folk traditions. But European pre-Christian traditions must have been extremely diverse—how did so many of them manage to culminate in an apparently widespread and uniform habit of dancing in churches? And if the lay public was so bent on performing its "pagan" dances, why not avoid ecclesiastical censure by doing so on secular turf?

The most likely explanation is that, despite the volume and duration of official condemnations, church dancing was in fact a long-standing Christian custom. We have already seen the evidence for liturgical dancing in the early Church, and there is far sturdier evidence of dancing within or around medieval churches. For example, a twelfth-century traveler in Wales described ecstatic dancing on St. Eluned's Day:

You can see young men and maidens, some in the church itself, some in the churchyard and others in the dance which wends its way round the graves. They sing traditional songs, all of a sudden they collapse on the ground, and then those who, until now, have followed their leader peacefully as if in a trance, leap up in the air as if seized by frenzy.[7]

In fact, there is ample evidence that priests themselves joined in or even led medieval church dancing. In the twelfth century, the rector of the University of Paris related that there were some churches in which bishops and even archbishops on certain occasions played games with their parishioners and danced openly. In other places, we learn that it was customary for deacons to dance on St. Stephen's Day, priests on St. John's Day, and choirboys on Innocents' Day.[8] In Limoges, the priests performed an annual ring-dance in the choir of the church. In some bishoprics, a new priest was expected to enliven his first mass by performing a sacral dance.[9] According to the medievalist Penelope Doob, the custom of dancing in churches was firmly enough engrained to be inscribed into the very architecture of medieval Catholicism. She offers evidence that labyrinths built into the pavements of church naves—a common feature of twelfth- and thirteenth-century French and Italian church architecture—were designed to serve as aids to a winding, circular dance performed by priests at Easter: "Labyrinth and dance together . . . constitute a celebratory dance performed by religious [i.e., priests and nuns] . . . a dance that incidentally imitates and invokes cosmic order and eternal bliss."[10]

Were there perhaps very different kinds of dances going on in the churches—decorous ones performed by clerics versus "indecent" ones indulged in by the laity? Possibly, but there is reason to believe that the clerics themselves were not always sober and restrained. Church discipline over its own priests was weak and unreliable; many lived openly with their mistresses, few were thoroughly literate in the official Church language, Latin. Priests were sometimes criticized not only for dancing in cathedrals but for certain unseemly activities involving choirboys and women that often accompanied it. Until late in the fourteenth century, newly inducted monks and nuns danced when they took their vows—an activity that was finally prohibited on account of the "wild behaviour" that ensued. So it is not really possible, Backman admitted, to clearly distinguish medieval "sacred" and "popular" forms of dancing.

But if dancing in churches was a venerable Christian tradition, why did so many powerful elements in the Church oppose it, or come to oppose it, in the thirteenth century? One motivation was probably a fear of the disorder that could be unleashed if whole congregations were moved to get up and engage in vigorous motion. When Church authorities in Wells, in England, banned dances and games from their cathedral in 1338, they cited the damage to church property, which suggests that dancing within churches was not a reliably decorous affair. And there was good reason for the Church to be fearful of the laity, especially its low-income majority: Christian doctrine upheld the virtues of poverty, but the late medieval Church had itself become a huge concentration of wealth, in the form of farmlands, monasteries and convents, as well as the visible luxury enjoyed by ecclesiastical higher-ups. Better, given this inherent paradox in medieval Christianity, for the laity to be kept as immobile as possible, at least in church.

Furthermore, the Church was determined to maintain its monopoly over human access to the divine. If religious dancing became ecstatic dancing—and the stories of dancers being "possessed" by the devil suggest that it sometimes may have—then ordinary people might get the idea that they could approach the deity on their own (as did, for example, the ancient worshippers of Dionysus) without the mediation of Catholic officialdom. Certainly the Church has a long history of suppressing enthusiasm, in the ancient Greek sense of being filled with, or possessed by, the deity. Consider the Church's vacillating attitude toward the flagellation fad that swept through the Italian and German lower classes in the thirteenth and fourteenth centuries. At first Church officials encouraged self-flagellation as a form of public penance, but as the movement grew it took on ecstatic—and often anticlerical— overtones. The flagellants moved in large groups from town to town, beating themselves in a rhythm set by religious songs sung, daringly enough, in the vernacular, and perhaps achieving—if only as an escape from the physical pain—altered states of conscious- ness. In 1349, a papal bull outlawed the flagellant movement, which had achieved the size and militancy of an insurrection.[11]

The most flamboyant form of what might be called "ecstatic dissent," however, was the dance manias that rocked parts of north- ern Europe in the thirteenth and fourteenth centuries and Italy a century later. The first outbreak sounds like another cautionary tale about the perils of dancing: In Utrecht in the summer of 1278, two hundred people started dancing on the bridge over the Mosel and would not stop until it collapsed, at which point all the dancers drowned.[12] A hundred years later, in the wake of the Black Death, a much larger outbreak of dance mania again struck Germany and spilled out into Belgium: "Peasants left their plows, mechanics their workshops, house-wives their domestic duties, to join the wild rev- els." Arriving in Aix-la-Chapelle (now the German town of Aachen), "they formed circles hand in hand, and appearing to have lost all control over their senses, continued dancing, regardless of the by-standers, for hours together in wild delirium, until they fell to the ground in a state of exhaustion."[13] We have, unfortunately, no testimonies from the dancers themselves, but contemporary ob- servers saw them in a condition ethnographers would now describe as a *possession trance*.

> While dancing they neither saw nor heard, being insensible to ex-
> ternal impressions [with the exception, one might guess, of the mu-
> sic they danced to] . . . but were haunted by visions, their fancies
> conjuring up spirits whose names they shrieked out . . . Others,
> during the paroxysm, saw the heavens open and the Saviour en-
> throned with the Virgin Mary.[14]

Hence the Church authorities' worry that the "manias" represented a new form of heresy: Nothing is more threatening to a hierarchical religion than the possibility of ordinary laypeople's finding their own way into the presence of the gods.

The dance manias of the late Middle Ages have fascinated scholars ever since, most of whom have inclined toward medical explanations of this baffling and sometimes self-destructive behavior. J. C. Hecker, the nineteenth-century physician who chronicled the dancing manias, proposed that the dancers were inspired by some "inward morbid condition which was transferred from the sensorium to the nerves of motion,"[15] and the search for an exact physical diagnosis has continued into the present time. A 1997 article, for example, describes the "Dancing Plague" as "a public health conundrum," the "etiology" of which remains a mystery.[16] In Italy, the dancing manias that broke out in the fifteenth through seventeenth centuries were often blamed on the bite of the tarantula, although the same kind of dance (called the tarantella, after the spider) was also believed to *prevent* the spider's bite and subsequent illness. Another favorite explanation is ergot poisoning caused by a fungus that grew on rye, a common grain in the German sites of dancing mania. But rye does not grow in Italy, nor do tarantulas menace Germans, and neither of these suspected agents of the "plague"— ergot or spider poison—has since been found to induce anything resembling dancing mania.

There is another reason to rule any form of toxin, whether ingested by or injected into the "victims" of dancing mania: The manias were contagious and could be spread by visual contact alone. Bystanders might first watch in amazement and then, overcome by the music provided by the bands of musicians who traveled with the dancers, find themselves swept up by the dance as well. As Hecker, still clinging to a disease model, put it, "Inquisitive females [in Italy] joined the throng and caught the disease, not indeed from the poison of the spider, but from the mental poison which they eagerly received through the eye."[17] At one point, eleven hundred people danced simultaneously in the city of Metz, utterly resistant to the priests' attempts to exorcise whatever demons were driving them. All this is reminiscent of the Dionysian revels described by Euripides: a contagious mania, pulling people away from their normal occupations, and indifferent to the disapproval of authorities. But in the medieval dancing manias, we can also discern faint political overtones, perhaps even a half-conscious form of dissent. It was the poor who were most likely to be stricken, and they often experienced their affliction as a cure for what Hecker describes as "a distressing uneasiness," marked by dejection and anxiety, or what we would now call depression. Moreover, the dancers often turned violently against the priests who tried to drive out the demons: "The possessed assembling in multitudes, frequently poured forth imprecations against them, and menaced their destruction."[18]

In at least one place—Italy—a public festivity seems to have been created as a way of institutionalizing and hence, to a degree, controlling dance manias. There, as Hecker reports, the mania associated with the tarantella "gradually became established as a regular festival of the populace, which was anticipated with impatient delight."[19] In other parts of Europe, the dance manias no doubt underscored to Church authorities that people, especially people hard-pressed by poverty and terrorized by plague, were going to seek relief in ecstatic rites, whether these rites were sanctioned by the Church or not. Having such rites take place inside churches was, as we have just seen, a decreasingly attractive option. Catholicism refused to embrace the kinds of ecstatic behavior that were the hallmark of so many ancient and indigenous religions; it could only tolerate them as a kind of sideshow.

Carnival Comes Together

Carnival, of course, involves much more than dancing. All sorts of things, ranging from the staid and pious to the thoroughly riotous, went on at a late medieval festival. The Church's direct contribution to the entertainment included a special mass and often a procession through town, which might be a huge affair including the local secular authorities (nobles and town council members) as well as contingents from the different guilds (tanners, coopers, plasterers, hosiers, butchers, and so forth). In addition, the Church might encourage or at least approve performances of dramas on religious themes, starring local people, like the German passion plays that have survived, in a few cases, right up to the present.

But the spectacles offered or sanctioned by the Church were probably the least of the attractions; laypeople creatively enriched the holiday experience with their own, often less edifying, rituals. In addition to the obligatory feasting, drinking, and dancing, there would be games and sports (bowling, handball, archery contests, darts, wrestling) as well as ritual forms of cruelty to animals, possibly rooted in ancient traditions of animal sacrifice (bear baiting, for example). More striking, from a modern point of view, were the ritual activities aimed at dissolving the normal social boundaries of class and gender. There would very likely be ribald humor enacted by a man dressed up as a "king of fools" or "lord of misrule" and aimed at mocking real kings and other authorities. People costumed as nuns and priests might engage in obscene parodies. As in some ancient Dionysian rites, cross-dressing was routine. The historian Natalie Zemon Davis reports that

> in sections of Germany and Austria, at carnival time, male runners, half of them dressed as women, jumped and leaped through the streets. In France it was on Saint Stephen's Day or New Year's Day that men dressed as wild beasts or as women and danced in public . . . The saturnalian Feast of Fools involved young clerics and laymen, some of them disguised as women, who made wanton and loose gestures.[20]

Whatever social category you had been boxed into—male or female, rich or poor—carnival was a chance to escape from it.

No aspect of carnival has attracted more scholarly attention than the tradition of mocking the powerful, since these customs were in some sense "political," or at least suggestive of underlying discontent. The use of public festivities as an occasion to send up the local secular and ecclesiastical authorities was by no means confined to late medieval Europe. The ancient Israelis had celebrated Purim with masking, drunkenness, and rituals ridiculing their rabbis; the Romans had their Saturnalia. Rituals of mockery were also indigenous to many parts of Africa, with a Dutch traveler, for example, describing an early-eighteenth-century carnival celebrated along the coast of Guinea as

> a Feast of eight days accompanied with all manner of Singing, Skipping, Dancing, Mirth, and Jollity; in which time a perfect lampooning liberty is allowed, and Scandal so highly exalted, that they may freely say of all Faults, Villainies, and Frauds of their Superiors, as well as Inferiours without punishment so much as the least interruption.[21]

In our own time, too, festivals miming class—or gender—struggle persist in traditional societies. Ecuadorian agricultural laborers celebrate a festival in which they dress up as and engage in parodies of their bosses. At the Holi festival in the Indian village of Kishan Garhi, women attack men, untouchables harass Brahmins, and even the resident American ethnographer might be forced to "dance in the streets, fluting like Lord Krishna, with a garland of old shoes around his neck."[22] In chapter 8, we will come across similar festivities—among African slaves in the Americas, for example—that also contained the latent threat of rebellion. The widespread occurrence of mocking rituals would almost suggest some human, or at least plebeian, instinct to playfully overthrow the existing order—whether as a way of harmlessly letting off steam or, at some level of consciousness, rehearsing for the real thing.

Many of the mocking rituals associated with European carnival centered on a king of fools, a costumed character who probably first appeared in the Church-sanctioned Feast of Fools. If anything illustrates the ambivalence of the Church toward festive behavior, it was this event, which was initiated by the lower-level clergy—deacons, subdeacons, and priests—who comprised the Church's internal lower class. This feast, described by Chambers as "largely an ebullition of the natural lout beneath the cassock," originally took place inside churches between Christmas and New Year's. The participating clergy dressed absurdly—in women's clothes or their own clothes worn inside out—and performed a noisy burlesque of the mass, with sausages replacing the priest's censer, or with "stinking smoke from the soles of old shoes" instead of incense, and "wanton songs" and gibberish substituting for the usual Latin incantations.[23] As one disapproving contemporary described the scene: "They run and leap through the church, without a blush at their own shame. Finally they drive about the town . . . and rouse the laughter of their fellows and the bystanders in infamous performances, with indecent gestures and verses scurrilous and unchaste."[24]

Ecclesiastical higher-ups were not amused and tried, in fits and starts, to stamp out the Feast of Fools. In 1207 Pope Innocent III ordered Polish churches to discontinue the rite, and in 1400 the rector of the University of Paris tried to ban it, complaining that the indecencies involved would "shame a kitchen or a tavern."[25] In 1436, the town council of Basle allowed the Feast of Fools, but only if it was conducted without irreverence. Apparently a reverent Feast of Fools was not possible, since Basle forbade the feast in 1439—only to permit it again four years later, on the condition that it be celebrated *outside* the church. In Sens, in 1444, local Church authorities contented themselves with limiting the number of buckets of water that could be poured over the king of fools during the rite—to three—and stipulating that the event be moved outside the church.

Church authorities often tried to "divert the energies of the revellers" from the Feast of Fools to the more uplifting spectacle of the ecclesiastical plays.[26] But these too had a tendency to get out of hand. As early as the twelfth century, Chambers reports there were complaints that the dramas were becoming too worldly and encouraging "license, buffoonery, and quarreling." Productions of religious plays easily descended into "shameless revel[s],"[27] no doubt abetted by the huge quantities of beer some towns budgeted for these occasions and even for the plays' rehearsals. Disorder was so common that the Church offered indulgences for attendance at plays, but only on condition that one did not engage in lewd or disorderly behavior at them, however that may have been defined. Even the Corpus Christi feasts honoring Christ's body had become, by the fourteenth century, an occasion for rioting.

Confronted with so much unruly behavior, sometimes at events once approved or initiated by clerics themselves, Church officials took the same approach they had taken with dancing: They sought again and again to expel the offending activities from their immediate property. The Feast of Fools, as we have just seen, was increasingly driven outdoors. Religious dramas followed it, many of them being abandoned by the Church and largely "secularized" in the thirteenth century. In England, the fund-raising festivities known as church ales were banned from Church property in the mid-thirteenth century. Corpus Christi processions came increasingly under secular control in the fifteenth century. The festivities that once added color and laughter to the Church usually proved to be more than it could handle.

The gradual expulsion of dancing, sports, drama, and comedy from the churches created a world of regularly scheduled festivity that is almost beyond our imagining today. The Church calendar featured dozens of holy days—including Epiphany, Ascension, Pentecost, and Corpus Christi, as well as the more familiar Easter and Christmas—on which all work was forbidden, and on most of which vigorous celebration was tolerated. In fifteenth-century France, for example, one out of every four days of the year was an official holiday of some sort, usually dedicated to a mix of religious ceremonies and more or less unsanctioned carryings-on. Weddings, wakes, and other gatherings furnished additional opportunities for conviviality and carousing. Then there were the various local ceremonial occasions, such as the day honoring a village's patron saint or the anniversary of a church's founding. In the north of France in the sixteenth century, the celebrations commemorating a local church's founding could last for a full eight days. So, despite the reputation of what are commonly called "the Middle Ages" as a time of misery and fear, the period from the thirteenth to the fifteenth century can be seen—at least in comparison to the puritanical times that followed—as one long outdoor party, punctuated by bouts of hard labor. As the British historian E. P. Thompson wrote:

> Many weeks of heavy labour and scanty diet were compensated for by the expectation (or reminiscence) of these occasions, when food and drink were abundant, courtship and every kind of social intercourse flourished, and the hardship of life was forgotten . . . These occasions were, in an important sense, what men and women lived for.[28]

The Sacred Versus the Profane

The festivities that crowded the late medieval calendar can be understood as the fragments of what might have been a more joyous and participatory religion. People once danced, drank, feasted, and performed dramas and burlesques within their churches; now they did so outside those churches in the festivities that still clung to, and surrounded, each holy day. Scholars often mark the transition with a change in terminology—using the word *ritual* for events held in the context of religious observance and the lighter-weight term *festivity* for those outside of it.

Inevitably, something was lost in the transition from ecstatic ritual to secularized festivities—something we might call meaning or transcendent insight. In ancient Dionysian forms of worship the moment of maximum "madness" and revelry was also the sacred climax of the rite, at which the individual achieved communion with the divinity and a glimpse of personal immortality. Medieval Christianity, in contrast, offered "communion" in the form of a morsel of bread and sip of wine soberly consumed at the altar—and usually saw only devilry in the festivities that followed. True, the entire late medieval calendar of festivities was to some degree sanctioned by the Church, but the uplifting religious experience, if any, was supposed to be found within the Church-controlled rites of mass and procession, not within the drinking and dancing. While ancient worshippers of Dionysus expected the god to manifest himself when the music reached an irresistible tempo and the wine was flowing freely, medieval Christians could only hope that God, or at least his earthly representatives, was looking the other way when the flutes and drums came out and the tankards were passed around.

The result of the Church's distancing itself from the festivities that marked its own holidays was a certain "secularization" of communal pleasure. After the festival's official religious rites—the mass, the procession, the various blessings and public prayers—were completed, the rest of the day's (or week's) activities lay at least in part outside the Church's spiritual framework and moral jurisdiction. On the one hand, this relative secularization may help account for the uglier side of the European carnival tradition. Without a built-in religious climax to the celebrations—the achievement, for example, of a trancelike state of unity with the divinity—they readily spilled over into brawling and insensate drunkenness. The Jews in particular, as Christian Europe's perennial scapegoats, knew better than to venture out when the gentiles were having fun. Shakespeare's Shylock warned his daughter:

What, are there masques? Hear you me Jessica:
Lock up my doors, and when you hear the drum
And the vile squealing of the wry-necked fife,
Clamber not you up to the casements then,
Nor thrust your head into the public street
To gaze on Christian fools with varnish'd faces.[29]

But if secularization drained festivities of moral content and ecstatic insight, it also gave people ownership of and control over them. Great passion and energy went into the planning of festivities, with special organizations, like the French confraternities of young men, dedicated entirely to preparations year-round. There were constant minor conflicts to resolve—between secular and religious authorities, peasant leagues and urban guilds—over the form and nature of festivities. And sometimes the revelers singled out for ridicule the very authorities who declaimed against the festivities and threatened to stamp them out. In 1558, for example—admittedly, well past the Middle Ages—the bishop of Fréjus's attempt to suppress the local Feast of Fools led to a riot and storming of his palace. Festivity—like bread or freedom—can be a social good worth fighting for.

Finally, with secularization, there had to be a realization that festivity, even when it occurred on religious holidays, was ultimately a product of human agency. Ancient Dionysian revelers and Christian glossolaliacs believed that their moments of ecstasy were the gifts of a deity. But when the church doors closed shut on festivity in the late Middle Ages, the revelers must have understood that whatever joys they found were of their own, entirely human, creation. Huge amounts of effort and expense went into a successful celebration: Costumes had to be sewed, dance steps and dramas rehearsed, sets built, special pastries and meats prepared. Pleasures crafted with so much creativity and forethought—pleasures that, moreover, were often barely tolerated by the ecclesiastical establishment—can hardly be said to come from God. In the secularized festivities of the late Middle Ages, people could discover the truth of Mikhail Bakhtin's great insight: that carnival is something people create and generate *for themselves*. Or, as Goethe wrote, carnival "is a festival that really is not given to the people, but one the people give themselves."[30]

5

Killing Carnival:
Reformation and Repression

At some point, in town after town throughout the northern Christian world, the music stops. Carnival costumes are put away or sold; dramas that once engaged a town's entire population are canceled; festive rituals are forgotten or preserved only in tame and truncated form. The ecstatic possibility, which had first been driven from the sacred precincts of the church, was now harried from the streets and public squares.

The suppression of traditional festivities, occurring largely in the sixteenth through the nineteenth centuries, took many forms. Sometimes it came swiftly and absolutely, when, for example, a town council suddenly broke with tradition by refusing to grant a permit for the celebrations or a church denied the use of its churchyard. Or the change might come slowly, with authorities first limiting festivities to Sundays, then, in a classic catch-22, prohibiting all recreations and sports on the Sabbath. In other places the festivities were attacked in a piecemeal fashion: Some German towns banned masking in the late fifteenth century;[1] in mid-sixteenth-century Béarn, the queen issued ordinances outlawing singing and feasting.[2] Dancing, masking, reveling in the streets—the ingredients of carnival, or festivities in general, could be outlawed one by one.

Church and state might act separately or together in suppressing festivities; in one French diocese, the local monsignor, finding himself "surrounded by dancers, cat-called by masked men," obtained from the king six sealed letters prohibiting the revelry.[3] In sixteenth-century Lyon, local church authorities disbanded the confraternities traditionally responsible for organizing festivities, replacing them with pious groups dedicated to organizing prayer vigils.[4] Often the attempts at suppression were more farcical than solemn. In one late-seventeenth-century English parish, a preacher denounced a newly erected maypole—the traditional signal for revelry. His wife went further and cut it down at night. Some youths put up another one, but as local authorities smugly observed, it was "an ugly thing . . . rough and crooked."[5] Other enemies of carnival were at first even less successful. "I could not suppress these Bacchanals," wrote the Reverend John William de la Flechere of the Shropshire Wakes, "the impotent dyke I opposed only made the torrent swell and foam."[6]

The wave of repression—or, as the instigators saw it, "reform"—extended from Scotland south to parts of Italy and eastward to Russia and Ukraine, sweeping through both town and countryside. It targeted not only the traditional festivities held on saints' days and the holy periods surrounding Christmas, Lent, and Easter, but almost every possible occasion for revelry and play. Traveling troupes of actors and musicians began to find themselves unwelcome in the towns, driven off or bribed by local authorities to go away. Church ales, festivities that had been used to raise money for English parishes, were denounced and often banned outright, along with the numerous fairs that served as festive gatherings as well as sites for commerce. Sports of every kind came under attack: bull running, bear baiting, boxing, wrestling, football. A 1608 order prohibiting football in Manchester speaks, for example, of the harm done by a "company of lewd and disordered persons usinge that unlawfulle exercise of playing with a footbale in ye streets."[7] The crackdown even extended to informal, small-scale fun, as in the English town of Westbury-on-Severn, where a group of young people who fell to "dancing, quaffing and rioting" on their way home from church found themselves facing charges for drunkenness, fornication, and various forms of impiety.[8]

There were all sorts of regional and temporal variations on the theme of repression. The Catholic south of Europe held on to its festivities more tightly than the north, though these were often reduced to mere processions of holy images and relics through the streets. In Germany, Protestantism rode in, as we shall see, on a wave of carnivalesque revolts, only to take a hard stance against public festivity or disorder in any form. England seesawed between repression and permissiveness for decades, with the Calvinists vigorously banning festivities and the Stuart kings—perhaps less out of fondness for the festivities than hostility to the Calvinists—repeatedly seeking to restore them. But everywhere the general drift led inexorably away from the medieval tradition of carnival. As Peter Stallybrass and Allon White summarize the change:

> In the long-term history from the 17th to the 20th century . . . there were literally thousands of acts of legislation introduced which attempted to eliminate carnival and popular festivity from European life . . . Everywhere, against the periodic revival of local festivity and occasional reversals, a fundamental ritual order of western culture came under attack—its feasting, violence, processions, fairs, wakes, rowdy spectacle and outrageous clamour were subject to surveillance and repressive control.[9]

The loss, to ordinary people, of so many recreations and festivities is incalculable; and we, who live in a culture almost devoid of opportunities either to "lose ourselves" in communal festivities or to distinguish ourselves in any arena outside of work, are in no position to fathom it. One young Frenchman told his reforming priest that he "could not promise to renounce dancing and abstain from the festivals . . . It would be impossible not to mingle and rejoice with his friends and relations."[10] A Buckinghamshire resident described the emptying of the common after the suppression of Sunday recreations as a depressing loss. While formerly the common "presented a lively and pleasing aspect, dotted with parties of cheerful lookers-on," it was now "left lonely and empty of loungers," leaving the men and boys with nothing to do but hang out in the pubs and drink.[11] To people who had few alternative forms of distraction—no books, movies, or television—it must have seemed as if pleasure itself had been declared illegal.

Why did it happen—this wave of repression, this apparent self-punishment undertaken by a huge swath of the world's population? If anything would have mystified the "converted Hottentot" whom nineteenth-century preachers liked to invoke in their diatribes against carnival, it would not be the persistence of a few festivities, kept alive largely as tourist attractions, but the disappearance, over the centuries, of so many more. The explanation offered by Max Weber in the late nineteenth century and richly expanded on by the social historians E. P. Thompson and Christopher Hill in the late twentieth is that the repression of festivities was, in a sense, a by-product of the emergence of capitalism. The middle classes had to learn to calculate, save, and "defer gratification"; the lower classes had to be transformed into a disciplined, factory-ready, working class—meaning far fewer holidays and the new necessity of showing up for work sober and on time, six days a week. Peasants had worked hard too, of course, but in seasonally determined bursts; the new industrialism required ceaseless labor, all year round.

There was money to be made from reliable, well-regulated, human labor—in the burgeoning English textile industry, for example—and to the men who stood to make it, the old recreations and pastimes represented the waste of a valuable resource. In France, economic concerns drove the administration of Louis XIV to reduce the number of saints' days from several hundred a year to ninety-two. In late-seventeenth-century England, an economist put forth the alarming estimate that each holiday cost the nation fifty thousand pounds, largely in lost labor time.[12] From an emerging capitalist perspective—relentlessly focused on the bottom line—festivities had no redeeming qualities. They were just another bad habit the lower classes would have to be weaned from, like the English workers' observance of "St. Monday" as a day to continue, or recuperate from, the weekend's fun.

Protestantism—especially in its ascetic, Calvinist form—played a major role in convincing large numbers of people not only that unremitting, disciplined labor was good for their souls, but that festivities were positively sinful, along with mere idleness. In part, its appeal was probably similar to that of much evangelical Christianity today; it offered people the self-discipline demanded by a harsher economic order: Curb your drinking, learn to rise before the sun, work until dark, and be grateful for whatever you're paid. In addition, ambitious middle-class people were increasingly repelled by the profligacy of the Catholic Church and the old feudal nobility—not only the lavish cathedrals and wealthy monasteries but the seasonal round of festive blowouts. Protestantism, serving as the ideological handmaiden of the new capitalism, "descended like a frost on the life of 'Merrie Old England,'" as Weber put it, destroying in its icy grip the usual Christmas festivities, the maypole, the games, and all traditional forms of group pleasure.[13]

But this account downplays the importance of festivities as a point of contention in their own right, quite apart from their perceived economic effects. Without question, industrial capitalism and Protestantism played a central role in motivating the destruction of carnival and other festivities. There was another factor, though, usually neglected in the economic-based accounts: To elites, the problem with festivities lay not only in what people were *not* doing—that is, working—but in what they *were* doing, that is, in the nature of the revelry itself. In the sixteenth century, European authorities (secular and ecclesiastical, Catholic as well as Protestant) were coming to fear and disdain the public festivities that they themselves had once played starring roles in—to see them as vulgar and, more important, dangerous.

Dangerous Dances

We saw in the previous chapter how medieval carnivals mocked the authorities with "rituals of inversion" that might feature a king of fools, obscene parodies of the mass, or dancers costumed as priests and nuns. To historians, such rude mockery highlights the political ambiguity of carnival: Did it serve as a "fundamental challenge to the status quo"[14] or as a mere safety valve for discontent—in Terry Eagleton's words, "a contained popular blow-off as disturbing and relatively ineffectual as a revolutionary work of art?"[15] Supporters of the "safety-valve" interpretation often quote a circular letter promulgated by the Paris School of Theology in 1444, arguing that festivities are necessary

> so that foolishness, which is our second nature and seems to be inherent in man, might freely spend itself at least once a year. Wine barrels burst if from time to time we do not open them and let in some air. All of us men are barrels poorly put together, which would burst from the wine of wisdom, if this wine remains in a state of constant fermentation of piousness and fear of God. We must give it air in order not to let it spoil.[16]

Similar sentiments can be found throughout the history of European carnival and carnival-like festivities. A writer in an English magazine opined in 1738 that "dancing on the Green at Wakes and merry Tides should not only be indulg'd but incourag'd: and little Prizes being allotted for the Maids who excel in a Jig or Hornpipe, would make them return to their daily Labour with a light Heart and grateful Obedience to their Superiors."[17]

There is probably no general and universal answer, though, to the question of whether carnival functioned as a school for revolution or as a means of social control. We do not know how the people themselves construed their festive mockeries of kings and priests, for example—as good-natured mischief or as a kind of threat. But it is safe to say that carnival increasingly gains a political edge, in the modern sense, *after* the Middle Ages, from the sixteenth century on, in what is known today as the early modern period. It is then that large numbers of people begin to use the masks and noises of their traditional festivities as a cover for armed rebellion, and to see, perhaps for the first time, the possibility of inverting hierarchy on a permanent basis, and not just for a few festive hours. In the French antitax revolt of 1548, for example, the rebellious peasant militias "were recruited on the basis of parishes from the *monstres*, or feast-day processions."[18] At the St. Blaise's Day festivity in 1579 in Romans, also in France, the lower-class people chose as their "carnival king" one of their actual political leaders. "They elected a chief not so much for the occasion," a conservative contemporary reported in alarm, ". . . as to embrace a cause which they called the rest and relief of the people."[19] It may also be relevant that in early-sixteenth-century England, the legendary outlaw philanthropist Robin Hood—or at least figures representing him—began to play a starring role as lord of misrule in annual summer festivities.[20]

The great social disruptions of the sixteenth century added to the danger of traditional festivities. The population was rising throughout Europe, forcing individuals off the land and into fast-growing, chaotic cities. For the fortunate, this was the Renaissance, a time when the artist, scholar, craftsperson, or adventurer could make his (or, very rarely, her) own way in the world, unconstrained by feudal obligations. But for every Erasmus or da Vinci, there were thousands of uprooted peasants for whom the relative freedom of the sixteenth century meant only vagrancy and destitution in a world where prices were rising and wages falling. Newly displaced people wandered in bands throughout the countryside, begging and stealing; they dispersed into the cities, where they formed a new urban underclass of prostitutes, laborers, and criminals. Imagine the violence that might have ensued if the London of 1600, with its approximately 250,000 disparate and often desperate residents, declared a several-day-long, citywide carnival, in which pickpockets and wealthy merchants were to revel together in the streets.

From the sixteenth century on, the carnivalistic assault on authority seems to become less metaphorical and more physically menacing to the elites. In Udine, Italy, the pre-Lent carnival of 1511 turned into a riot that ended with the sacking and looting of more than twenty palaces and the murder of fifty nobles and their retainers.[21] Two years later, hundreds of peasants seized the occasion of some June festivities to march on the city of Berne and sack it.[22] During the Shrove Tuesday celebration in 1529, gangs of armed men overran the city of Basle.[23] In the most thoroughly documented carnival uprising of the period—at Romans in 1580—the insurgents announced their intentions by dancing aggressively with swords, brooms, and flails used for threshing wheat. "They held street dances through the town," a local notable, who was himself a target of the insurgency, wrote, ". . . and all these dances were to no other end than to announce that they wanted to kill everything."[24]

To what extent these carnival uprisings were spontaneous—fueled by alcohol and inspired by the fleeting excitement of the occasion—we cannot know, but some, like the revolt at Romans, were certainly planned in advance. Anyone with a mind for rebellion could see the advantages of the carnival setting, with its routine disorder, masks to conceal the perpetrators' faces, and enough beer or wine to confound the local constabulary. And if there was no convenient holiday in the offing, people again and again dressed up their rebellions in the trappings of carnival: masks, even full costumes, and almost always the music of bells, bagpipes, drums. It is no coincidence that the confraternities and "youth abbeys" responsible for organizing festivals in parts of rural France became bastions of sedition, or that peasant militias in the antitax revolt of 1548 were drawn from the groups of men who organized feast-day processions.

Similarly, the maypole, around which so many traditional French and English festivities revolved, became a signal of defiance and a call to action. Well into the eighteenth century, the political aspirations of the common people were expressed, as E. P. Thompson writes of England, in "a language of ribbons, of bonfires, of oaths and the refusal of oaths, of toasts, of seditious riddles and ancient prophecies, of oak leaves and of maypoles, of ballads with a political *double-entendre*, even of airs whistled in the streets."[25] In England, even football could provide an excuse for assembling and a cover for violence; in 1740, "a Mach of Futtball was Cried [announced] at Ketring of five Hundred Men of a side, but the design was to Pull Down Lady Betey Jesmaine's Mills."[26] "It is in fact striking," write Stallybrass and White, "how frequently violent social clashes apparently 'coincided' with carnival . . . to call it a 'coincidence' of social revolt and carnival is deeply misleading, for . . . it was only in the late 18th and early 19th centuries—and then only in certain areas—that one can reasonably talk of popular politics *dissociated* from the carnivalesque at all."[27]

Protestants and Guns

Without question, Protestantism was responsible for stiffening the spines of people like the minister's wife mentioned above, whose response to a maypole was to reach for an ax. But it is worth noting that Protestantism did not begin as a puritanical, anticarnival movement. In fact, it is probably better to speak of two Protestant Reformations: one led by Martin Luther in the early sixteenth century, and a second, far more puritanical one, led by John Calvin a few decades later. Luther's Reformation probably even appeared to many, at first, as a possible source of relief from the Catholic

Church's attacks on festivities, which seem to have been mounting to a crescendo on the very eve of the Reformation.

In Florence in the 1490s, for example, the crusading monk Girolamo Savonarola raged against worldly extravagance and folly in all forms, not least of them carnival, preaching that "boys should collect alms for the respectable poor, instead of mad pranks, throwing stones and making floats [for carnival.]"[28] In Germany, during the years when young Luther was quietly agonizing over his relationship to the pope and the deity, reforming priests were already inveighing against Church festivals, arguing that the attendant drinking, dancing, and gaming were "the ruin of the common people."[29] Of particular concern to early-sixteenth-century Catholic reformers was the mockery of religious ritual common to so many festivities. The late fifteenth century had seen a growing number of mandates against such parodies, as well as against people costuming themselves for carnival as priests and nuns.[30] One target for early-sixteenth-century Catholic "reform," for example, was the Strasbourgers' custom of *Roraffe*, in which a buffoon sang and clowned in the cathedral all through the Pentecost service.[31]

Luther did aim to abolish the "superstitious" worship of saints, which meant the end of saints' days and the festivities that had grown up around them. But he found nothing intrinsically evil in the traditional communal pleasures, stating in a sermon:

> Because it is the custom of the country, just like inviting guests, dressing up, eating, drinking, and making merry, I can't bring myself to condemn it, unless it gets out of hand, and so causes immoralities or excess. And even though sin has taken place in this way, it's not the fault of dancing alone. Provided they don't jump on the tables or dance in church . . . But so long as it's done decently, I respect the rites and customs of weddings . . . and *I* dance, anyway![32]

Luther even introduced a powerful new experience of community solidarity and uplift into the Christian service, in the form of hymn singing, many of the hymns being of his own composition, and to Christians accustomed to silence and passivity at the Catholic mass, this must have seemed an exceedingly lively innovation.

Like other popular insurgencies at the time, the early Protestant movement made good use of the carnival tradition. At the very beginning of the Reformation, when Luther publicly burned the papal bull condemning him, his supporters did not respond with prayer and hallelujahs; instead they paraded through the streets of Wittenberg accompanied by musicians and someone costumed as the pope, singing and laughing. The procession, the music, the mock pope—all this is traditional carnival fare; the difference being that at Wittenberg, the revelers were going well beyond parody. The historian Bob Scribner found evidence of twenty-three additional incidents in sixteenth-century Germany in which Protestants used carnivals and carnival themes to advance their cause. At scheduled carnivals throughout the century, Protestants (or perhaps I should say proto-Protestants, since the followers of Luther had not yet, in all these cases, developed an alternative Church) performed traditional carnival activities such as parodying Catholic ritual and offering lewd impersonations of monks and nuns. They also burned mock papal bulls, smashed statues, dragged paintings from churches and burned them, extorted food and drink from a monastery, even defecated on altars.

Sometimes the local secular authorities sought to control the anti-Catholic revelry, and sometimes they participated in it. Scribner describes carnival in Hildesheim in 1543, where, after the usual days and nights of dancing, iconoclasm, and reviling people dressed as the pope and other religious dignitaries and "the mayor led the entire crowd of reveling men, women and children to the cathedral. They were refused entrance to the church itself, but they led a dance through the cloisters and profaned the graves in the churchyard."[33] If Protestantism was supposed to be dour, no one knew that in the beginning. In Luther's Germany, Protestantism made its first appearance, in town after town, as the fulfillment of the populist threat to the Catholic Church that had been implicit in centuries of carnival revelry.

All too soon, Luther's Protestantism severed its connection with the tradition of carnivalesque revolt. When German peasants, inspired in part by Luther's teachings, rebelled in 1524—sometimes using carnivalesque props like masks[34]—a horrified Luther called for their extermination. Similarly, Scribner reports that even where they supported the Reformation, town magistrates were alarmed by carnival-based attacks on the Catholic Church, fearing, as one official put it, that these might "go beyond mere matters of religion."[35] In Basle, the Reformation had been ushered in by a carnival rebellion on Shrove Tuesday of 1529, with demands for the democratization of the town government as well as for the reform of religious ritual. But the political demands went unmet, and, in the Protestant order that followed, carnival itself was increasingly tamed and curtailed, leading one citizen to complain in 1568 of Protestantism itself as a devilish "new popedom": *"Der tüfel het uns mit den nüwen Bapsttum beschissen!"* (The devil has shat on us with a new papacy!)[36]

Calvin's version of Protestantism, of course, condemned all forms of festive behavior, including leisure activities of any kind. While Luther had danced, Calvin banned dancing, along with gambling, drinking, and sports. As Michael Walzer writes, Calvinism "obviously missed by some distance any transcendence of anxiety. It offered no sense of human freedom or brotherly love . . . It is not even unfair to suggest that [Calvin] sought to maintain a certain fundamental anxiety."[37] To the Calvinist, who spent his or her life in a lonely internal struggle to determine whether he or she was "saved," not only was pleasure in any form a distraction; it was the devil's snare.

But Protestantism, whether seen as a revolt against the old order or a new form of pacification, was only one factor affecting the fate of carnival in the sixteenth century. Another was the availability of firearms. The historian Emmanuel Le Roy Ladurie notes that "things had changed between 1566 and 1584. The Dauphinois [people of the southeastern French province the Dauphiné] had developed a taste for arms, or at least gotten into the habit of using them after more than ten years of civil war."[38] A primitive gun, the arquebus, began to make its appearance in peasant rebellions and— what were often overlapping events—carnivals and other festivities.[39] In sixteenth-century Romans, the archery contests that accompanied many festive occasions were replaced by contests with firearms; Jean Serve, the leader of the rebellion in Romans in 1580, bore the title "king of the Arquebus," apparently because of his markmanship.[40]

Throughout Europe, guns became a prominent feature of carnival: guns carried proudly by men processing through the streets, shaken at effigies of unpopular individuals, or fired in multigun salutes. For example, an English charivari or "skymmington"—a traditional festivity aimed at mocking, and sometimes threatening, some person or people—was conducted in 1618, according to a contemporary account, by "three or four hundred men, some like soldiers armed with pieces and other weapons," and reached an ear-shattering crescendo when "the gunners shot off their pieces, pipes and horns were sounded, together with lowbells and other smaller bells which the company had amongst them."[41] To the noble listening from his manor house or the cleric hidden away in his rectory, the sound of armed revelry must have been profoundly unnerving.

The French Revolution showed, if nothing else, what guns could do for the traditional carnivalesque revolt. Common people armed themselves—in the most famous case, by storming the Bastille to seize the guns stored within it. Less often noted is that they also "armed" themselves with carnival motifs that directly expressed their revolutionary aspirations. Although traditional festivities had been largely vitiated or expunged by the Church by the end of the eighteenth century, rural people were still in the habit of announcing their political intentions by setting up a maypole. Such maypoles served a political purpose, as a "call to riotous assembly, a sort of visual tocsin bell," the French historian Mona Ozouf writes, and might bear slogans such as "No more rents"[42] along with the traditional ribbons and flowers. The message was not lost on the feudal authorities, who often met the erection of maypoles with violence.[43]

Even as it was politicized, the maypole continued to play its traditional role as a signal for public festivity. There is "no doubt," according to Ozouf, of "the privileged link between the maypole and collective joy"[44]—or, we might add, between collective joy and spontaneous revolution from below. In Perigord in July 1791, according to a report drawn up by local revolutionary clubs, peasants attacked weathercocks and church pews—symbols of feudal and religious authority respectively—"both with some violence and in the effusion of their joy . . . they set up maypoles in the public squares, surrounding them with all the destructive signs of the feudal monarchy."[45]

Dancing, costuming, and other forms of festive behavior often accompanied these rural uprisings during the French Revolution, especially in parts of France that still retained some remnant of a carnival tradition. The carnival themes of mockery and inversion, which had amused and perhaps pacified the lower classes for centuries, now signified serious political intent: Pigs dressed up to resemble nobles, a monkey wearing a bishop's miter on its head, feudal insignia pulled through the streets by goats are among the festive jokes of the French Revolution. "We see women flogging saints' statues," Ozouf reports. "Priests' soutanes drop to reveal the dress of the sans-culottes; nuns dance the carmagnole. A cardinal and a whore walk on either side of the coffin of Despotism."[46] News of revolutionary victories was often greeted with firecrackers, drums, singing, and dancing in the streets. "They are like madmen who ought to be tied up, or rather like bacchantes," the mayor of Leguillac remarked of the local revolutionaries, while the seigneur de Montbrun observed with distaste that "they danced around like Hurons and Iroquois."[47]

The Withdrawal of the Upper Class

Well before the French Revolution, the first response of nervous elites—nobles and members of the emerging urban bourgeoisie—was simply to withdraw from public festivities into parallel festivities of their own. At least into the fifteenth century, they had participated as avidly as the peasants and urban workers, and the mixing of classes no doubt enhanced the drama and excitement of the occasion. Fifteenth-century Castilian festivals, for example, brought the local nobility, including contingents of knights costumed as Moors, together with lower-class revelers: "The music of trumpets, drums, and other musical instruments and the unpredictable behavior of fools and buffoons served as counterpoint to, and inversion of, the martial splendor of the knights."[48] Nor can it be said that the upper classes always behaved in a dignified manner, perhaps especially when their identities were concealed by masks. "Any account of Carnival," according to British medievalist Meg Twycross, "has to accommodate the facts that in Ferrara the Duke, in Rome the cardinals, and in France the King and his minions behaved in just as riotous a way as the temporarily liberated underclasses."[49]

In fact the class conflicts that went on at festive occasions were sometimes initiated by the elite participants, who might ride their horses into the crowds of townspeople or harass the local women. Mostly, though, members of the elite seem to have been thoroughly welcome; in fourteenth-century Holland, for example,

> a town increased its status in the eyes of neighboring towns when it succeeded in making the ruler take part in the town's festivities. By his presence the duke revealed his power and authority. He took part in the meals and dances; he listened sympathetically to reciters and the town's actors; he showed his generosity to all those and to the numerous minstrels and buffoons.[50]

To an extent the upper classes had always preferred to reserve some parts of the celebration for their own exclusive enjoyment. In late-fifteenth-century Castile, for example, where carnival served as a site for the festive mingling of the classes, the ruling noble family and its retinue actually moved back and forth during important feasts, enjoying the ribaldry of the public celebrations and then retiring for "more courtly forms of entertainment" in their private lodgings.[51] But a century later, the classes were in the process of separation. In France, Ladurie reports, the increasing use of festivities as an occasion for protest sometimes led communities to "organize two separate Carnivals, even two separate Maypoles, one for the poor and one for the rich," so as to diminish the possibility of violence.[52] In Romans, in 1580, the rich organized their own carnival, choosing as their symbols a more noble-seeming set of animals than those representing the peasants and workers; a partridge, for example, as opposed to the plebeians' hare. But in this case, the separation was ineffective. Fighting broke out between the classes, climaxing in the slaughter of the insurgent peasants and artisans by the nobles.

From the sixteenth century on, festivities served largely to drive a wedge between the classes.* In eighteenth-century prerevolutionary Nice, rich and poor partied together on important holidays until *"une certaine heure de la nuit,"* when it was customary for everyone to remove their masks—at which point the rich hastily retired for the night, presumably still safely incognito.[53] A more dramatic retreat took place in Germany, where, by the nineteenth century, the celebrations of local elites "increasingly took place at home or in private clubs."[54] And in eighteenth-century England, the novelist Henry Fielding observed that two entirely separate cultures had emerged.

---

*Some separation of the classes can be found in many kinds of festivities around the world. At carnival time in Rio de Janeiro in the late twentieth century, the upper classes were likely to leave the city for the quiet of the countryside. On the Swahili coast of Africa in the nineteenth century, major holidays were celebrated mostly by "persons of low status," while "powerful Arabs . . . generally stayed out of holiday rituals altogether, except as occasional patrons." (Glassman, p. 170.)

Whilst the people of fashion seized several places to their own use, such as courts, assemblies, operas, balls, &c., the people of no fashion . . . have been in constant possession of all hops, fairs, revels, &c . . . So far from looking on each other as brethren in the Christian language, they seem scarce to regard each other as of the same species.[55]

At least in the earlier part of the early modern period, the private festivities of elites had often been as uninhibited as the celebrations of the poor. The historian Edward Muir reports that the wedding parties of wealthy burghers often featured "clowns, musicians, acrobats, even prostitutes . . . the reciting of obscene poems and the wild dancing in which the men would swing young women about so lifting their skirts (underwear had not yet been invented)."[56] But by the late eighteenth century, in France, according to an anonymous bourgeois chronicler of life in Montpellier, traditional festivities were definitely déclassé, whether held indoors or out.

Such amusements have completely gone out of favor in this city and have given way to a concern for making money. Thus no more public *fêtes*, no more Perroquet archery contests or general merry-making. If any take place from time to time, it is only among the common people. *Les hônnetes gens* [the "better" class of people] do not take part.[57]

The historian Robert Darnton comments that the poor and working class "had all the fun," while the elite could only "parade about solemnly in *processions générales*."

Hell-raising had even gone out of wedding feasts, except in the "Third Estate" [the working class]. In the upper estates, one invited only the immediate family, not the whole neighborhood. There was no more drunkenness, no more brawling at table, no invasions from a rowdy counter-ceremony (*trouble-fête*) or bawdiness exploding from a charviari or cabaret.[58]

As another historian observes of England in the same period: "A solid barrier" had arisen "between the culture of gentility and the culture of the people."[59]

There was something besides fear driving the aristocrats and the rich merchants who aped them away from the public festivities, something more like contempt. The medieval nobleman who had treated his vassals to meat and drink on holidays, who had plunged into the dancing or even stripped to his waist to wrestle with the blacksmith, was a man secure in his social function and what he believed to be his innate superiority. He was a warrior and, along with his retinue of knights, the only protection the common people had from the incursions of other predatory nobles. But as guns replaced swords and mass armies replaced bands of mounted knights, the noble was deprived of his old military role and left emasculated in more ways than one. Power became more centralized, shifting to kings, who alone had the authority to tax huge populations and thus support armies numbering in the tens of thousands—and kings did not look kindly on the exercise of violence by their subordinates, even in the relatively innocuous form of dueling. The nobleman was now required, lest he plot against the king, to take up residence at the royal court for a certain number of months per year, where he was confined, more or less, to making small talk and otherwise amusing the royals. Once a warrior, he became a courtier.

With this reduction in status came a change in the aristocratic personality, away from spontaneity and self-assertion, toward guardedness and self-restraint. The old warrior way of life, according to the chronicler of this transformation, Norbert Elias, permitted the nobleman "extraordinary freedom in living out his feelings and passions, it allow[ed] savage joys, the uninhibited satisfaction of pleasure from women, or of hatred in destroying and tormenting anything hostile."[60] In the court of his superior, the king, the noble's swashbuckling ways would no longer do. Though seldom violent, Elias relates, life in this circle [the court] is in no way peaceful. Very many people are continuously dependent on each other. Competition for prestige and royal favour is intense . . . If the sword no longer plays so great a role as the means of decision, it is replaced by intrigue, conflicts in which careers and social success are contested with words. They demand and produce other qualities than did the armed struggles that had to be fought out with weapons in one's hand. Continuous reflection, foresight, and calculation, self-control, precise and articulate regulation of one's own effects, knowledge of the whole terrain, human and non-human, in which one acts, become more and more indispensable preconditions of social success.[61]

One way of charting the personality change required by court life is through the emergence of "manners." The old nobleman-as-warrior had no need of good manners, had such a concept even been clearly defined. Since his nobility inhered in his blood, whatever he did was by definition admirable, and late medieval guidebooks suggested that he did many things that would be judged, within a few centuries, as thoroughly disgusting. "Do not clean your teeth with your knife. Do not spit on or over the table . . . Do not let yourself go [fart or urinate?] at table . . . Do not clean your teeth with the tablecloth . . . Do not fall asleep at table."[62] These are, to the say the least, very minimal restrictions, suggesting a culture of far greater physical intimacy between individuals than anything we can comfortably imagine today. Medieval people ate together, "taking meat with their fingers from the same dish, wine from the same goblet," and still needed to be reminded, in the early sixteenth century, that "it is impolite to greet someone who is urinating or defecating"—in a corridor, for example, or on the sidewalk. What medieval culture lacked, according to Elias, was "the invisible wall of affects which seems now to rise between one human body and another, repelling and separating."[63]

It is in the tense, competitive setting of the early modern royal court that etiquette, in the form we know it, is forged, throwing up a barrier between individuals and at the same time, inevitably, between the classes. Court society is the first to adopt utensils for eating, along with individual plates to eat from, and chairs, rather than benches, to sit on. In this setting, urges that a medieval noble would have indulged without thinking—to belch or scratch or reach across the table—are carefully repressed; courtiers must learn to drink more moderately, to avoid jostling and elbowing one another. And it should be emphasized that the new concern to separate eating from excreting, and one human body from another, had nothing to do with hygiene: Bathing was still an infrequent, even—if indulged in too often—eccentric, practice; the knowledge that contact with others and their excreta can spread disease was still at least two centuries away. The notion of "personal space" and the horror of other people's bodily processes that set limits on human physical interaction in our own time arose, originally, out of social anxiety and distrust.

Courtiers have amusements too—in fact they have no other way to pass the time, since work, even of a scholarly or professional nature, is beneath them—but their amusements diverge radically, from the sixteenth century on, from those of the poor or even of aristocrats in an earlier time. Instead of the shouted boasts and jests that enlivened a medieval baron's table, there is "conversation," decorated with flowery circumlocutions and admired as a kind of art form. Courtiers still dance, but theirs is a new form of dancing, stately and restrained, and almost always performed indoors. Baldesar Castiglione, in his famous early-sixteenth-century advice book, councils the aspiring courtier to master the fashionable dances, but when performing a particularly challenging one in public, he should wear a mask lest he disgrace himself with a misstep.[64] Even when supposedly enjoying himself, the courtier never for a moment lets down his guard.

Increasingly, the aristocracy creates its own culture, featuring innovations like "classical" music and ballet—strained and, by plebeian standards, no doubt tedious entertainments to be consumed, ideally, in silence while sitting or standing still. By the same token, the exuberance and solidarity of traditional festivities begin to look—to the lord or lady of the court, as well as to the businessmen and professionals who aped the noble's manners—unseemly, vulgar, perhaps even revolting. As in the class and racial prejudices of our own time, contempt mixes easily with fear: The "vulgar" carnival participant was, in the eyes of his social betters, also a violent lout. To the wealthy, carnival could only evoke what the historian Stephen J. Greenblatt describes as "the great ruling class nightmare of the Renaissance: the marauding horde, the many-headed multitude, the insatiate, giddy, and murderous crowd."[65]

6

A Note on Puritanism and Military Reform

Almost two hundred years after the Protestant Reformation in Europe, something strikingly similar occurred in a very different setting. A Muslim scholar, Muhammad ibn Abd al-Wahhab, launched a crusade to reform and purify Arabian Islam, which had been corrupted, in his view, by such practices as the veneration of saints and shrines and ecstatic forms of worship involving dancing, singing, and chanting. Wahhab went about axing holy trees (much as English puritans had attacked maypoles), smashing shrines, and attempting to crush traditional ecstatic rituals. His view of religious practice was every bit as austere as John Calvin's: There were to be no decorations or music in the mosques, no route to salvation except through prayer and obedience to religious teaching, in the Islamic case, sharia law. And like Calvin, Wahhab and his followers aimed at the establishment of a theocratic state with strict control over individual behavior—no hashish, for example, no "sexual perversions" or female immodesty—a goal still pursued by his ideological descendants, the militant Islamists of our own time.

The parallel between the Protestant Reformation and the Wahhabi movement within Islam has been noted before. Samuel P.

Huntington, for example, writes that "both are reactions to the stag-nation and corruption of existing institutions; advocate a return to a purer and more demanding form of their religion; preach work, or-der, and discipline."[1] In the Islamic world, the role of Catholicism was played by Sufism—a current of Islam dating from the eighth or ninth century and offering a richly diverse, in some ways even florid, set of spiritual possibilities. Like Catholicism, Sufism had its intel-lectuals, mystics, and poets; like Catholicism, it was open to a prolif-eration of saints and popular festivities, some of which may have originated in pagan practices. In both the Islamic and Christian cases, the "reformers" claimed to be returning to the foundations of their religion—stripping away the gaudy excrescences, the sensory delights, the carnivals and color, and arresting the slide toward poly-theism as represented by the veneration of saints. The idea, in both cases, was to achieve a "purified" form of religion focused on the struggle for holiness within the individual soul.

What is baffling about this parallel is the apparent lack of any parallel conditions within the societies involved. The Protestant Reformation took place in a Europe already possessed of large cities and teetering on the verge of the industrial revolution. Wah-habism, in contrast, found its first converts in the central part of the Arabian Peninsula, a place still occupied by tribal nomads based around oasis settlements. Capitalism and industrialism, for all their alleged role in the Protestant Reformation, were at best distant ru-mors in the tiny town of Ad Dir'iyyah, where Wahhab made his base. And while sixteenth-century Europe was beginning to expand into Africa, Asia, and the Americas, eighteenth-century Arabia was a backwater within the Ottoman Empire, which was itself already in decline. Anyone looking for a "materialist" explanation of both Islamic and Protestant puritanism—that is, one based on concrete economic circumstances—can only throw up her hands in despair.

Possibly there were no common conditions underlying the two "reformations," Protestant and Islamic. After all, Wahhab was hardly the first puritanical reformer within Islam. The conflict between a cold and legalistic form of Islam, centered on sharia, and the more accessible Sufist tendency goes back many centuries. What distinguished Wahhabism from most earlier Islamic "reform" movements was the patronage of a tribal chief, Muhammad ibn Saud, who transformed it from a theological challenge into an armed campaign. One attraction of Wahhab's teachings to the Saudi leader was that they justified raids on neighboring tribes, which could be judged as "infidels" according to Wahhab's rigorous standards. Thus Wahhabism provided a loophole in the Muslim prohibition against attacking fellow Muslims: If they did not accept a purified Islam in the form of Wahhabism, they could be killed— or offered the opportunity to convert. According to one of the best-known historians of Saudi Arabia, "Wahhabism was an ideology of military expansion and raids from the outset,"[2] and it spread throughout the Arabian Peninsula at sword point.

Though perhaps not entirely at sword point. There is one clue suggesting a possible common thread between the religious reform movements in sixteenth-century Europe and eighteenth-century Arabia. According to an Arabic text dating from at least the nineteenth century, it was Wahhab who introduced the use of guns to the Saudi tribe: "They [the Saudi tribe] followed Wahhab in religion and in worldly affairs as in managing wars, interests, and hostilities . . . and he ordered the people of Dir'iyyah to learn how to shoot guns. He [Wahhab] was the one who obtained for them the guns that they now have."[3] Firearms were not new to Arabia, of course, but until Wahhab, the nomadic Arabians fought largely with swords and bows and arrows. He may have been a traditionalist, aiming to restore a pure and original form of Islam, but he was also a modernizer.

Clockwork Armies

Within Europe, guns have been credited with redressing the imbalance of power between mounted aristocrats and the common people.

One lowly fellow with a gun could potentially bring down an armored nobleman with a sword, and it was this possibility, in part, that made carnival seem increasingly dangerous to the powerful. But used in war, guns had a very different effect—grinding down the individual soldier to the level of a cog in a giant war machine—and this process drew enthusiastic support from the new puritans of the Protestant Reformation.

The pre-Reformation, medieval European style of fighting, featuring mounted aristocrats armed with bladed weapons, had always allowed for plenty of downtime among the foot soldiers, much of it devoted to revelry. Guns, which became the weapon of choice in the sixteenth century, required far greater discipline among the rank and file, in part because of the very primitiveness of the available firearms. Since muskets and harquebuses could not be aimed with any precision, they worked best when fired in volleys by a great many men at the same time. And since they took several minutes to reload, the men had to be adept at the process and trained to spend every moment when they were not actually firing preparing to fire again. This was a job not for "warriors" in the old-fashioned, individualistic sense, but for men who should perhaps be considered the first true proletarians—the rigidly disciplined, dully obedient soldiers of the new mass armies. Any discussion of the suppression of carnival in Europe would be incomplete without mentioning the disciplining of Europe's fighting men, who had to be forcibly restrained from the drinking and carousing that had once enlivened military service for so many reluctant conscripts.

It was a Calvinist, the Dutch aristocrat Maurice of Orange, who first applied the spirit of Calvinism to the business of war. In the early 1600s, three hundred years before the American efficiency expert Frederick Winslow Taylor transformed factory work by breaking it down into a series of repetitive gestures, Maurice devised a detailed schedule of motions—thirty-two in all—for each soldier to follow while firing, reloading, and firing again.[4] His new system required endless practice, marching, and reloading, to the point

where the necessary motions were automatic enough to be performed in the stress of battle. But in Maurice's system, the "drill,"
as it came to be known, went well beyond what was necessary for
practice; the point was to fill the soldier's time entirely, and when he
was not drilling, he was assigned tasks formerly disdained by fighting men, like digging trenches and constructing fortifications. "Idleness," as the historian William H. McNeill writes, "was banished
from military life. This was a great departure from earlier custom,
since waiting for something to happen occupies almost all of a soldier's time, and when left to their own devices, troops had traditionally escaped boredom by indulging in drink and other sorts of
dissipation."[5] As the military historian M. D. Feld observed, "The
changes instituted in the Dutch armed forces corresponded strikingly with the outlook expected of a middle-class society," and he
was referring to a middle-class *Calvinist* society.[6]

Another Calvinist, the English revolutionary Oliver Cromwell,
took the new military discipline a step further, banning outright all
the soldier's usual diversions: drinking, gambling, looting, woman-
izing, even cursing. War had always been a dangerous and uncom-
fortable occupation for the common man, but it had also offered a
break from routine, a chance to travel and carouse. But Cromwell's
"New Model Army" offered no carnivalesque entertainments, only
the effort of functioning as one tiny part of a vast, smooth-running
machine. This was a prospect that, however appalling to a fun-
loving peasant boy, thrilled Calvinist ideologues, and not only on
account of its potential military advantages. "Above all creatures
[God] loves soldiers," according to one English Calvinist preacher,
referring to the drilled and disciplined Calvinist type of soldier.[7]
Even without the threat of war, even for civilians, the drill seemed
to Calvinists an admirable use of time. "Abandon your carding, dic-
ing, chambering, wantonness, dalliance, scurrilous discoursing and
vain raveling out of time," urged another preacher, "to frequent
these exercises."[8]

The new Calvinist armies were hugely successful. Maurice used his to defeat the Spanish troops occupying Holland; Cromwell won out over the aristocratic Cavaliers, who practiced a non-Puritan form of Protestantism and still fought in the old, disorderly, aristocratic style. Soon monarchs and generals all over the Western world were imposing the drill and the new Calvinist discipline on their own armies, regardless of whether these armies were Catholic, Protestant, or Orthodox. Thus, with the help of reformed and reforming religions, Europe adjusted to the imperatives of gun-based warfare, and the changes have been with us ever since.

European historians in the Marxist tradition have tended to look to the "means of production" as a determining social force, omitting what the anthropologist Jack Goody terms the "means of destruction." Thus they are more likely to see the industrial revolution as the change underlying the Protestant Reformation than to consider the role of the *military* revolution wrought by guns. But gun-based warfare, no less than industrialization, required social discipline on an unprecedented scale—huge numbers of men (and in our own time, women too) trained to obedience and self-denial, and the new Protestantism helped to provide it. Wahhabism may have served the same function in tribal Arabia, which—thanks to Wahhab himself—was making its own adjustment to gun-based warfare.

Drilling with Dromedaries

Was military discipline linked to religious puritanism in the mind of Wahhab or his patron, Muhammad ibn Saud? Unfortunately, we have no way of knowing. What we do know, however, is that Saud was, like Wahhab, a military innovator. According to a Frenchman who had been on Napoleon's expedition to Egypt and served as French consul in Aleppo at the time when the Wahhabis invaded Syria:

It was at Diriyah that Ibn Saud began to realize his designs of conquest, neglecting nothing in order to ensure their success. His soldiers, who were already accustomed to fatigue, became even stronger and more indefatigable through the drilling which he instilled in them. He did away with horses, replacing them with dromedaries. This animal is as swift as the horse, but stronger; nature created it for the desert which would be uninhabitable without it. Ibn Saud ordered that each dromedary should be mounted by two soldiers. He rationed not only the soldiers' food, but also that of the animals.[9]

The reference to "drilling" provides a startling link to the puritan-led military reforms of seventeenth-century Europe. It is unlikely that Saud's men, who numbered about six thousand, drilled by repetitive marching, as the Europeans did, because they were not foot soldiers but what Europeans would call cavalry. Possibly, the shift from horses to two-man dromedaries was an adaptation to the use of guns that Wahhab insisted on. The guns available at the time—probably muskets—would have been of little use to a single man on horseback: It was hard enough to reload a musket on the ground, much less from the back of a moving animal. But with two men on a dromedary's back, one could manage the animal while the other devoted himself to the tricky business of shooting. Thus the drilling instituted by Saud may have been practice in shooting and reloading from the back of a moving dromedary.

But drilling is not just a matter of forcing men to master a particular military technology; its universal goal is to inculcate an iron level of discipline. Saud wanted his men to be "indefatigable"; he even hardened them by limiting their rations. These concerns are entirely consistent with the asceticism and self-denial demanded by puritanical religious reforms. In both the European and the Arabian cases, one real function of religious puritanism was to make fighting men internalize the discipline that the new gun-based mode of fighting required: Not only the generals insisted on sobriety and obedience among their troops; according to the puritanical reformers, so did God.

By the nineteenth century, military modernization and religious puritanism were clearly linked in other parts of the Muslim world. In 1826, the Ottoman sultan Mahmud II destroyed his own army of janissaries, about one hundred thousand elite foot soldiers, who were resisting military reforms. The janissaries may have been condemned by their record of palace coups, but it is interesting to note that they were also closely associated with a particularly ecstatic stream of Sufism. In Egypt, Mehmet Ali Pasha, who governed throughout the early nineteenth century, introduced European-style military reforms along with a wide-ranging attempt to discipline his population. He cracked down on Sufism generally and attempted to outlaw the *mulid*, a saint's day festival similar to European carnival. In "modernized," early-nineteenth-century Egypt, the anthropologist Michael Gilsenan writes, "military parades, marching in new time to the new drum rhythm, were approved, productive and expressive of order and hierarchy; Sufi processions and banners were violently attacked, as they still are, as productive and expressive of precisely the opposite, as well as being denounced by some authorities as un-Islamic."[10]

Could there have been a connection between the repression of festivities and the need for disciplined mass armies in other parts of the world? The Roman Empire, for example, relied on a rigidly drilled infantry, and it would be interesting to know whether the Romans' intermittent hostility to ecstatic religions could be traced, in any way, to this aspect of the Roman military.

Then there is the intriguing case of China. Max Weber observed that the Chinese had abandoned their ecstatic traditions very early, so that by the time of large-scale empire, "dances are not to be found—the old war dance had vanished—nor are sexual, musical, or other forms of toxic orgies found."[11] According to Weber, "all orgiastic elements were strictly eliminated" from the state religious cult, which deemed ecstatic rituals "as dangerous as the Roman nobility once considered the cult of Dionysos."[12] It may be relevant that ancient China had undergone its own military revolution, beginning in the seventh century BCE, when foot soldiers armed with crossbows began to replace aristocratic warriors in chariots. Quite possibly—and I leave it to the appropriate historians to explore this further—the crossbow played a role in the culture of ancient China similar to that of the gun in early modern Europe or eighteenth-century Arabia. The project of disciplining large numbers of ordinary men to the repetitive use of an action-at-a-distance weapon—the crossbow or gun—may have required a level of social discipline that is incompatible with traditional festivities and ecstatic rites.

7

An Epidemic of Melancholy

Beginning in England in the seventeenth century, the European world was stricken by what looks, in today's terms, like an epidemic of depression. The disease attacked both young and old, plunging them into months or years of morbid lethargy and relentless terrors, and seemed—perhaps only because they wrote more and had more written about them—to single out men of accomplishment and genius. The puritan writer John Bunyan, the political leader Oliver Cromwell, the poets Thomas Gray and John Donne, and the playwright and essayist Samuel Johnson are among the earliest and best-known victims. To the medical profession, the illness presented a vexing conundrum, not least because its gravest outcome was suicide. In 1733 Dr. George Cheyne lamented "the late frequency and daily increase of wanton and uncommon self-murders, produced mostly by this distemper," and speculated that the English climate, combined with sedentary lifestyles and urbanization, "have brought forth a class of distemper with atrocious and frightful symptoms, scarce known to our ancestors, and never rising to such fatal heights, and afflicting such numbers in any known nation. These nervous disorders being computed to make almost one-third of the complaints of the people of condition in England."[1] A hundred years later, little had changed: "[Nervous] complaints prevail at the present day," claimed a contemporary, "to an extent unknown at any former period, or in any other nation."[2]

Samuel Johnson, the intellectually prodigious son of impecunious parents, first fell prey to depression in 1729 at the age of twenty, shortly after being forced to leave Oxford for a lack of funds. According to his friend and biographer James Boswell, himself a victim of depression, Johnson's "morbid melancholy" began to "afflict him in a dreadful manner" upon his return to his parents' home.

> He felt himself overwhelmed with an horrible hypochondria, with perpetual irritation, fretfulness, and impatience; and with a dejection, gloom, and despair, which made existence misery. From this dismal malady he never afterwards was perfectly relieved; and all his labours, and all his enjoyments, were but temporary interruptions of its baleful influence.[3]

Without a degree or much possibility of a career, he spent hours sitting and staring at the town clock without seeming to notice the time. He took long walks, pondering suicide. But it was not only the prospect of poverty and failure that rendered him vulnerable, because years later, at the height of his success as a writer and popularity as a conversationalist, the illness struck again. *"My terrors and perplexities have so much increased,"* he wrote in his early fifties, "that I am under great depression . . . Almighty and merciful Father look down upon my misery with pity."[4]

To the English, the disease was "the English malady," described in Timothie Bright's *Treatise of Melancholie* in the late sixteenth century, and exhaustively analyzed by the Anglican minister Robert Burton in his 1621 classic, *The Anatomy of Melancholy*. But the rainy northern island was not the only site visited by the disease; all of Europe was afflicted. According to Andrew Solomon, the concern with melancholy originated in Italy and was carried back to England by English tourists.[5] It seemed primarily a Spanish problem, however, to the Italian political theorist Giovanni Botero, who observed in 1603 that the men of that country "have more than a bit of melancholy, which makes them severe in manner, restrained and sluggish in their undertakings," and the problem was rampant in the court of Philip III.[6]

By the eighteenth century, melancholy was as much a German disease as an English one,* presenting later historians of that nation with the paradox that "the era of dawning light, the Enlightenment" should also be characterized by "black gall and melancholy persons"—such as the editor Karl Philipp Moritz, who "could sit all day, without any thoughts, scribbling on paper, and could loathe himself for the loss of time, without having the energy to use this time any better."[7] In France, which produced the famous melancholic Jean-Jacques Rousseau,[8] the disorder did not become a major literary theme until the mid-nineteenth century, when it afflicted, among others, the poet Charles Baudelaire. From the nineteenth century on, depression figures prominently in the biographies of the notable: the Russian novelist Leo Tolstoy, the German social scientist Max Weber, the American psychologist William James.

The disease grew increasingly prevalent over the course of the twentieth century, when relatively sound statistics first became available, and this increase cannot be accounted for by a greater willingness on the part of physicians and patients to report it. Rates of schizophrenia, panic disorders, and phobias did not rise at the same time, for example, as they would be expected to if only changes in the reporting of mental illness were at work.[9] According to the World Health Organization, depression is now the fifth leading cause of death and disability in the world, while ischemic heart disease trails in

---

*The historian Robert Kinsman states that "melancholy in Renaissance art, both pictorial and literary, became a central point of reference," and offers a number of German examples, including the work of Dürer. (Kinsman, p. 310.)

sixth place.[10] Fatalities occur most dramatically through suicide, but even the mild form of depression—called *dysthemia* and character- ized by an inability to experience pleasure—can kill by increasing a person's vulnerability to serious somatic illnesses such as cancer and heart disease. Far from being an affliction of the famous and suc- cessful, we now know that the disease strikes the poor more often than the rich, and women more commonly than men.

Just in the last few years, hundreds of books, articles, and televi- sion specials have been devoted to depression: its toll on the individ- ual, its relationship to gender, the role of genetic factors, the efficacy of pharmaceutical treatments. But to my knowledge, no one has sug- gested that the epidemic may have begun in a particular historical time, and started as a result of cultural circumstances that arose at that time and have persisted or intensified since. The failure to con- sider historical roots may stem, in part, from the emphasis on the celebrity victims of the past, which tends to discourage a statistical, or epidemiological, perspective.* But if there was in fact a begin- ning to the epidemic of depression, sometime in the sixteenth or seventeenth century, it is of obvious concern here, confronting us as it does with this question: Could this apparent decline in the abil- ity to experience pleasure be in any way connected with the decline in *opportunities* for pleasure, such as carnival and other traditional festivities?

There is reason to think that something like an epidemic of de- pression in fact began around 1600, or the time when Burton

---

*This is a limitation of Kay Redfield Jamison's fascinating book *Touched with Fire*, which en- deavors to link manic-depressive disease to artistic creativity, chiefly by enlisting a long line of highly creative sufferers. To begin with, she does not clearly distinguish manic-depressive, or bipolar, disease from "unipolar" depression, throwing a number of unipolar victims—like Samuel Johnson—into her mix. Then, to establish that depression in any form was more common among eighteenth-century writers and poets than other people, she compares its rate among the poets of that time to rates among the general population today (p. 73). But what were the rates of depression among the general population in the eighteenth century? And why should we count as poets and "highly creative" people only those who achieve pub- lication and subsequent fame? At any rate, she never comments on the fact that none of the celebrated victims whose cases she discusses lived earlier than the seventeenth century.

undertook his "anatomy" of the disease. Melancholy, as it was called until the twentieth century, is of course a very ancient problem, and was described in the fifth century BCE by Hippocrates. Chaucer's fourteenth-century characters were aware of it, and late medieval churchmen knew it as *acedia*, which was technically a sin, since it often led to the neglect of religious obligations. So melancholy, in some form, had always existed—and, regrettably, we have no statistical evidence of a sudden increase in early modern Europe, which had neither a psychiatric profession to do the diagnosing nor a public health establishment to record the numbers of the afflicted. All we know is that in the 1600s and 1700s, medical books about melancholy and literature with melancholic themes were both finding an eager audience, presumably at least in part among people who suffered from melancholy themselves. Samuel Johnson, for example, was an admirer of Burton's *Anatomy of Melancholy*, asserting it "was the only book that ever took him out of bed two hours sooner than he wished to rise."[11]

Increasing interest in melancholy is not, however, evidence of an increase in the prevalence of actual melancholy. As the historian Roy Porter suggested, the disease may simply have been becoming more stylish, both as a medical diagnosis and as a problem, or pose, affected by the idle rich, and signifying a certain ennui or detachment. No doubt the medical prejudice that it was a disease of the gifted, or at least of the comfortable, would have made it an attractive diagnosis to the upwardly mobile and merely out-of-sorts. Nervous diseases in general, Dr. Cheyne asserted, "never happen, or can happen to any but those of the liveliest and quickest natural parts whose Faculties are the brightest and most spiritual, and whose Genius is most keen and penetrating, and particularly when there is the most delicate Sensation and Taste, both of pleasure and pain."[12]

By the mid-eighteenth century, melancholy did indeed become a stylish stance among the affluent English, inspiring the insipid sentiments expressed in poems like Thomas Warton's "The Pleasures of

Melancholy" and Elizabeth Carter's "Ode to Melancholy," which reads in part: "COME, Melancholy! silent power/Companion of my lonely hour . . . / Thou sweetly sad ideal guest."[13] In fact the notion that melancholy was an exclusively elite disease was common enough to be a subject for satire. In a mid-eighteenth-century English play, a barber complains of melancholy and is told: "Melancholy? Marry, gup, is *melancholy* a word for a barber's mouth? Thou shouldst say heavy, dull, and doltish: melancholy is the crest of the courtier's arms!"[14] For their part, physicians probably were eager to diagnose melancholy, or, as it was sometimes called, "spleen," among their better-off patients and, in general, to wrest the treatment of nervous disorders away from the clergy.

But melancholy did not become a fashionable pose until a full century after Burton took up the subject, and when it did become stylish, we must still wonder: Why did this particular stance or attitude become fashionable and not another? An arrogant insouciance might, for example, seem more fitting to an age of imperialism than this wilting, debilitating malady; and enlightenment, another well-known theme of the era, might have been better served by a mood of questing impatience. Even when melancholy became popular as a poetic theme and social affectation, there were individual sufferers, like the poet William Cowper, who could hardly have chosen their affliction. He first fell prey in his twenties, when anxiety about an exam led to a suicide attempt that necessitated an eighteen-month stay in an asylum. Four more times in his life he was plunged into what he called "a melancholy that made me almost an infant"[15] and was preserved from suicide only by institutionalization. And it is hard to believe he could have been feigning when he wrote to a friend, toward the end of his life, "I have had a terrible night—such a one as I believe I may say God knows no man ever had . . . Rose overwhelmed with infinite despair, and came down into the study execrating the day I was born with inexpressible bitterness."[16]

Nor can we be content with the claim that the apparent epidemic of melancholy was the cynical invention of the men who profited by writing about it, since some of these were self-identified sufferers themselves. Robert Burton confessed, "I writ of melancholy, by being busy to avoid melancholy."[17] George Cheyne was afflicted, though miraculously cured by a vegetarian diet of his own devising. The Englishman John Brown, who published a best-selling mid-nineteenth-century book on the subject of the "Increase of low Spirits and nervous Disorders," went on to commit suicide.[18] *Something* was happening, from about 1600 on, to make melancholy a major concern of the reading public, and the simplest explanation is that there was more melancholy around to be concerned about.

There remains the question of whether melancholy, as experienced by people centuries ago, was the same as the disease we now know as depression. Even in today's *Diagnostic and Statistical Manual of Mental Disorders*, the definitions of mental illnesses always seem a little fuzzy around the edges; and there was not even an attempt, until the eighteenth century, at a scientific or systematic nomenclature. "Melancholy," in Burton's account, sometimes overlaps with "hypochondria," "hysteria," and "vapors"—the last two being seen as particularly feminine disorders.[19] But on the whole, his descriptions of melancholy could, except for the prolix language, substitute for a modern definition of depression: "Fear and Sorrow supplant [those] pleasing thoughts, suspicion, discontent, and perpetual anxiety succeed in their places" until eventually "melancholy, this feral fiend," produces "a cankered soul macerated with cares and discontents, a being tired of life . . . [who] cannot endure company, light, or life itself."[20]

If we compare the accounts of melancholics from the past with one of the best subjective descriptions of depression from our own time—William Styron's 1990 book *Darkness Visible*—we find what certainly looks like a reasonable concordance. Styron found himself withdrawing from other people, even abandoning his own guests at a dinner party, while Boswell said of Johnson during one of his episodes of melancholy, "He was so ill, as, notwithstanding his remarkable love of company, to be entirely averse to society, the most fatal symptom of that malady."[21] Styron listed "self-hatred" as a symptom, while the highly productive Johnson repeatedly upbraided himself for leading "a life so dissipated and useless."[22] More flamboyantly, John Bunyan bewailed what he called his "original and inward pollution": "That was my plague and my affliction. By reason of that, I was more loathsome in my own eyes than was a toad."[23]

Another symptom mentioned by Styron is a menacing change in the appearance of the nonhuman world. Terror is externalized, like a toxin coating the landscape and every object within it. Styron found that his "beloved home for thirty years, took on . . . an almost palpable quality of ominousness."[24] Similarly William James, no doubt drawing from his own long struggle with the illness, wrote that to "melancholiacs," "the world now looks remote, strange, sinister, uncanny. Its color is gone, its breath is cold."[25] These perceptions fit neatly with the sixteenth- and seventeenth-century melancholics' notion that the natural world was itself in a state of deterioration—crumbling, corrupt, and doomed. As John Donne put it—and I cannot think of a more apt image of the world as it appears to a depressive—"*colour is decai'd*" (my emphasis).[26] Hence, no doubt, Styron's sense of immersion in a "gray drizzle of horror," and Johnson's repeated references to "the distresses of terrour."[27]

So I think we can conclude with some confidence that the melancholy experienced by men and women of the early modern era was in fact the same disorder we know today as depression, and that the prevalence of melancholy/depression was actually increasing in that era, at least relative to medieval times—though admittedly we have no way of knowing how substantial this increase was in statistical terms. We can return, then, to the question of the relationship between this early "epidemic of depression" and the larger theme of this book: the suppression of communal rituals and festivities. Very likely, the two phenomena are entangled in various ways.

It could be, for example, that, as a result of their illness, depressed individuals lost their taste for communal festivities and even came to view them with revulsion. But there are other possibilities: First, that both the rise of depression and the decline of festivities are symptomatic of some deeper, underlying psychological change, which began about four hundred years ago and persists, in some form, in our own time. The second, more intriguing possibility is that the disappearance of traditional festivities was itself a factor contributing to depression.

The Anxious Self

One approaches the subject of "deeper, underlying psychological change" with some trepidation, but fortunately, in this case, many respected scholars have already visited this difficult terrain. "Historians of European culture are in substantial agreement," Lionel Trilling wrote in 1972, "that in the late 16th and early 17th centuries, something like a mutation in human nature took place."[28] This change has been called *the rise of subjectivity* or *the discovery of the inner self*, and since it can be assumed that all people, in all historical periods, have some sense of selfhood and capacity for subjective reflection, we are really talking about an intensification, and a fairly drastic one, of the universal human capacity to face the world as an autonomous "I," separate from, and largely distrustful of, "them." As we saw in chapter 5, the European nobility had undergone this sort of psychological shift in their transformation from a warrior class to a collection of courtiers—away from directness and spontaneity and toward a new guardedness in relation to others. In the late sixteenth and seventeenth centuries, the change becomes far more widespread, affecting even artisans, peasants, and laborers. The new "emphasis on disengagement and self-consciousness," as Louis Sass puts it,[29] makes the individual potentially more autonomous and critical of existing social arrangements, which is all to the good. But it can also transform the individual into a kind of walled fortress, carefully defended from everyone else.

Historians infer this psychological shift from a number of concrete changes occurring in the early modern period, first and most strikingly among the urban bourgeoisie, or upper middle class. Mirrors in which to examine oneself become popular among those who can afford them, along with self-portraits (Rembrandt painted over fifty of them) and autobiographies in which to revise and elaborate the image that one has projected to others. In bourgeois homes, public spaces that guests may enter are differentiated, for the first time, from the private spaces—bedrooms, for example—in which one may retire to let down one's guard and truly "be oneself." More decorous forms of entertainment—plays and operas—requiring people to remain immobilized, each in his or her separate seat, begin to provide an alternative to the promiscuously interactive and physically engaging pleasures of carnival.[30] The very word *self*, as Trilling noted, ceases to be a mere reflexive or intensifier and achieves the status of a freestanding noun, referring to some inner core, not readily visible to others.

The notion of a self hidden behind one's appearance and portable from one situation to another is usually attributed to the new possibility of upward mobility. In medieval culture, you were what you appeared to be—a peasant, a man of commerce, or an aristocrat—and any attempt to assume another status would have been regarded as rank deception; sumptuary laws often barred the wealthy commoner, for example, from dressing in colors and fabrics deemed appropriate only to nobles. According to the historian Natalie Zemon Davis: "At carnival time and at other feast days, a young peasant might dress as an animal or as a person of another estate or sex and speak through that disguise . . . But these were temporary masks and intended for the common good."[31] But in the late sixteenth century, upward mobility was beginning to be possible or at least imaginable, making "deception" a widespread way of life. The merchant who craved an aristocratic title, the craftsman who aspired to the status of a merchant—each had to learn to play the part, an endeavor for which the system of etiquette devised in royal courts came to serve as a convenient script. You might not be a lord or a lofty burgher, but you could find out how to act like one. Hence the popularity, in seventeenth-century England, of books instructing the would-be member of the gentry in how to comport himself, write an impressive letter, and choose a socially advantageous wife.

Hence, too, the new fascination with the theater, with its notion of an actor who is different from his or her roles. This is a notion that takes some getting used to; in the early years of the theater, actors who played the part of villains risked being assaulted by angry playgoers in the streets. Within the theater, there is a fascination with plots involving further deceptions: Shakespeare's Portia pretends to be a doctor of law; Rosalind disguises herself as a boy; Juliet feigns her own death—to give just a few examples. Writing a few years after Shakespeare's death, Robert Burton bemoaned the fact that acting was no longer confined to the theater, for "men like stage-players act [a] variety of parts." It was painful, in his view, "to see a man turn himself into all shapes like a Chameleon . . . to act twenty parts & persons at once for his advantage . . . having a several face, garb, & character, for every one he meets."[32] The inner self that can change costumes and manners to suit the occasion resembles a skilled craftsperson, too busy and watchful for the pleasures of easygoing conviviality. As for the outer self projected by the inner one into the social world: Who would want to "lose oneself" in the communal excitement of carnival when that self has taken so much effort and care to construct?

So highly is the "inner self" honored within our own culture that its acquisition seems to be an unquestionable mark of progress—a requirement, as Trilling called it, for "the emergence of modern European and American man."[33] It was, no doubt, this sense of individuality and personal autonomy, "of an untrammeled freedom to ask questions and explore," as the historian Yi-Fu Tuan put it, that allowed men like Martin Luther and Galileo to risk their lives by defying Catholic doctrine.[34] Which is preferable: a courageous, or even merely grasping and competitive, individualism, versus a medieval (or, in the case of non-European cultures, "primitive") personality so deeply mired in community and ritual that it can barely distinguish a "self"? From the perspective of our own time, the choice, so stated, is obvious. We have known nothing else.

But there was a price to be paid for the buoyant individualism we associate with the more upbeat aspects of the early modern period, the Renaissance and Enlightenment. As Tuan writes, "the obverse" of the new sense of personal autonomy is "isolation, loneliness, a sense of disengagement, a loss of natural vitality and of innocent pleasure in the givenness of the world, and a feeling of burden because reality has no meaning other than what a person chooses to impart to it."[35] Now if there is one circumstance indisputably involved in the etiology of depression, it is precisely this sense of isolation or, to use the term adopted by Durkheim in his late-nineteenth-century study of suicide: *anomie.* Durkheim used it to explain the rising rates of suicide in nineteenth-century Europe; epidemiologists invoke it to help account for the increasing prevalence of depression in our own time.[36] As Durkheim saw it: "Originally society is everything, the individual nothing . . . But gradually things change. As societies become greater in volume and density, individual differences multiply, and the moment approaches when the only remaining bond among the members of a single human group will be that they are all men [human]."[37] The flip side of the heroic autonomy that is said to represent one of the great achievements of the early modern and modern eras is radical isolation, and, with it, depression and sometimes death.

But the new kind of personality that arose in sixteenth- and seventeenth-century Europe was by no means as autonomous and self-defining as claimed. For far from being detached from the immediate human environment, the newly self-centered individual is continually preoccupied with judging the expectations of others and his or her own success in meeting them: "How am I doing?" this supposedly autonomous "self" wants to know. "What kind of an impression am I making?" Historians speak of the *interiorization* that marks the new personality, meaning "the capacity for introspection and self-reflection," but it often looks as if what has been "interiorized" is little more than the human others around one and their likely judgments of oneself.

It is no coincidence that the concept of *society* emerges at the same time as the concept of *self:* What seems to most concern the new and supposedly autonomous self is the opinion of others, who in aggregate compose "society." Mirrors, for example, don't show us our "selves," only what others can see, and autobiographies reveal only what we want those others to know. The crushing weight of other people's judgments—imagined or real—would help explain the frequent onset of depression at the time of a perceived or anticipated failure: Johnson's forced exit from Oxford, Cowper's approaching exam. In the nineteenth century, the historian Janet Oppenheim reports, "severely depressed patients frequently revealed totally unwarranted fears of financial ruin or the expectation of professional disgrace."[38] This is not autonomy but dependency: The emerging "self" defines its own worth in terms of the perceived judgments of others.

If depression was one result of the new individualism, the usual concomitant of depression—anxiety—was surely another. It takes effort, as well as a great deal of watchfulness, to second-guess other people's reactions and plot one's words and gestures accordingly. For the scheming courtier, the striving burgher, and the ambitious lawyer or cleric of early modern Europe, the "self" they discovered is perhaps best described as an awareness of this ceaseless, internal effort to adjust one's behavior to the expectations of others. *Play* in this context comes to have a demanding new meaning, unconnected to pleasure, as in "playing a role." No wonder bourgeois life becomes privatized in the sixteenth and seventeenth centuries, with bedrooms and studies to withdraw to, where, for a few hours a day, the effort can be abandoned, the mask set aside.

The Tormented Soul

But we cannot grasp the full psychological impact of this "mutation in human nature" in purely secular terms. Four hundred—even two hundred—years ago, most people would have interpreted their feelings of isolation and anxiety through the medium of religion, translating *self* as "soul"; the ever-watchful judgmental gaze of others as "God"; and *melancholy* as "the gnawing fear of eternal damnation." Catholicism offered various palliatives to the disturbed and afflicted, in the form of rituals designed to win divine forgiveness or at least diminished disapproval; and even Lutheranism, while rejecting most of the rituals, posited an approachable and ultimately loving God.

Not so with the Calvinist version of Protestantism, which by the seventeenth and eighteenth centuries had spread beyond such hardcore Calvinist denominations as Presbyterianism and the Reformed Church of Holland to infect, in varying degrees, Lutheranism, Anglicism, and even, through the Counter-Reformation, Catholicism. Instead of offering relief, Calvinism provided a metaphysical framework for anomie: If you felt isolated, persecuted, and possibly damned, this was because you actually were. Robert Burton understood the role of Calvinism in promoting melancholy, singling out *religious melancholy* as an especially virulent form of the disease, and his book can be read, at one level, as a polemic against that harsh, puritanical religion.

> The main matter which terrifies and torments most that are troubled in mind is the enormity of their offences, the intolerable burthen of their sins, God's heavy wrath and displeasure so deeply apprehended that they account themselves . . . already damned . . . This furious curiosity, needless speculation, fruitless meditation

about election, reprobation, free will, grace . . . torment still, and crucify the souls of too many, and set all the world together by the ears.[39]

With Calvinism, the sense of isolation purportedly rampant in early modern Europe is ratcheted up to an intolerable degree. Christianity requires that every soul ultimately confront God alone, at least at the moment of death, but the Calvinist soul wanders forever in solitude. Friends may turn out to be false—enemies and competitors in disguise—as illustrated by what Weber calls "the strikingly frequent repetition, especially in the English Puritan literature, of warnings against any trust in the aid and friendship of men."[40] Even family deserves no lasting loyalty. In that great Puritan epic, John Bunyan's *Pilgrim's Progress*, Christian flees his home in the "City of Destruction," despite the fact that "his Wife and Children . . . began to cry after him to return; but the man put his fingers in his ears, and ran on crying, 'Life Life Eternal Life.' So he looked not behind him, but fled towards the middle of the Plain."[41] Bunyan's own inner domain, to judge from his spiritual autobiography, *Grace Abounding to the Chief of Sinners*, was rarely visited by another human or brightened by a glimpse of the physical world. In over eighty claustrophobic pages recounting alternating fits of despair and moments of hope, one finds few pronouns other than *I* or animate beings other than Satan and God. When Bunyan does mention some fellow humans at one point, it is to express his disillusionment about these people, whom he had taken as reliable fellow Calvinists: "[They were] much distressed and cast down when they met with outward losses, as of husband, wife, child, etc. Lord, thought I, what a do is here about such little things as these!"[42]

One of Max Weber's greatest insights was to see the compatibility between Calvinism and capitalism, or, we might just as well say, to sense the terrible sense of psychic isolation—"the unprecedented inner loneliness"[43]—that a competitive, sink-or-swim economy imposed. Just as the soul struggled along its solitary path toward damnation or grace, the self toiled and schemed along a parallel trajectory in the material world. But if that trajectory was to slope upward toward wealth or merely security, much more was required than a cold indifference to others. One had to engage in an endless project of self-discipline and self-denial, deferring all gratification, except perhaps for the pleasure of watching one's assets mount. "The most urgent task" of Calvinism, Weber wrote, was "the destruction of spontaneous, impulsive enjoyment."[44] A late-eighteenth-century Scottish medical handbook confirms this view of Calvinism, advising that

> many persons of a religious turn of mind behave as if they thought it a crime to be cheerful. They imagine the whole of religion consists in certain mortifications, or denying themselves the smallest indulgence, even of the most innocent amusements. A perpetual gloom hangs over their countenances, while the deepest melancholy preys upon their minds. At length the fairest prospects vanish, every thing puts on a dismal appearance, and those very objects which ought to give delight, afford nothing but disgust.—Life itself becomes a burthen, and the unhappy wretch, persuaded that no evil can equal what he feels, often puts an end to his miserable existence.[45]

John Bunyan seems to have been a jolly enough fellow in his youth, much given to dancing and sports in the village green, but with the onset of his religious crisis these pleasures had to be put aside. Dancing was the hardest to relinquish—"I was a full year before I could quite leave it"[46]—but he eventually managed to achieve a fun-free life. In *Pilgrim's Progress*, the Bunyan-like hero Christian finds that any time he lets down his guard and experiences a moment of rest or even just diminished anxiety, he has lost ground or been sorely taken advantage of. The only thing Christian encounters resembling festivity, "Vanity Fair," turns out to be a death trap for the virtuous, the place where Christian's high-minded companion, Faithful, is seized, tortured, and finally burned to death by the wanton fairgoers. Carnival, in other words, is the portal to hell, just as pleasure in any form—sexual, gustatory, convivial—is the devil's snare. Nothing speaks more clearly of the darkening mood, the declining possibilities for joy, than the fact that, while the medieval peasant created festivities as an escape from work, the Puritan embraced work as an escape from terror.

Oliver Cromwell experienced a psychological crisis very similar to Bunyan's. Born to a Puritan family in the rural English gentry, he enjoyed a youth marked by "wilnesses and follies" as well as "love of horseplay and of practical jokes in something less than the best of taste."[47] At the age of twenty-eight, however, he fell into a condition diagnosed by a physician as *valde melancholicus*, meaning "extreme melancholy," apparently occasioned by reflection on his youthful sins. As he later wrote to a cousin, echoing Bunyan: "You know what my manner of life hath been. Oh, I lived in and loved darkness, and hated the light. I was a chief, the chief of sinners."[48] After what we might now call a "born-again" experience, Cromwell abandoned the worst of his sins—whatever they were—though, unlike Bunyan, he continued to enjoy music and drink ale and wine.

Whether Weber succeeded in establishing a seamless link between Calvinism and capitalism is open to question, but his own life provides vivid evidence of the connection between Calvinism and depression. A thoroughly secular thinker himself, Weber was raised by a Calvinist mother to see pleasure in almost any form as a danger to be fended off through ceaseless self-discipline and work. His biographer and wife, Marianne, wrote of his using work to "rescue" himself from the "danger of becoming comfortable." Of his student life in the late 1800s, she reported, "He continues the rigid work discipline, regulates his life by the clock, divides the daily routine into exact sections for the various subjects, saves in his way, by feeding himself evenings in his room with a pound of raw chopped beef and four fried eggs."[49] A few months after their marriage, he wrote to her, "I can't risk allowing the present composure—which I enjoy with the feeling of a really new happiness—to be transformed into relaxation."[50]

In his mid-thirties, at a time of enviable academic success, Weber experienced a total breakdown, lasting for months and marked by back pain, trembling hands, insomnia, feelings of worthlessness and despair, and—perhaps most tragically for him—a complete inability to work. Another biographer tried mightily to fit Weber's problems into a Freudian mold, attributing the breakdown to tensions between Weber and his rather easygoing and self-indulgent father.[51] But Robert Burton would no doubt have blamed the mother's Calvinism and diagnosed Weber, whatever his personal beliefs, as another victim of religious melancholy.

We do not have to rely on psychological inference to draw a link between Calvinism and depression. There is one clear marker for depression—suicide—and suicide rates have been recorded, with varying degrees of diligence, for centuries. In his classic study, Durkheim found Protestants in the nineteenth century—not all of whom, of course, were of the Calvinistic persuasion—about twice as likely to take their own lives as Catholics, and this was not just a matter of regional difference, since the same ratio prevailed in regions in which adherents of the two religions were intermixed.[52] More strikingly, a recent analysis finds a sudden surge of suicide in the Swiss canton of Zurich, beginning in the late sixteenth century, just as that region became a Calvinist stronghold. Some sort of general breakdown of social mores cannot be invoked as an explanation, since homicides fell as suicides rose. Nor did the suicides reflect a failure to adjust to the Calvinist regime, with its many prohibitions on gambling, dancing, and sexual misbehavior. The historian R. Po-Chia Hsia reports that the plurality of the dead received postmortem praise as "honorable, God-fearing, bible-reading, diligent, and quiet Christians in life." In fact a majority—61 percent—came from families "that constituted the backbone of the Calvinist regime."[53]

The Lost Cure

So if we are looking for a common source of depression, on the one hand, and the suppression of festivities, on the other, it is not hard to find. Urbanization and the rise of a competitive, market-based economy favored a more anxious and isolated sort of person—potentially both prone to depression and distrustful of communal pleasures. Calvinism provided a transcendent rationale for this shift, intensifying the isolation and practically institutionalizing depression as a stage in the quest for salvation. All this comes together in a man like John Bunyan, a victim of severe depression—or so we would say in secular language—and a fierce opponent, in his years as a preacher, of traditional festivities, not to mention pleasure in any form. At the level of "deep, underlying psychological change," both depression and the destruction of festivities could be described as seemingly inevitable consequences of the broad process known as modernization. But could there also be a more straightforward link, a way in which the death of carnival contributed directly to the epidemic of depression?

Certainly, in some instances, the destruction of carnival left a residue of sadness and regret. The nineteenth-century French historian Jules Michelet bemoaned a childhood devoid of festivals: "My childhood never blossomed in the open air, in the warm atmosphere of an amiable crowd, where the emotion of each individual is increased a hundredfold by the emotion felt by all."[54] The writer Jean Rhys recalled her childhood envy, in around 1900, of the lower-class celebrants she was forbidden to join.

> The three days before Lent were carnival in Roseau. We couldn't dress up or join in but we could watch from the open window and not through the jalousies. There were gaily masked crowds with a band. Listening, I would give up anything, anything to be able to dance like that, the life surged up to us sitting well-behaved, looking on.[55]

There is no evidence, though, of an innate human need for communal pleasure, which, if thwarted, leads to depression or other mental diseases. Obviously, millions of people forgo such pleasures without developing clinically recognized disorders, and it would trivialize the torments of a man like a Bunyan, for example, to ascribe them to his abandonment of dancing and games. But I am not the first to suggest that the suppression of festivities could have played a role in the etiology of the nervous disorders that so plagued European culture from the early modern era on. Speaking of hysteria, which had been viewed in the seventeenth and eighteenth centuries as the female equivalent of melancholy, the historians Stallybrass and White note that "carnival debris spills out of the mouths of those terrified Viennese women in Freud's 'Studies on Hysteria.' 'Don't you hear the horses stamping in the circus?' Frau Emmy von N. implores Freud at a moment of particularly abject horror."[56] Freud was so determined to find a purely sexual source for mental illness that he was not prepared to pick up on such clues. "In one way or another," Stallybrass and White remark, "Freud's patients can be seen as enacting desperate ritual fragments from a festive tradition, *the self-exclusion from which* had been one of the identifying features of their social class."[57]

If the destruction of festivities did not actually cause depression, it may still be that, in abandoning their traditional festivities, people lost a potentially effective *cure* for it. Robert Burton suggested many cures for melancholy—study and exercise, for example—but he returned again and again to the same prescription: "Let them use hunting, sports, plays, jests, merry company . . . a cup of good drink now and then, hear musick, and have such companions with whom they are especially delighted; merry tales or toys, drinking, singing, dancing, and whatsover else may procure mirth."[58] He acknowledged the ongoing attack on "Dancing, Singing, Masking, Mumming, Stage-plays" by "some severe Catos," referring to the Calvinists, but heartily endorsed the traditional forms of festivity: "I . . . was ever of that mind, those May-games, Wakes, and

Whitsun-Ales, &c., if they be not at unseasonable hours, may justly be permitted. Let them freely feast, sing and dance, have their Puppet-plays, Hobby-horses, Tabers, Crowds, Bag-pipes, &c . . . , play at Ball, and Barley-breaks, and what sports and recreations they like best."[59] In his ideal world, "none shall be over-tired, but have their set times of recreations and holidays, to indulge their humour, feasts and merry meetings . . . like that Sacred Festival amongst the Persians, those Saturnalia in Rome."[60] His views accorded with treatments of melancholy already in use in the sixteenth century. While the disruptively "mad" were confined and cruelly treated, melancholics were, at least in theory, to be "refreshed & comforted" and "gladded with instruments of musick."[61]

A little over a century after Burton wrote *The Anatomy of Melancholy*, another English writer, Richard Browne, echoed his prescription, backing it up with a scientific (for the time) view of the workings of the human "machine." Singing and dancing could cure melancholy, he proposed, by stirring up the "secretions." Thanks, he said, to "the prevailing Charms of Musick, etc. that attend it, (without which Dancing would be insipid) the Mind is fill'd with gay enlivening Ideas, the Spirits flow with Vigour and Activity through the whole Machine."[62] But if such traditional pleasures were under attack in Burton's time, they seemed to be on their way to extinction in Browne's: "Thus we may see what a vast Influence Singing has over the Mind of Man, and with Pleasure reflect on its joyful Consequences, and at the same time be amaz'd that it should be a Diversion or Exercise so little practis'd, since the Advantages that may be reap'd from it are so very numerous."[63] Reflecting a more puritanical era, Browne recommended no "Saturnalia"—only regular doses of dancing "in a due and regular time," preferably "an Hour or more at a convenient time after every Meal."[64]

And a century later, even Adam Smith, the great prophet of capitalism, was advocating festivities and art as a means of relieving melancholy.

The state, by encouraging, that is by giving liberty to all those who for their own interest would attempt, without scandal or indecency, to amuse and divert the people by painting, poetry, music, dancing . . . would easily dissipate, in the greater part of them, that melancholy and gloomy humour which is almost always the nurse of popular superstition and enthusiasm.[65]

Burton, Browne, and Smith were not the only ones to propose festivity as a cure for melancholy, and there is reason to believe that—whether through guesswork, nostalgia, or personal experience—they were on to something important. I know of no attempts in our own time to use festive behavior as treatment for depression, if such an experiment is even thinkable in a modern clinical setting. There is, however, an abundance of evidence that communal pleasures—ranging from simple festivities to ecstatic rituals—have served, in a variety of cultures, as a way of alleviating and even curing depression. Almost two thousand years ago, the Greek musicologist Aristides Quintilianus observed, "This is the purpose of Bacchic [Dionysian] initiation, that the depressive anxiety [*ptoiesis*] of less educated people, produced by their state of life, or some misfortune, be cleared away through the melodies and dances of the ritual in a joyful and playful way."[66] Similarly, a fifteenth-century Italian writer—Marsilio Ficino—who was himself a depressive, recommended exercise, alterations of diet, and music.[67]

The ecstatic rituals of non-Western peoples often have healing, as well as religious, functions (if the two kinds of functions can even be reliably distinguished), and one of the conditions they appear to heal seems to be what we know as depression. To give a few examples drawn from very different sorts of cultures: The !Kung people of the Kalahari Desert use their ecstatic nocturnal dances to treat "the full range of what in the West would be called physical, psychological, emotional, social, and spiritual illnesses," according to an ethnographer who actually participated in these rituals.[68] Far to the north of the !Kung, in Islamic Morocco, rituals involving music, dance, and trance are used to cure "paralysis, mutism, sudden blindness, severe depressions, nervous palpitations, paraesthesias, and possession."[69] In Christian Uganda in the 1990s, danced rituals were used to help rehabilitate severely withdrawn children traumatized by their experience as captives of the murderous guerrilla movement known as the Lord's Resistance Army.[70]

Italian folk tradition provides another example of the use of public festivity as a cure for depression. In chapter 4, we saw that the tarantula was blamed for dancing manias in Italy. In some accounts, the supposed effect of the spider bite was actually a melancholic syndrome, marked by lassitude to the point of stupefaction, for which the only remedy, according to the nineteenth-century historian J. F. C. Hecker, was dancing, preferably outdoors and for days on end. At the sound of the appropriate musical instruments, he reports, the afflicted "awoke as it were by enchantment, opened their eyes, and moving slowly at first, according to the measure of the music, were, as the time quickened, gradually hurried on to the most passionate dance." These exertions cured them—at least for a while, because a year later whole villages full of sufferers "again grew dejected and misanthropic, until, by music and dancing, they dispelled the melancholy."[71] As mentioned earlier, the therapeutic celebrations were eventually institutionalized as regular, seasonal festivities featuring the kind of tune known generically as the tarantella.

Hecker reports a similar syndrome and cure in nineteenth-century Abyssinia, or what is now Ethiopia. An individual, usually a woman, would fall into a kind of wasting illness, until her relatives agreed to "hire, for a certain sum of money, a band of trumpeters, drummers, and fifers, and buy a quantity of liquor; then all the young men and women of the place assemble at the patient's house," where they dance and generally party for days, invariably effecting a cure.[72] Similarly, in twentieth-century Somalia, a married woman afflicted by what we would call depression—often precipitated by her husband's stated intention to take a second wife—would call for a female shaman, who might diagnose possession by a *sar* spirit. Musicians would be hired, other women summoned, and the sufferer cured through a long bout of ecstatic dancing with the all-female group.[73] In his description of this phenomenon, I. M. Lewis emphasizes the sufferer's potential material gains, since the shamans often recommend, as part of the cure, that the husband shower the afflicted wife with expensive gifts. But this seems to me an overly instrumental view of the situation. To believers, it is the danced ritual that exorcises the *sar* spirit, and their view deserves some respect.

We cannot be absolutely sure in any of these cases—from seventeenth-century England to twentieth-century Somalia—that festivities and danced rituals actually cured the disease we know as depression. But there are reasons to think that they might have. First, because such rituals serve to break down the sufferer's sense of isolation and reconnect him or her with the human community. Second, because they encourage the experience of *self-loss*, that is, a release, however temporary, from the prison of the self, or at least from the anxious business of evaluating how one stands in the group or in the eyes of an ever-critical God. Friedrich Nietzsche, as lonely and tormented an individual as the nineteenth century produced, understood the therapeutics of ecstasy perhaps better than anyone else. At a time of almost universal celebration of the "self," he alone dared speak of the "horror of individual existence,"[74] and glimpsed relief in the ancient Dionysian rituals that he knew of only from reading the classics—rituals in which, he imagined, "each individual becomes not only reconciled to his fellow but actually at one with him—as though the veil of Maya had been torn apart and there remained only shreds floating before the vision of mystical Oneness . . . He feels himself to be godlike and strides with the same elation and ecstasy as the gods he has seen in his dreams."[75]

The immense tragedy for Europeans, I have argued, and most acutely for the northern Protestants among them, was that the same social forces that disposed them to depression also swept away a traditional cure. They could congratulate themselves for brilliant achievements in the areas of science, exploration, and industry, and even convince themselves that they had not, like Faust, had to sell their souls to the devil in exchange for these accomplishments. But with the suppression of festivities that accompanied modern European "progress," they had done something perhaps far more damaging: They had completed the demonization of Dionysus begun by Christians centuries ago, and thereby rejected one of the most ancient sources of help—the mind-preserving, lifesaving techniques of ecstasy.

8

Guns Against Drums:
Imperialism Encounters Ecstasy

The reader might justifiably accuse me of eurocentrism in my emphasis, so far, on European developments—except for one thing: It was the Europeans—not the Chinese or Aztecs or Zulu—who forcibly imposed their culture and beliefs on people throughout the world. The centuries, roughly the sixteenth through the nineteenth, in which Europeans discarded and suppressed their festive traditions are the same ones in which Europeans fanned out all over the globe conquering, enslaving, colonizing, and in general destroying other peoples and their cultures. Technological advances—in navigation and of course in weaponry—made the European campaign of global conquest possible; perhaps the psychological changes discussed in the previous chapter—toward a more driven and individualistic type of personality—helped make it seem necessary and appealing. No doubt there are many reasons (economic, demographic, ideological, even sexual) to explain why Europe's embrace of the new puritanism coincided with such a frantic burst of expansionism—a drive, it almost seems, to get *away*.

But it is the immediate consequence, rather than the sources, of European expansionism that concerns us here: The Europeans who explored and conquered and colonized were, certainly from the late sixteenth century on, fresh from their own experience of harsh cultural "reform" and had little tolerance for the exuberant rituals of other peoples. For example, a historian of Tahiti described the Protestant missionaries who settled on that sunny island in the early nineteenth century as followers of a "dour and cheerless creed," who routinely dressed in black and "never laughed, never made a joke or understood anyone else's, never enjoyed what they condemned as unseemly levity, and never let themselves forget for a moment the awful burden of the sins of the world."[1] Even in milder forms, the Christianity Europeans attempted to export to the world frowned on anything that looked to them like "emotionalism." As an early-twentieth-century American professor wrote in condemnation of "primitive" religiosity, "The mature fruit of the Spirit is not the subliminal uprush, the ecstatic inflow of emotion, the rhapsody, the lapse of inhibition, but rational love, joy, peace, long-suffering, kindness, goodness, faithfulness, meekness—*self-control.*"[2]

Sometimes the Europeans' destruction of "native" rites was incidental to the physical destruction of the natives themselves: It would be shortsighted to complain about the abolition of Tasmanian or Carib traditions, for example, when the people who might have been carriers of these traditions no longer exist, having succumbed centuries ago to European weapons and diseases. In Australia, the missionaries' efforts to uplift and "civilize" the Aboriginals were often overwhelmed by the more pressing business of burying them. One missionary outpost was abandoned with the explanation that "the termination of the Mission has arisen solely from the Aboriginals becoming extinct in these districts."[3]

On the whole, though, there was nothing "incidental" about the European campaign against the communal rituals of other societies. Most Europeans had little use for any aspects of non-European culture; African religions, for example, were described by an English promoter of the missionary effort as "little more than loose collections of ideas, vague and puerile, arising from a superstitious devotion to the life of Nature around."[4] Especially repellent to Europeans were the rituals of indigenous peoples, since these almost invariably featured dancing, singing, masking, and even the achievement of trance states. In large parts of Africa, for example, the identification between communal dance and music, on the one hand, and what Europeans might call "religion," on the other, was profound. The term the Tswanas of southern Africa use for dance (*go bina*) also means "to venerate,"[5] and in the Bantu language group of southern, central, and eastern Africa, the word *ngoma* can mean "ritual," "cult," "song-dance," or simply "drum."[6]

The anthropologist Jean Comaroff noted that of all the "native" customs and traditions in southern Africa, "collective song and dance were especially offensive to Christians."[7] As we saw in the introduction, Europeans tended to view such activities, wherever they found them, as outbreaks of devil worship, lasciviousness, or, from a more "scientific" perspective, hysteria. For example, a Jesuit missionary among the Yup'ik people of late-nineteenth-century Alaska wrote:

> I have great hopes for these poor people, even though they are so disgusting on the exterior that nature itself would stand up and take notice . . . In general their superstitions are a fearful worship of the devil. They indulge profusely in performances and feasts to please their dead but in fact to please and corrupt themselves, in dancing and banqueting.[8]

So whether the goal was to pacify indigenous peoples in a military and administrative sense or, more generously, to impose upon them the supposed benefits of civilization, Europeans generally found themselves in furious opposition to the communal pleasures and rituals of the people whose lives they intruded upon.

The existence of a widespread European campaign against indigenous ritual is beyond dispute; some scholars mention it almost in passing, as if little elaboration were required. The anthropologist

Jon P. Kirby, for example, tells us that missionaries in West Africa "were too busy suppressing traditional rituals and beliefs" to find out what they were and meant,[9] while another anthropologist, Beverly Stoeltje, explains that the distinction between ritual and festival "evolved as a consequence of modern religious systems' attempts to obliterate native religions."[10] Apparently, if native religious rituals could not be tolerated, they could still sometimes survive as "secular" festivities.

But it is frustratingly difficult to find blow-by-blow accounts of conflicts over specific native practices. One exception is Hawaii, where a three-way conflict—among white missionaries, white sailors, and native Hawaiians—has been documented. The Hawaiians, for the most part, wanted to continue their traditional pleasures; the sailors wanted to drink and exploit local women; the missionaries wanted to establish a kind of puritanical theocracy. Although the Hawaiians were organized into socially complex kingdoms, the white American missionary Hiram Bingham saw them as "almost naked savages," having "the appearance of destitution, degradation, and barbarism."[11] He and succeeding missionaries fought, with mixed success, to suppress both the sailors' carousing and such Hawaiian customs as surfing, canoe racing, lei wearing, and that "depraved native dance," the hula.[12]

I could find only sketchy and scattered accounts of the encounters between high-minded Europeans and native "devil worshippers" elsewhere. What they suggest is that the global campaign against festivities and ecstatic rituals in many ways resembled the post-Reformation campaign against festivities within Europe: It was a sporadic undertaking, carried out by both secular and religious authorities, and subject to frequent setbacks. In some settings, repression had the force of law, taking the form of edicts against drumming, dancing, and masking, for example, with penalties of flogging or even mutilation. As Kirby notes, "Most missionaries considered the colonial administrations as allies in the essential task of destroying existing structures,"[13] just as religiously motivated reformers within Europe could generally count on the assistance of secular authorities.

In other settings, where the colonial administration was still underdeveloped, individual missionaries usually attempted to halt the "devilish" native practices single-handedly, much like the puritanical preachers who took it upon themselves to tear down maypoles and disrupt festivities in their native England. Missionary accounts include many tales of such courageous, reckless, and, from a non-European point of view, surely ridiculous behavior. Early Catholic missionaries in Africa reported that, at the first sound of drums, they would "immediately run to the place to disturb the hellish practice."[14] A Capuchin friar in the Portuguese fort at Massangano, in what is now Angola, was almost stoned to death by an angry crowd "for endeavoring to oppose these people in their wicked ceremonies."[15] In the mid-nineteenth century, a Presbyterian missionary found black Jamaicans engaged in what they called a *myal* dance, and rushed out to stop them, only to be told that the dancers were not, as he supposed, "mad." "You must be mad yourself," they told him, "and had best go away."[16]

Again, as in Europe, collective rituals became what Comaroff called an "arena of contest" between the contending cultures—sites for the exchange of insults and threats, if not actual violence. Colonized peoples might use their rituals to mock the European intruders or, as the Europeans usually suspected, to whip up armed resistance. Or they might be attracted by Christian teachings, only to be repelled by Christian forms of worship. Nxele, a nineteenth-century Xhosa diviner, was originally drawn to Christianity, then decided that the right way to worship was not "to sing M'Dee, M'Dee, M'Dee all day and pray with their faces on the ground and their backs to the almighty—but to dance and enjoy life and to make love, so that the black people would multiply and fill the earth."[17] For their part, the Europeans "focused their challenge on communal rites"[18] and often judged the progress of their "civilizing" efforts by their success in suppressing such rites. A Methodist missionary in southern Africa, S. Broadbent, wrote in 1865: "I feel happy also in saying that the Bechuana customs and ceremonies are considerably on the wane. The native dance is, in some instances, kept up; but I frequently go at the time of the dance, oppose it, and preach to those who are willing to hear."[19] Among the Namaquas of South Africa, it was said of someone who converts to Christianity that "he has given up dancing."[20]

European observers sometimes noted the parallel between the crackdown on native rites worldwide and the crackdown on carnival and other festivities within Europe. Recall their tendency, as mentioned earlier, to equate the "savages" of "new" worlds with the lower classes of the old world, and the occasional analogy drawn between European carnival and the ecstatic rites of distant peoples. The parallel extends, in part, to the motive for repression: One of the goals of the crackdown within Europe was to instill the work ethic into the lower classes and apply the time "wasted" in festivities to productive labor. Similarly, European colonizers were often appalled both by the apparent laziness of the natives and by the energy they invested in purely "superstitious" ritual activities, and to such a degree that their irritation sometimes extended to the flora that supported the supposedly easygoing, native way of life. The poet Samuel Coleridge, for example—surely a liberal by nineteenth-century British standards—once suggested that the South Sea Islanders' breadfruit trees be destroyed, so that the islanders would be forced to learn hard work.[21] Along the same lines, the historian Thomas Carlyle was incensed by the West Indian pumpkin: "Where a Black man, by working about half-an-hour a-day . . . can supply himself, by aid of sun and soil, with as much pumpkin as will suffice, he is likely to be a little stiff to raise into hard work!"[22] Short of eliminating these psychologically debilitating plants, Christianity could solve the problem, as proposed by the English promoter of missions quoted above: "One of the chief difficulties experienced by employers of labour in Africa is the unstable and undisciplined character of the native labourer. Christian teaching and industrial training can do much to remove this trouble."[23]

But the parallel between repression within Europe and the cultural repression visited by Europeans on their colonial subjects in distant places goes only so far. Within Europe, elites recognized the human objects of repression—generally peasants, laborers, and artisans—as fellow Christians and, increasingly over time, as people who shared with them a sense of nationhood. Not so with the "savages," whose skin color and facial features combined with their unfamiliar beliefs and customs to render them almost entirely "other"—to the point where their very status as humans was open to question. English settlers in Australia thought of the original occupants of that subcontinent as "a species of tail-less monkeys" or, if human in any sense, clearly the kind of human "nearest of all to the monkey or orang-outang."[24] Georges Cuvier, the noted early-nineteenth-century Swiss comparative anatomist, judged that "the negro race . . . manifestly approaches to the monkey tribe. The hordes of which this variety is composed have always remained in a state of complete barbarism."[25] This attitude helped justify a casual, even lighthearted, approach to genocide. "I took no more notice of a hundred armed Indians than I would have of a handful of flies," wrote a Spanish conquistador,[26] while an English bush ranger boasted he would just "as leave shoot [Tasmanians] as so many sparrows."[27]

Within Europe, the intent of post-Reformation cultural "reform" was not to destroy the celebrants, only the celebrations. There, the overriding political-economic context was the rise of absolutism and, later, industrialization, within each of which emerging systems the European lower classes had an important part to play: as soldiers in the mass armies of absolute monarchs, and as workers in manufacturing enterprises. Their fate was to be disciplined, not necessarily to die. But the colonial context was, in large portions of the world, unabashedly murderous, comprising, as Tom Engelhardt wrote, a "single, multicentury, planetwide exterminatory pulse."[28] The analogue of the European worker was the colonial slave, and in places like South America and the Caribbean, slaves who were worked to death could readily enough be replaced. In settings where the conquerors and colonizers had no use for the indigenous population even as laborers—in Australia or the western part of the United States, for example—the natives were simply in the way, and the progress of "civilization" could be measured by their disappearance. In a recent book, Mark Cocker puts the death toll from four centuries of European imperialism at 50 million, an impressive figure even by twentieth-century standards of genocide.[29]

In this context, the missionaries who almost everywhere accompanied the conquerors sometimes appear almost as noble and altruistic as they imagined themselves to be. Their mission, after all, rested on the belief that native peoples had souls to save, meaning that they were in fact human. British missionaries often opposed the slave trade and sometimes slavery itself; in Australia they protested settler rapes and massacres of Aboriginals. In South America, Jesuit missionaries were seen by colonial authorities as too protective of the mission Indians they had converted, and were expelled from the entire continent in the late eighteenth century. For their part, secular authorities sometimes opposed missionary efforts, particularly those directed at African slaves in the Americas, out of the fear that slaves might take the liberatory themes of Christianity to heart. Until the religious revival of the mid-eighteenth century, many North American slave owners vigorously resisted the conversion of their slaves, who could be flogged for attending Christian prayer meetings or even praying in private.[30] Or they offered their slaves only a twisted form of Christianity, as in this sample from a "catechism" devised for North American slaves:

Q. What did God make you for?
A. To make a crop.
Q. What is the meaning of "Thou shalt not commit adultery"?
A. To serve our heavenly father, and our earthly master, obey our overseer, and not steal anything.[31]

In some instances, secular authorities irritated missionaries by failing to suppress "heathen" collective rites with sufficient consistency and vigor: In Jamaica and Brazil, slave owners often permitted nocturnal dancing on the grounds that it kept the slaves content and, given its evident "lasciviousness," possibly encouraged them to reproduce.[32] In India, English colonial administrators initially opposed the entry of Christian missionaries, fearing that any challenge to Hinduism would threaten stability and hence imperial profits.[33]

But what is striking, in any overview of colonialism as a global enterprise, is the degree of concordance between conquerors and missionaries, between those who would exploit non-European peoples, their habitats, and their resources, and those who would "merely" destroy their cultures.[34] "Imperialism is a matter of religion," argued the English promoter of the missionary effort. "We need a Christian imperialism and a Christian commercialism. We also need an imperial Christianity and an economic religion."[35] Slave owners and colonial administrators may have cared little what gods, if any, their slaves and subjects worshipped, but they shuddered at the collective strength such rituals invoked and represented. Dance was "particularly distasteful to the Europeans, not only for its 'salacious[ness],'" Comaroff writes, but because of the sheer "vitality of the system it represented," a vitality that directly defied the aims of the white exploiters.[36] And while individual missionaries may have had little concern for the profits of their fellow countrymen, they shared their dismay at the group unity so powerfully embodied in native ritual. John Mackenzie, sent to southern Africa by the London Missionary Society, wrote enthusiastically of "weakening the communistic relations of members of a tribe among one another and letting in the fresh, stimulating breath of healthy individualistic competition.'"[37]*

---

*For more on the complex, and often antagonistic, relationship between missionaries and the colonial effort, see Elbourne.

Black Carnival

The victims of European expansionism did not usually relinquish their traditions as swiftly and completely as the Europeans would have liked. Even under the crushing weight of imperialism and slavery, under circumstances of the most minute surveillance by colonial authorities, subject peoples sometimes found ways to preserve bits and pieces of their communal rituals and to invent new ones. The African diaspora to the Americas provides particularly striking cases of such cultural resistance, traces of which persist to this day, in the form, for example, of African-derived American music: blues, rock and roll, hip-hop, and jazz.

Between the seventeenth and nineteenth centuries, at least 10 million Africans were forcibly transported to the Americas under conditions that would seem to have precluded the preservation of any cultural traditions at all: They arrived in the "new" world virtually naked, stripped of all cultural artifacts and kinship connections, thrown together with Africans of entirely different national groupings and languages: Yoruba, Dahomeans, Ibo, and others. Once settled on the plantations of white European and North American slave owners, they were worked almost ceaselessly and often forbidden to engage in any of their "heathen" practices, including dancing and drumming. Yet these tormented peoples managed, with great courage and ingenuity, to preserve some of their traditional forms of communal celebration and, beyond that, to use them as springboards for rebellion against white rule, much as the European lower classes had deployed carnival as an occasion for armed resistance to their rulers and landlords.

For the most part, Africans of the diaspora carried out this work of cultural preservation under cover of European institutions. Carnival, for instance, transported to the Americas by Catholic French, Spanish, and Portuguese settlers, was originally a white-only event, but appropriated by slaves for their own purposes. Christianity itself provided another disguise for African traditions and—when combined with remnants of African worship—a vehicle for ecstatic ritual. Both the secularized tradition of carnival and the Africanized versions of Christianity that arose in the Americas—Vodou,* Santeria, Candomblé, and so on—became sites of black defiance and, inevitably, targets of white repression.

Let us begin with carnival and other, somewhat secular festivities brought by Europeans to the Americas. These celebrations, which Europeans expected to carry on as vigorously—if not more vigorously—in the "new" world as in the old, posed an immediate problem in the colonial setting: What about the slaves? When Europeans caroused or simply feasted, there were always dark faces watching, waiting for some particle of generosity to come their way, or waiting perhaps for some moment of weakness to present an opportunity for revolt. In Protestant settings, such as Jamaica and the southern United States, where Christmas was the highlight of the social calendar, slaves used it as an opening to establish their own, probably African-derived festivity: Jonkonnu. As early as 1688, Jamaican slaves were celebrating Jonkonnu with costuming and dancing with "Rattles ty'd to their Legs and Wrists."[38] A little over a century later, they had won a measure of white respect for Jonkonnu, with whites agreeing to do their own chores during this brief period of black celebration. A white contemporary reported that during the holidays "the distance between [masters and slaves] appears to be annihilated for the moment, like the familiar footing on which the Roman slaves were with their masters at the feast of the Saturnalia, to which a West Indian Christmas may be compared."[39] In the Carolinas, where Jonkonnu had spread by the nineteenth century, slaves marched to the big house, where they danced and demanded money and drinks from their masters. Thus a moment of white weakness—Christmas—was transformed into a black opportunity.

In Catholic settings, slaves encountered, and quickly exploited,

---

*Colloquially, *Voodoo*. I avoid that term because of its implications of black magic and "irrationality" generally, as in the expression *voodoo economics*. Other versions of the word include *Vudun* and *Voudun*.

a more robust version of the European festive tradition: a carnival period extending from Christmas not just to New Year's Day but nearly to Ash Wednesday. The case of Trinidad is particularly well documented. There, carnival was initially a white celebration, imported by French settlers, and an occasion for so much uninhibited revelry that from 1800 on, martial law was imposed at Christmastime in order to contain the white mischief.[40] People of color—slave or free—were barred from participation or confined to their own celebrations away from public spaces.

> The free persons of Colour were subject to very stringent Regulations and although not forbidden to mask, yet compelled to keep to themselves and never presume to join in the amusements of the privileged class. The Indians kept entirely aloof, and the slaves, except as onlookers . . . had no share in the Carnival which was confined exclusively to the upper class of the community.[41]

For slaves who dared to break the law by wearing masks at carnival time, the prescribed sentence was "one hundred stripes . . . and it being in the night time, the punishment is doubled."[42] Perhaps these dire prohibitions were not entirely necessary: Slaves and freed blacks may have been sufficiently repelled by the peculiar white carnival custom of dressing as slaves—as "mulatresses" (slave women) or *Négue jadin* (male field hands).[43]

No doubt unwittingly, the Trinidadian whites had broken the rule propounded almost two millennia earlier in Rome: that elites do not engage in uninhibited celebration in front of their social inferiors without compromising their legitimacy as rulers. In the early decades of the nineteenth century, Trinidadian blacks showed their disrespect by moving in on the white institution of carnival, finally achieving full participation in 1834, on the eve of emancipation, with an event transformed to suit their own culture and purposes. Blacks brought their own music to the celebration, along with African-derived symbolic imagery and their own mocking rituals of inversion. In the 1834 carnival, black Trinidadian marchers presented a parody of the island's (white) militia—which whites, newly sensitive to racial caricature, found to be "in very bad taste."[44]

A similar takeover of carnival took place later in Brazil, where, beginning in the 1880s, blacks used drums and tambourines to "initiate a new kind of carnival parading," apparently derived from the slaves' earlier practice of dancing at the funerals of African princes who died in slavery.[45] In both Trinidad and Brazil, whites responded to black participation just as elites had responded to the disorderly lower-class celebrations of carnival in Europe: by retreating indoors to their own masked balls and dinner parties, which were invariably described as "elegant" by the local newspapers, in contrast to the "barbarous" celebrations of the blacks.

One strains to imagine the vitality and color of the great black-dominated carnivals of the nineteenth-century Caribbean. Unfortunately, we have only the disapproving accounts of white observers to go by, and these downplay the artistic creativity that went into costume making and choreography, to focus instead on the perceived violence, disorder, and lewdness of the events. A Trinidadian newspaper account from the early 1870s, for example, mentions the "brutish cries and shouts" of the celebrants, as well as the "horrid forms running to and fro about the town with flaming torches in their hands, like so many demons escaped from a hot place not usually mentioned in polite society."[46]

We cannot even discern, in white accounts, what aspects of carnival were derived from Africa rather than Europe, since, as they grew more and more estranged from the festivities, whites tended to label any disagreeable elements "African." In reality, some of the features of black carnival that whites found most disturbing would have been thoroughly familiar, at least in form and intent, to a celebrant of French medieval carnival—notably the rituals of inversion and mocking attacks on authority. Gender inversion, in the form of cross-dressing, seems to have been a common pleasure of Trinidadian carnival, with a (white) newspaper reporting in 1874: "As for the number of girls masked and in men's clothing, we cannot say how many hundred are flaunting their want of shame. As many men, also generally of the lowest order, are in like manner strutting about in female dress, dashing out their gowns as they go."[47] In a more directly threatening way, black carnival participants used the occasion to insult the virtue of well-known white ladies and send up the entire plantocracy. As one historian reports, "Elaborately costumed revellers impersonated the Governor, the Chief Justice, the Attorney General, well-known barristers and solicitors, socially prominent cricketers, and other props of society."[48]

In another striking parallel to the European festive tradition, Caribbean slaves and freed blacks put carnival to service as an occasion for armed uprisings. The historian Elizabeth Fenn reports that 35 percent of all known slave plots and rebellions in the British Caribbean were planned for the Christmas period, noting that "in this regard the slaves of the Americas differed little from the French peasants and laborers studied by Emmanuel Le Roy Ladurie and Natalie Zemon Davis."[49] An early Trinidadian slave revolt, on Christmas 1805, was blamed on slave societies, called *convois*, organized "for the purpose of dancing and innocent amusement."[50] In Cuba, similar groups known as *cabildos*, which were responsible for organizing carnival processions, hatched uprisings in 1812 and 1835.[51] Even gentle Jonkonnu aroused white fears of rebellion. An 1833 novel by a former resident of Jamaica described the pre-Christmas military preparations undertaken in Kingston "in case the John Canoes should take a small fancy to burn or pillage the town, or to rise and cut the throats of their masters, or any little innocent recreation of the kind."[52]

In Trinidad, carnival and any form of public black festivity came in for harsh repression in the 1880s. Fearful of the black response to an outright ban on carnival, the British attacked it piecemeal, itemizing their prohibitions on drumming, parading, dancing, masking, and even the carrying of lighted torches. Attempts to enforce these rules often led to violent clashes between revelers and the police, as at a celebration in Princes Town where dancing women mocked the police while others in the crowd of five hundred hurled missiles, "some containing foul-smelling substances." The police opened fire, killing two, and a few months later attacked another festivity celebrated by East Indian immigrants as well as blacks, killing "many."[53]

The Preservation of Ecstasy

Carnival provided one vehicle for the preservation of African traditions, religion another. How much of African theology and religious ritual survived the Middle Passage is a subject of keen scholarly debate. Uprooted from their shrines and holy places, deprived of opportunities for collective worship, slaves could not have brought much more than memories of their West African religious ideas and practices. Yet uprooted Africans, who were intended to occupy much the same spiritual—and often physical—space as domestic animals, cobbled together bits of Christianity and remembered fragments of their original religions to create entirely new ones: Candomblé in Brazil; Vodou, Santeria, Obeah, and Shango in the Caribbean. Even North American black Protestantism, to the extent that it offered (and continues to offer) a rhythmically engaging variation on the white version, served to keep alive African musical and communal approaches to worship.

Theologically, the larger "syncretic," or hybrid, religions— Vodou, Candomblé, and Santeria—are defined by their use of the Catholic saints as a cover for a pantheon of African-derived deities. But it is the collective *practice* of these religions that concerns us, and this was, and remains, Dionysian, if we understand that word in the most ancient religious sense. These are ecstatic, danced religions, in which music and the muscular synchrony of dance are employed to induce a state of trance interpreted as possession by, or transcendent unity with, a god. To most European observers, the danced rituals leading to possession trance looked like madness, complete abandon, or sexual frenzy. A 1929 novel about Haiti, for example, offered the following overwrought description of a Vodou ritual.

> In the red light of torches which made the moon turn pale, leaping, screaming, writhing black bodies, blood-maddened, sex-maddened, god-maddened, drunken, whirled and danced their dark saturnalia, heads thrown weirdly back as if their necks were broken, white teeth and eyeballs gleaming, while couples seizing one another from time to time fled from the circle, as if pursued by furies, into the forest to share and slake their ecstasy.[54]

For all their ambivalence about ecstatic experience, anthropologists agree that the rites of religions like Vodou and Candomblé are in fact quite disciplined and focused. Alfred Métraux, the ethnographer of Vodou, whom we encountered in the introduction fretting over whether Vodou rites represented a form of hysteria, more accurately observed that

> they are more like difficult exercises to which one applies one's whole being, never allowing oneself to succumb to disorderly gestures. Ritual dictates that the gods be present at various times during the ceremony, and they never fail to turn up at the appropriate moment. Possession is therefore a controlled phenomenon obeying precise rules. It is considered to be unseemly for a god to "mount" a person who does not belong to the family giving the fete, and if he does so he is asked to go away.[55]

Participants know under what circumstances trance states should appropriately occur, and achieve them only through practice and training. As a scholar of Caribbean literature writes, again of the Vodou rites: "This experience of election [possession trance], its shock of communion, is not evidence of psychic disruption, or proof of pathology, but rather a result of the most intense discipline and study. Not everyone can be possessed, for not everyone can know how to respond to the demands and expectations of her god."[56] So the ecstatic rites of these diaspora religions were not mad orgies, as whites often perceived them, but deliberately nurtured *techniques* of ecstasy, derived from ancient traditions.

For the most part, it was West African religions that inspired the rites of blacks in the Americas.[57] In the Caribbean, the ecstatic tradition preserved in diaspora religions is almost entirely African, since African slaves were imported only as the indigenous Caribs and Arawaks rendered themselves unfit for labor by dying off from European diseases and mistreatment. Brazilian Candomblé, however, also draws on certain indigenous Brazilian Indian ecstatic rites observed by Europeans when they first started arriving in the sixteenth century. For example, an early French traveler found Brazilian Indian women (of what locality or tribe I do not know) gathering to dance and sing in a circle, after which they would begin to foam at the mouth and "suddenly become possessed with the devil."[58] But the African connection remains strong in Brazil, where particular candomblés (meaning religious subcommunities) are sometimes distinguished by their Yoruban or Dahomean roots and possession is believed necessary to physically summon the gods from their homes in Africa.[59] If the slave could not escape back to Africa, her religion could bring Africa to her—or, at the very least, the memory of freedom. As one nineteenth-century observer put it, "In dancing and singing, they forget their ills and servitude, and only remember their native country and the time that they were free."[60]

Like carnival, diaspora religions provided a springboard for rebellions throughout the nineteenth century. Some of the reasons for this are obvious even in the most rationalist European terms: Religious rituals offered an excuse for slaves to congregate; religious institutions fostered organization among slaves belonging to different owners; religious training nurtured leadership, often among women as well as men. So we find the candomblés serving as "centers for insurrection" in early-nineteenth-century Brazil[61] and

Santeria gatherings in Cuba linked to slave revolts on that island. In Trinidad, where Obeah prevailed, some revolts were led by religious leaders, or obeah men.[62] Haiti provides the most spectacular—and successful—case of insurrection inspired in part by diaspora religion.[63] The nocturnal danced rituals of Vodou served to rally slaves to the cause and were, until the achievement of independence in 1803, a constant target of French repression. Samba Boukman, one of the revolution's first leaders, was himself a *houngan* (Vodou priest) guided by a *loa* (spirit) of African derivation. As the case of Haiti demonstrates, the memory of freedom—kept alive in ecstatic dances and visions—could also be its source.

Ecstatic Revolution

But the response of subjugated peoples to colonialism was not only conservative, in the sense of keeping old traditions alive. As anthropologists have often noted, imperialism seemed, perversely, to encourage the emergence of new and often defiant ecstatic religious cults. Perhaps we should count diaspora religions like Vodou among the "new," since these involved creative amalgams of African and European religions, but there were many more such inventions—often short-lived and usually at least implicitly opposed to white rule. Imagine the distress of the missionary who had, with the help of colonial authorities, stamped out indigenous religious practices, demolished local shrines, pulled the children into his mission schools—only to find the "natives" forsaking Christianity for some fresh form of "deviltry." The explanation often given by anthropologists is that collective ecstasy serves as a form of escapism: Sorely stressed by colonialism, the colonized people sought, through ecstatic forms of worship, a fleeting alternative to the horrors of their actual situation.

Whatever the explanation, we find ecstatic and millenarian cults springing up from the era of first contact almost into the present time. In Africa, some of these took institutional form in the so-called

Independent Churches, which, like the diaspora religions of the Americas, drew on Christianity as well as indigenous religions. Frequently led by women, these were "often contrasted to the mission-founded Churches by their wearing of flowing white garments and headgear, their use of drums and responsive chanting, and their emphasis on spiritual healing."[64]

Ecstatic responses to white conquest were a global phenomenon, arising in Indonesia, Melanesia, and North America as well as Africa. In North America, the Menomini Indians of upper Wisconsin launched their "Dream Dance" cult in 1879, in which the central rite was a dance revolving around a large drum embodying the Great Spirit: "The rhythmic beating, gradually speeding up to a climactic pitch, produces a state of excitement and frenzy strongly imbued with the dancers' feeling of oneness."[65] Better known is the Ghost Dance, which arose in the late 1860s among the Paiute and spread from them to the Cheyenne, Shoshone, Sioux, and others. Here, too, the central ritual was a dance leading to trance states.

> The Ghost dancers, women as well as men, paint their bodies to indicate the revelations they have received, and arrange themselves in concentric circles, the arms of each dancer resting on the shoulders of both neighbors, so that the vibrant rhythm of the dance sways the worshippers as if they were a single body. The mood quickly created by the dance is conducive to collective exaltation and trance, the dance being usually performed at night.[66]

For a more explicitly revolutionary case, consider the Maori Hau-hau cult that arose under British rule in 1864, a time when many of the Maori had converted to Christianity. The British settlers, irritated by the continuing Maori presence on land that could be more profitably used for farming, had begun to behave in a decidedly un-Christian fashion—driving the Maori from their villages so that thousands died of exposure and starvation. The Maori responded by taking up arms against the whites and deconverting from Christianity en masse. In its stead, they embraced the new Hau-hau cult, which combined traditional religious themes with bits of missionary learning, or at least songs sung in "an extraordinary jumble of Hebrew, English, German, Greek and Italian." Here again, the central ritual was a danced one, performed, the Italian ethnographer Vittorio Lanternari reports, "for the purpose of producing a state of ecstasy in the participants."[67] Candidates for initiation into the cult assembled around a sacred pole, where,

> because of the strain, combined with the heat of the day, the shouting of the worshippers, and the furious pace of the dancers going round and round, the candidates for initiation were hypnotized; their bodies were then seized by others and tossed repeatedly into the air until they became unconscious. As soon as they recovered, they were considered initiated into the cult, and were pushed summarily into the march [against the British].[68]

Anthropologists and other scholars have often tended, in recent decades, to view such rites with impatience, if not disgust. Dancing in circles does not, after all, as was claimed in some cases, make men immune to bullets or cause colonizers to depart in their ships. From a modern European vantage point, this is "irrational" behavior, akin to mental illness.[69] Thus the anthropologist Lucy Mair saw similarities between the visions of millenarian (and often ecstatic) cults and the "fantasies" and "hysterical phenomena" common to mental patients.[70] Even the deeply sympathetic Lanternari described the ecstatic rites of colonized people as "collective psychoses" and a "means of evasion."[71] More recently, the sociologist Bryan Wilson notes condescendingly:

> Cargo cults, and other movements among simpler peoples, are frequently attended by manifestations of what observers might call "hysteria" or "frenzy." Undoubtedly, these responses can be induced in some circumstances, but there is no reason to suppose that they

are not usually spontaneous . . . The psychic benefit from such exercises, we may note parenthetically, is, sociologically speaking, the only sort of salvation that is really to be attained.[72]

But it is this smug Western vantage point, rather than the rituals of "simpler peoples," that cries out for psychological interpretation. The danced rituals of rebellious colonized peoples would probably not, after all, have seemed so strange to a medieval European carnival rebel or, for that matter, to one of the sixteenth-century German Anabaptists who danced triumphantly through the streets of Munster until more orthodox Protestants subdued them. What had changed between the sixteenth and the twentieth centuries was the Western idea of revolution. Medieval European peasants, like nineteenth-century colonized peoples throughout the world, seem to have imagined revolution as a fairly sudden transformation, coming up from below and leading swiftly to abolition of the hated hierarchy, to a "world turned upside down." But European revolutionaries of the post-Reformation era faced absolutist monarchs who possessed vast armies and police apparatuses. In this situation, revolution appeared to be a painstaking project, requiring many months or years, and similar to war in its demand for discipline and planning.

The historian Michael Walzer has argued that modern revolution was a task for the kind of ascetic, single-minded, self-denying personality that Calvinism sought to inculcate, and certainly some of the successful revolutionaries of the West would seem to fill the bill. As we have seen, the English revolutionary leader Oliver Cromwell, a Calvinist himself, railed perpetually against the festive inclinations of his troops. The Jacobin leader Robespierre despised disorderly gatherings, including "any group in which there is a tumult"—a hard thing to avoid during the French Revolution, one might think.[73] His fellow revolutionary Louis de Saint-Just described the ideal "revolutionary man" in terms that would have been acceptable to any Puritan: "inflexible, but sensible; he is frugal; he is simple . . .

honorable, he is sober, but not mawkish."[74] Lenin inveighed against "slovenliness . . . carelessness, untidiness, unpunctuality" as well as "dissoluteness in sexual life,"[75] seeing himself as a "manager" and "controller" as well as a leader.[76] For men like Robespierre and Lenin, the central revolutionary rite was the *meeting*—experienced in a sitting position, requiring no form of participation other than an occasional speech, and conducted according to strict rules of procedure. Dancing, singing, trances—these could only be distractions from the weighty business at hand.

We might respond in many ways to this Calvinist model of revolution, which has served to reinforce Western disdain for the ecstatic rituals of oppressed and colonized peoples. We could point out that the ascetic and militaristic Western model of revolution—though successfully applied to anticolonial struggles in the midtwentieth century—carries a considerable risk of dictatorship as the outcome. Fear of disorderly or "irrational" behavior readily masks a fear of the people, and a leader who sees himself as a "controller" is well on his way to becoming a tyrant. Alternatively, we might make a utilitarian argument for the importance of ecstatic ritual within otherwise "Western" revolutions. What is achieved through such rituals, in a purely functional sense, is an intense feeling of solidarity among the participants—at least all accounts suggest as much—and solidarity is the basis of effective political action from below. Even the "fantasies" entertained by participants, or apprehended in trance, surely have an empowering effect. The field hand who achieves unity with a god through a Vodou possession trance, and the market woman who leads a second life as a priestess—these are potentially formidable adversaries.

Furthermore, if ecstatic rites were only a frivolous distraction from "real" politics in the Western sense, how are we to explain the zeal with which white authorities sought to repress them? The only explanation we would be left with is that the white authorities were themselves being "irrational" and that *white* hysteria was a persistent feature of the colonial effort—for wherever they sprang up, the syncretic religions and mystically motivated movements of native peoples were met with harsh repression. In Africa, colonial authorities crushed any religious movement they saw as heterodox, overly enthusiastic, or simply too "African." The first leader of an "independent" African-Christian movement—a Congolese woman who took the name of Donna Beatrice—was burned to death by the Belgians in 1706.[77] As recently as the 1920s, the Belgians sentenced another independent African prophet, Simon Kimbangu, to life imprisonment, and the British even harassed the African version of the Watchtower movement, which featured long nights of drumming, hymn singing, and speaking in tongues.[78] In the Americas at the end of the eighteenth century, the British governor of Trinidad launched "a kind of inquisition" against Obeah, in which suspected adherents of that religion were burned, hanged, or subjected to amputations of their ears or noses.[79] Napoleon Bonaparte instigated an effort to eradicate Vodou in Haiti;[80] Portuguese colonial authorities harassed and suppressed the candomblés.[81]

In some cases, pure hysteria—or at least overreaction—does seem to have motivated the repression of native rituals. The Ghost Dance religion, for example, presented no immediate threat to whites; in fact, its moral code included the precepts: "Do no harm to anyone" and "You must not fight!"[82] But apparently unaware of the cult's pacifism, U.S. authorities suppressed the cult vigorously and ended up blaming it for the Sioux uprising of 1890, which culminated in the massacre at Wounded Knee. After all, Ghost Dancers were subversive enough to imagine the imminent return of all the Indian dead, who would have amounted, by the end of the nineteenth century, to an impressive army.

But can the European repression of ecstatic rites everywhere be ascribed to irrational overreaction, or can we credit the whites with some ability to discern a real threat? In the Caribbean, the colonial authorities' long-standing hostility to the African-style drum does seem to have been based on a realistic assessment of that instrument's subversive uses. British authorities in Trinidad banned drums in 1884, with a newspaper expressing the usual dismay over "the state of civilization of people whose members can be set in movement by the repetition of such barbarous sound."[83] But we can infer a more rational and military motive, since the authorities simultaneously banned dancing, processions, and "any assemblage or collection of persons armed with sticks or other weapons of offence and numbering ten or more."[84] In Cuba, U.S. occupying forces banned "drums of African origin" in 1902, later expanding the prohibition to include "all Afrocuban ceremonial dances" as "symbols of barbarity and disturbing to the social order."[85] Military considerations played a role in the prohibition of drums in mid-eighteenth-century South Carolina, in part because slaves were using them as a means of long-distance communication.

Finally, even supposing that the danced rituals and religions with which people worldwide responded to enslavement and colonization were entirely frivolous, nonthreatening, and politically pointless, who are we—as people operating within the Western tradition of rationality and scholarship—to judge them? If the oppressed gained nothing more from their ecstatic rituals and cults than a "psychic benefit," to use Wilson's phrase, we must still concede that—to people who had lost their traditions, their land, and often their freedom—a psychic benefit is no small thing. As the anthropologist I. M. Lewis wrote: "What we find over and over again in a wide range of different cultures and places is the special endowment of mystical power given to the weak. If they do not quite inherit the earth, at least they are provided with means which enable them to offset their otherwise crushing jural disabilities."[86]

Consider a fairly recent ecstatic religion, the Full Witness Apostolic Church of Zion, started by a Zulu mine worker under South African apartheid in 1956. The church's central ritual is a circular leaping dance derived from a precolonial initiation ritual: "The whirling circle builds up a unitary momentum, like a dynamo generating the spiritual energy . . . The ever closer coordination of physical gestures under the driving beat and the physiological effects of the circling motion seem to dissolve the margins between individual participants, who act and respond as one body."[87] These dancers might have been better advised, by a left-leaning anthropologist, for example, to join the African National Congress, and possibly some of them did. But if all they found in their religious ritual was a moment of transcendent joy—well, let us give them credit for finding it. To extract pleasure from lives of grinding hardship and oppression is a considerable accomplishment; to achieve ecstasy is a kind of triumph.

Such triumphs become rarer and rarer, though, as we move from the age of conquest to the present. Despite all the efforts to preserve traditional rites—and all the flare-ups of ecstatic and defiant religious movements—the overall story is necessarily one of cultural destruction and gathering gloom. Ancient rituals were suppressed; syncretic religions marginalized and driven underground; religiously inspired revolutionary cults destroyed. To return to the Tahitians with whom we began this chapter: In the late eighteenth century, they had used one of their traditional festivities to make fun of the two Spanish priests who had come to convert them, denouncing the poor Christians as thieves, fools, and (although this insult may have lost some of its potency in translation) "shellfish."[88] A few decades later, though, the Tahitians were sufficiently worn down that the dour Protestant missionaries who replaced the priests could boast of having "restrained the natural levity of the natives" and prevailed on them to abandon their danced rituals.[89]

When the Russian navigator Baron Thaddeus Bellingshausen visited the island in 1820, he found that the Tahitians now wore European clothes and that both men and women had shaved their heads since, as the historian Alan Moorehead writes, "that lovely gleaming black hair which once fell to the girls' waists was apparently regarded by the missionaries as unsanitary." Tattooing had been discouraged; liquor officially banned; and "where there had once been unashamed free love there now existed Christian guilt." The missionaries must have been especially proud that "no one danced any more or played Tahitian music. Even the weaving of garlands of flowers was forbidden."[90] Defeated, converted, and "re-formed," the Tahitians had little to do but drink.

Such were the *tristes tropiques* lamented by Claude Lévi-Strauss in the mid-1950s—scene of broken cultures, wrecked economies, and melancholic populations disposed to suicide and alcoholism.[91] In the face of so much destruction, it may seem petty to focus on the obliteration of communal ritual and festivity. But in any assessment of the impact of European imperialism, "techniques of ecstasy"—ways of engendering transcendence and joy from within the indigenous group itself, without any recourse to the white man's technologies or commodities—must at least be counted among the losses.

9

Fascist Spectacles

In this, the modern—or, we might say, postfestive—era, people still come together in large numbers from time to time, expecting an experience of unity, uplift, or, at least, diversion. The occasion may be a sporting event, a concert, theatrical production, parade, or public ceremony such as the funeral of an important personage. Of all the mass gatherings of the modern era, though, the most notorious—and certainly the most disturbing—were the giant rallies and public rituals staged in the 1930s by the Nazis and the Italian fascists. And of these, none was more notorious than the annual Nazi party congress held in Nuremberg, where hundreds of thousands of the party's faithful gathered for an experience often characterized by observers as "ecstatic."

It was at the 1934 Nuremberg congress that the American journalist William Shirer began to "comprehend . . . some of the reasons for Hitler's success. Borrowing a chapter from the Roman church, he is restoring pageantry and colour and mysticism to the drab lives of twentieth-century Germans."[1] The congress, which went on for a week, included no debates or deliberations to interfere with the "mystic" effects, only parades (chiefly of soldiers and

Nazi leaders), military drills, and exhortatory speeches. For the climactic nighttime events, the Nazi architect Albert Speer had designed a huge stone stadium crowned with a giant eagle, decked out with thousands of swastika banners, and illuminated by 130 high-power antiaircraft searchlights.[2] There, "in the flood-lit night," Shirer believed that the congress-goers "achieved the highest state of being the Germanic man knows: the shedding of their individual souls and minds . . . until under the mystic lights and at the sound of the magic words of the Austrian they were merged completely in the German herd."[3]

The Austrian was of course Adolf Hitler, whose entrances and speeches were staged for the maximum dramatic effect. Upon his arrival at the rally site, Shirer reported, the band would stop playing and a hush would fall over the crowd. Then the band would strike up the Badenweiler March, which was used only for Hitler's entrances, followed by an orchestra playing Beethoven's Egmont Overture, while "great Klieg lights played on the stage."[4] The speech itself might be little more than a string of slogans about "blood and soil," "our fallen heroes," et cetera, but it was delivered with a mounting passion, approaching fury, to repeated choruses of full-throated "Sieg heils" from the crowd. Under these circumstances, even the thoroughly hostile ambassador from France, André François-Poncet, could not help marveling at "the atmosphere of collective enthusiasm that permeated the ancient city, the singular exaltation that seized hundreds of thousands of men and women, the romantic fever and the mystic ecstasy and the sacred delirium, as it were, that possessed them!"[5]

This image of ecstatic crowds Sieg heil–ing their mad leader—always juxtaposed in our minds with the mass graves and starved bodies of his victims—has become, in our own time, emblematic of collective excitement in any form. It altered the outlook of the social sciences, making Durkheim's enthusiasm for what he called collective effervescence begin to look, as Charles Lindholm wrote, "terribly naive." Lindholm reported that the field of social psychology was so "traumatized by the direction mass movements have taken in the contemporary era" that it came to see collective excitement as "synonymous with evil."[6] The historian William H. McNeill added that "since World War II, repugnance against Hitlerism has discredited rhythmic muscular expressions of political and other sorts of ideological attachment throughout the western world."[7] Or, as some revisionist social psychologists put it very recently, the effect of fascism was to convince social scientists that "groups are inherently dangerous."[8]

In less academic circles too, the very word *Nuremberg* evokes crowds driven to hysteria by cunning stagecraft and charismatic speakers—primed for any atrocities they may be called on to commit. Search the Internet for the words *Nuremberg rally* and you will find references not only to the historical event but to almost any kind of gathering charged with group excitement: "Nuremberg" as a pejorative applied to the Super Bowl, to rock concerts, to the Academy Awards show. A left-winger describes a right-wing pro-Israel rally as a "Jewish Nuremberg";[9] a critic says of the audience for a less-than-witty stand-up comic, "It feels like I am at the Nuremberg rally and everyone is Sieg heil-ing in the form of laughs."[10] In a 1968 *New York Times* article, a critic described a Rolling Stones concert as "pure Nuremberg!"[11] Reflecting on sports fandom, including his own enthusiasm for baseball, the novelist Leslie Epstein writes:

> Dissolution of the self, transcendence, the feeling of oneness, wholeness, unity: Who can draw the line between, on the one hand, such innocent joy, the return to childhood in the adult, the jump toward manhood in the boy; and, on the other, the echo of a Nuremberg rally . . . ? Between, finally, the tolerated commonplace, *Kill the ump!* and the no less sanctioned urge to *Kill the Jews?*[12]

Epstein refrains from taking credit for this insight, attributing it to long-standing general knowledge: "Long before Freud wrote on the subject . . . everyone knew that membership in a crowd was a permit to regress to a more primitive form of the instinctual life."

But the intellectuals' condemnation of crowds originates no more than 150 years before Nuremberg, and in an entirely different, if not opposite, political situation: the French Revolution. While the fascist rallies celebrated tyranny, the French revolutionaries sought its permanent overthrow. While fascism epitomizes the political right at its cruelest extreme, the French Revolution gave birth to the modern idea of the *left*—not to mention the very categorization of political stances into *right* and *left*. If there was any similarity between, say, the events at Nuremberg and the decisive actions of the French Revolution, such as the storming of the Bastille, it is a seemingly superficial one: Both involved large outdoor gatherings of people, in other words, *crowds*.

The insurgent French crowds may seem relatively benign to us now—even heralds of an age of democracy—but they had sent a shock wave throughout the palaces and manor homes of Europe: Here were shabbily dressed people, many of them hungry or at least demanding bread, and they had succeeded in demolishing the Bourbon monarchy. Looking back from the late nineteenth century, the amateur French social scientist Gustave Le Bon declared that the revolutionary crowds could not be understood in terms of any rational motives, such as hunger or disgust with the Old Regime. They were simply insane, and they were so because insanity is an inherent feature of crowds. Within one, individuals enter a "special state, which much resembles the state of fascination in which the hypnotised individual finds himself in the hands of the hypnotiser." The proximity of large numbers of other people causes the brain to become "paralysed," so that the individual "becomes the slave of all the unconscious activities of his spinal cord."[13] What you have, in effect, is a crowd not of individuals but of spinal cords, and there could be nothing more "primitive" than that.

Le Bon's 1895 book, *The Crowd*, became the one of the world's all-time best-selling works of social science, despite the fact that Le Bon did not witness the revolution he freely described as if he had been watching it all from a balcony, nor did he see the necessity of citing either historians or eyewitness accounts. His book consists of a string of assertions, most of which we would dismiss today as simple prejudices. For example, crowds are "like women," he insists, in their irrationality and tendency to go to extremes.[14] As for the lower classes whose energy drove the revolution, he was opposed to the kind of egalitarianism the French revolutionaries fought for, as well as all forms of democracy, writing that "the masses" of his own time were motivated by "nothing less than a determination to utterly destroy society as it now exists."[15] But these failings did not disqualify Le Bon from being the sole source for Freud's reflections on collective behavior, and hence entering into the canonical mainstream of Western thought.

Thus in what has been the conventional intellectual view, "the crowd"—whether obediently cheering Hitler at Nuremberg or rising up to demand bread in revolutionary Paris—resembles nothing so much as the bands of "savages" colonialists encountered performing their ecstatic rituals. Early missionaries understood the ecstatic "savages" to be possessed by the devil; later psychologists described people caught up in crowds as "de-individuated" or as having "regressed" into a highly suggestible, emotionally labile, childlike state. Not that the devil went entirely out of style, even with the scientifically minded: Commenting on street crowds he had witnessed as a young man in Paris, Freud wrote, "I believe they are all possessed of a thousand demons . . . They are the people of psychical epidemics, of historical mass convulsions."[16] Individually, we may be reasonable and civilized people, but—the thinking goes—put us together and some primitive evil churns up. Nuremberg in 1934 and Paris in 1789, the Holocaust and the Reign of Terror—all merge with the war dances of the Mohawk and the initiation rites of Australian Aboriginals into a single category of wild and potentially homicidal behavior.

But were the fascist rallies of the 1930s really examples of collective ecstasy, akin to carnivals and Dionysian rituals? And if so, does the threat of uncontrollable violence stain every gathering, every ritual and festivity, in which people experience transcendence and self-loss?

We begin with an important distinction: The mass fascist rallies were not festivals or ecstatic rituals; they were spectacles, designed by a small group of leaders for the edification of the many. Such spectacles have a venerable history, going back at least to the Roman Empire, whose leaders relied on circuses and triumphal marches to keep the citizenry loyal. The medieval Catholic Church used colorful rituals and holiday processions to achieve the same effect, parading statues of saints through the streets, accompanied by gorgeously dressed Church officials. In a mass spectacle, the objects of attention—the marchers or, in the Roman case, chained captives and exotic animals in cages—are only part of the attraction. Central to the experience is the knowledge that hundreds or thousands of other people are attending the same spectacle—just as, in the age of television, the announcer may solemnly remind us that a billion or so other people are also tuned in to the same soccer game or Academy Awards presentation.

In the case of Nuremberg, we have a record of the proceedings in the form of Leni Riefenstahl's documentary *Triumph of the Will*, and it bears witness to a distinctly unfestive experience. Most of the "action" consists of uniformed men marching in columns through streets or across open spaces. Occasionally civilians are featured: Women in traditional folk costumes briefly walk by; thousands of members of the national work brigades march. The latter are also uniformed and carry their shovels over their shoulders like rifles. Other than that, there is speech making, mostly at night, by lengthy lineups of dignitaries, and a good deal of music, mostly from marching bands. That is the sum total of the entertainment, if we can call it that. At Nuremberg, as at countless other rallies in Nazi Germany and fascist Italy, the only spectacle on display was the military, the only legitimate form of motion the march.

And what is there for the nearly two hundred thousand people who have come to Nuremberg for the event to do? They line the streets as Hitler's motorcade comes through—smiling, cheering, giving the Nazi salute. They line the streets again as the various columns of men march through. They assemble in the evening for the speeches. Their sole role, in other words, is to watch and applaud.

It could be argued that the crowds in *Triumph of the Will* have a further role as part of the spectacle themselves—after all, a movie is being made of the proceedings, not to mention the fact that Hitler and his henchmen get to enjoy the view of the assembled masses from on high. But even as a part of the overall spectacle, the individual's role is limited to being one tiny element of the mass. His or her movements are restricted to the occasional straight-armed salute; even the slight forward surge of the crowd as Hitler passes in an open car is quickly and firmly arrested by the line of policemen. Day after day as the party congress proceeds, the crowds wait and watch, reassemble at a new spot where they again wait and watch. They could be theatergoers deprived of seats. But they are too well-behaved and immobilized to be mistaken for, say, a late-twentieth-century crowd of sports fans or rock concert–goers. "They are actors," the historian George L. Mosse observed, "in carefully staged liturgical rites."[17]

An audience is very different from a crowd, festive or otherwise. In a crowd, people are aware of one another's presence, and, as Le Bon correctly intuited, sometimes emboldened by their numbers to do things they would never venture on their own. In an audience, by contrast, each individual is, ideally, unaware of other spectators except as a mass. He or she is caught up in the speech, the spectacle, the performance—and often further isolated from fellow spectators by the darkness of the setting and admonitions against talking to one's neighbors. Fascist spectacles were meant to encourage a

sense of solidarity or belonging, but in the way that they were performed, and in the fact that they *were* performed, they reduced
whole nations to the status of an audience.

The Festivals of the French Revolution

The prototype for the fascist rallies of the twentieth century was,
ironically enough, forged in the French Revolution, though in a
kind of event unnoted by Le Bon. He fantasized and obsessed
about the spontaneous actions of crowds but paid no attention to
the well-organized, and for the most part quite staid, mass patriotic
spectacles staged by whatever faction held power or was intent on
capturing it. At least in the case of the French Revolution, there is
little danger of confusing the officially staged spectacles with more
spontaneous types of festivities. The official "festivals of the revolution," as these patriotic spectacles were called, did not build on or
reinforce either traditional, carnivalesque festivities or the excitement of crowds in the streets. They were designed in no small part,
in fact, to counter and replace such livelier forms of festivity.

And within the revolution itself, there was a great deal of festive
crowd behavior to counter. Nineteenth-century historians—of
whatever political sympathies—invariably commented on the revolution's "maenadic" or "Saturnalian" qualities. Here, in the years
from 1789 to about 1794, the European lower-class tradition of festive uprisings reached a historic climax: People deployed traditional
festive occasions and symbols, like the maypole, to advance the revolutionary cause. Or they used political uprisings as occasions for
festive behavior: dancing the carmagnole in the streets, singing revolutionary songs, feasting, and drinking. Even the carnival tradition
of costuming makes an appearance, with citizens wearing the tri-
color badge of revolution or affecting the simple garments of the
lower classes. The largely female crowd that marched on Versailles
in 1789, which, legend has it, had been summoned by a little girl
beating a drum, turned the return trip into a traveling celebration:

"The fishwives seated on the cannon, others wearing grenadiers' caps; wine barrels next to powder kegs; green branches attached to butts of rifles; joy, shouting, clamor, gaiety, . . . noise, the image of the ancient Saturnalia, nothing could describe this convoy."[18]

Power, during the years of the revolution, was a slippery thing, and whichever group grasped for or briefly held it faced a vexing problem: how to harness the collective energy of ordinary people without letting that energy turn against the group itself. The more or less spontaneous actions of *le menu peuple* (the simple people) had toppled the king and brought the National Assembly to power, but there was always the danger, especially in times of great hunger, that the same sorts of spontaneous actions would be used against the National Assembly or factions within it. Decades earlier, Rousseau had suggested public festivals as a means of unifying people, and revolutionary intellectuals were well aware of the need for something to replace the discredited rituals of the royalty and the Catholic Church. The idea behind the revolutionary festivals, insofar as they lend themselves to generalization, was that instead of running and marching in the streets, people would stand on the sidewalks and watch the officially selected groups march by: battalions of old men and little boys, elaborately painted floats, columns of soldiers. Instead of entertaining themselves by dancing, drinking, and flirting, people would listen to speeches and perhaps recite the Declaration of the Rights of Man in chorus. Instead of wildness and spontaneity, there would be serenity and order.

We can discern something of the intentions of the men who designed the official revolutionary festivities from their attitude toward traditional festivities, such as carnival, and this was an attitude of relentless hostility. In part, the intellectual leaders of the revolution, the men who populated the National Assembly, were repelled by the "traditional" per se, along with any reminder of the old regime. They abolished the traditional Church calendar, replacing it with a series of months of their own invention—Prairial, Thermidor, and so on—and a ten-day week culminating in a kind of Sunday called Décadi. To the revolutionary authorities, carnival was "that season that the peculiar prejudices of the ancien régime once devoted to noisy pleasures," an event fraught with superstition, and a breeding ground for "religious tricksters."[19] All of this had to be swept away to make room for the revolutionary program of rationality and unwavering virtue.

But it was not only the urge to modernize, or the fear of further political upheaval, that inspired hostility to traditional festivities. The revolutionary leadership represented a different social class than the *menu peuple* and carried within it an elitist disdain for the amusements of the masses. Among the Jacobins, for example, whose coming to power brought the revolution to a hideously bloody climax, one finds lawyers and journalists drawn from the emerging educated middle class—a very different kind of people than the workers and peasants who provided the revolution with muscle: "The middle-class Jacobins preached the virtues of monogamous marriage and deplored libertine manners, drinking, gambling and prostitution. By contrast, the *menu peuple* found enjoyment in cheap wineshops, and gambling filled their hours with a modicum of relief from their monotonous jobs."[20] Like the Calvinists in Protestant parts of Europe, the Jacobins saw traditional festivities as "barbarous" and a waste of time that could be devoted to labor. To them, as the historian Mona Ozouf writes: "The popular [traditional] festival meant the senseless din of coal shovels and pans; crowds obstructing the streets and public squares; barbarous 'sports' like shooting birds or tearing a goose limb from limb; the veiled threat of masks; the disgusting spectacle of people fighting over loaves of bread or sausages. In short, popular excitement disconcerted, or worse 'offended,' reason."[21] The Jacobin leader Louis de Saint-Just, whom the historian Christopher Hibbert describes as "a hard, unsmiling, remorseless, dislikeable, clever young man,"[22] saw nothing to do but "put an end to all this orgiastic filth."[23]

Short of applying the guillotine—as they did with so many

other problems they faced—the Jacobins did their utmost to eliminate what they saw as wasteful, undignified, and atavistic festivities.
Having thrown out the familiar calendar of saints' days, Easter,
Christmas, and so on, they proceeded to ban cross-dressing—an
age-old feature of carnival—and discouraged the use of maypoles
even for revolutionary purposes. They sent special commissioners
out to the provinces to investigate traditional festivities; the same
commissioners were charged with the task of setting up official festivals in their *départements*. But these efforts failed to reform popular tastes. Ozouf cites a contemporary observer to the effect that
"the organizers of the [official] festivals were always in search of a
public, whereas each year, in the name of Saint John, Saint Martin,
or Saint Benedict, the people required no summons to converge in
large numbers"[24] for their usual dancing, drinking, and costuming.
To explain their failure, the commissioners recalled the prior failure of the Church to curb traditional festivities: "Even the terrifying eloquence of the preachers had been unable to shake the reign
of carnival."[25]

This is a surprising admission, considering how much the Jacobins hated the Church. At least on the issue of festivities, the revolutionary commissioners were acknowledging that they were on
the same side as puritanical Counter-Reformation Catholicism.
The Jacobins may have been "revolutionaries" in a conventional
political sense, but when it came to the life of the senses and the
possibility of disorderly collective pleasure, they were part of the
long tradition of repression from on high. The historian Madelyn
Gutwirth likens them to the Theban king who crushes the Maenads
in Euripides' play: "The Revolutionaries . . . garbed in their tu-
nics of moral virtue, bear a startling resemblance to the censorious
Pentheus."[26]

But if the underlying aim of the official revolutionary festivals
was repressive, this does not mean that they were homogeneous
and uniformly boring. They were, in fact, incredibly diverse,
offering—aside from patriotism and appeals to unity—no single

unifying political or philosophical theme, but rather a plethora of themes representing a changing lineup of factions. Conservatives staged festivals stressing law and order; atheists carried off the "Festival of Reason"; the Jacobins' highly didactic fetes were designed to encourage civic virtue. As public entertainment, these festivals ranged from the stiff and tedious to what seems, at least in one case, to have been a truly thrilling event. This was the festival in 1790 commemorating the storming of the Bastille on July 14, 1789—the first "Festival of Federation"—which, more than any of the succeeding festivals, grew out of popular demand.

The revolutionary authorities acceded to the idea of a celebration commemorating the fall of the Bastille only reluctantly, fearing that mass gatherings could lead to unpredictable outbreaks of violence. "When you undertake to run a revolution," Mirabeau warned his fellow revolutionary leaders, "the difficulty is not to make it go; it is to hold it in check."[27] Hence the Festival of Federation was designed to "seal" the revolution and mark the end of disorderly mass participation. For the main celebration in Paris, the planners rejected all proposals they found unseemly or potentially disruptive—such as female participation in the official events—and sought to confine the festival to a long, entirely military parade.

But the event spilled over the confines imposed by the officials. Thousands made the pilgrimage to Paris, where people of all classes—from bourgeois ladies in silks to common laborers—worked together to prepare the Champs de Mars for the celebration. This was, according to the nineteenth-century British historian Thomas Carlyle, "a true brethren's work; all distinctions confounded, abolished,"[28] and the same spirit of harmonious enthusiasm prevailed throughout the nation. In Paris, people not only attended the official parade on July 14—which at two hours in duration dismayed even the revolutionary firebrand Camille Desmoulins—but staged their own carnivalesque parties, parodies, and dances in the days that followed. The nineteenth-century historian Jules Michelet described the events in the town of Saint-Andéol.

[The people] rushed into each other's arms, and joining hands, an immense farandole [a kind of dance], comprising everybody, without exception, spread throughout the town, into the fields, across the mountains of Ardèche, and towards the meadows of the Rhône; the wine flowed in the streets, tables were spread, provisions placed in common, and all the people are together in the evening, solemnising this love-feast, and praising God.[29]

Michelet has been accused of romanticizing the revolution, but he was probably right that, for at least a few days of festivity in the summer of 1790, "no one was a mere spectator; all were actors."[30] With the shared wine and food, the dancing that wound through whole cities and out into the fields, this has to have been one of the great moments, in all of human history, to have been alive.

At the stiffer end of the festive spectrum was the 1794 Festival of the Supreme Being, instigated by the Jacobin leader Maximilien Robespierre to counter the prior and, he felt, overly atheistic Festival of Reason. There was a long procession, led by the gorgeously dressed Robespierre—no proletarian sans culotte–style trousers for him—and including battalions of children and mothers with babies at their breasts and, in some cities, members of various trades marching with their tools in hand. There were instructive *tableaux vivants*, depicting, among other things, the ideal French family. There was some singing of patriotic songs, an artillery salute, and a total of three lengthy speeches by Robespierre, which provoked a certain amount of grumbling and guffawing from the crowd. In all of this, Ozouf emphasizes, there was no room for individual creativity: "Every attempt was made to regulate it [the festival] down to the smallest detail . . . Instructions were issued on how the little girls' hair was to be arranged, what bouquets of flowers were to be given to them, where the rosette was to be tied."[31]

The festivals of the French Revolution, with their varying and often conflicting political messages, are probably best understood as a medium, rather than as events adding up to a single propaganda campaign. There was of course no television at the end of the eighteenth century, no radio, and only a nascent newspaper industry (although printed speeches circulated widely). To reach large numbers of people with any kind of message, it made sense to gather them in outdoor venues and address them with speeches, selected symbols (for example, a pretty girl representing Liberty or the Goddess of Reason), and interludes of uplifting orchestral music. Here, in the French Revolution, the elements of all succeeding nationalist rallies and spectacles were assembled—the parade or procession, the music, the speeches—and these have survived the emergence of powerful electronic media, becoming in fact the occasional content of such media. A fascist rally in Rome or Nuremberg, the British queen's jubilee celebration in 2002, a small-town American Fourth of July celebration—all owe their basic form to the official festivals of the French Revolution.

The Military as Entertainment

A central part of the official French Revolutionary festivals, whatever their political flavor, was the military parade, accompanied by marching music. The idea of military marches as an entertaining spectacle goes back to well before the revolution; in the late seventeenth century, Louis XIV had built military reviews and maneuvers into the rituals of his court.[32] The more democratic Swiss opened military parades to the view of the general public in the 1760s—a form of "patriotic celebration" that Rousseau had urged the French to reproduce.[33] This the revolutionaries did with enthusiasm, as we have just seen, helping develop the military procession into one of the central appurtenances of nationalism.

What made the military a potentially edifying spectacle was the highly disciplined drilling introduced more than two centuries before the revolution by the Dutch prince Maurice of Orange. There would have been little entertainment value in watching the disorderly troops of the late Middle Ages shamble through the streets, but the drill produced men capable of marching synchronously, with great precision, with or without musical accompaniment. Marching bands transformed the military procession into a potentially exciting event for the spectators, despite their immobilization on the sides of the street or arena. In earlier times, European armies had relied on fifes and drums for musical encouragement; the full marching band was an import from the Muslim world and began to take hold in Europe only in the early eighteenth century. From Turkey, Europeans acquired the bass drum, cymbals, and tambourines, as well as visual effects supplied by the presence of black musicians dressed in silk turbans and brightly colored uniforms, adding, according to the historian Scott Myerly, "a dash of the exotic oriental to the show."[34]

If the drill created the possibility of the military as public spectacle, the Napoleonic Wars created the demand for it. Napoleon's armies carried with them the central tenet of the French Revolution: that "the people" were no longer subjects of a king but citizens of a nation. And what was a nation? Not, as Benedict Anderson convincingly argued, a population united by ties of blood, language, and common traditions, since many aspiring nations—such as Italy and Germany in the nineteenth century—lacked some or all of these sources of unity. Rather than growing "naturally" out of shared geography and genetics, the nation required effort to create. It was, and remains, a mystic *idea* of unity, an imaginary collectivity defined by certain symbols (flags, for example), monuments, shared experiences (of revolution or war, for example), even songs. As part of what we might call their "nation-building" effort, the Jacobins called on composers to come up with new forms of martial music for the patriotic festivals. Interestingly, it was not the popular, infectiously danceable, revolutionary song "Ça Ira" ("It Will Succeed") that the French government chose as the national anthem in 1795, but "La Marseillaise," which is suitable only for marching.

Nationalism was the feeling induced by this imagined collectivity—or, more commonly, by the symbols representing it—a feeling so fraught with the ideas of sacrifice and spiritual transcendence that scholars have often likened it to religion. What better ritual with which to observe this new "religion" than one that could inspire, however briefly, strong feelings of bonding with one's fellow countrymen? This had been the aim, of course, of the official festivals of the French Revolution. Stripped of revolutionary paraphernalia—the recitations of patriotic oaths, the floats carrying young women representing Liberty—what remained of the revolutionary festivals was a military parade, and it was this ultimately menacing spectacle that the Napoleonic Wars popularized throughout much of Europe. As Myerly observes, in the wake of the Napoleonic Wars, military spectacle became "an important entertainment genre" in England, competing with earlier, more participatory, and less martial kinds of gatherings.[35]

In keeping with their new status as performers, soldiers began to dress for the part. Uniforms had been difficult to impose before the nineteenth century, if only because armies were made up largely of mercenaries, who found uniforms a serious obstacle to desertion. In the wake of the Napoleonic Wars, uniforms became almost universal, and not only because they served military functions, such as distinguishing one side from the other. In fact, the highly polished brass buttons of nineteenth-century uniforms could make a man an easy target, but this disadvantage was apparently outweighed by theatrical considerations, since a man might spend more time marching for an audience than he did in battle.

Naturally, the most brilliant men on display were the officers, with their brightly colored uniforms and extravagant headgear. In the Musée de l'Armée in Paris today, one finds scores of nineteenth-century officers' helmets and bearskins topped with feathers that could add a foot or more to a man's height. Not only were such costumes dangerously cumbersome in battle; they could occasionally disrupt the spectacles they were designed to enhance. Myerly reports that "when wearing the nearly two-foot-high regulation First Life Guards' bearskin cap with its enormous swan feather while attending a review . . . [the Duke of Wellington] was literally blown off his horse by a gust of wind in front of tens of thousands of spectators and soldiers."[36]

Britain embraced the military spectacle with at least as much enthusiasm as France had. An 1811 military review at Wimbledon attracted two hundred thousand spectators to watch twenty thousand soldiers go through their paces; a royal review staged in honor of the king in 1830 drew crowds that were "immense beyond description."[37] In addition to the deliberately staged military spectacles, even mundane tasks such as the changing of the guard attracted eager audiences. "We were all soldiers, one way or another," an Edinburgh lawyer recalled of the wartime year 1803. "The parade and the review formed the staple of men's talk and thoughts."[38] Women were drawn to the spectacle of the gorgeously uniformed young officers on horseback; everyone responded to the martial music, which, as one spectator noted, "cause[s] the pulse to pound and fire[s] the imagination."[39] Even the socialist Robert Blatchford hailed the public military drills for fostering a sense of solidarity among the viewers, "a feeling of strength through unity and *esprit de corps*," though not without observing sourly "that in reality this sense of solidarity was directed not by its members but by the state."[40]

In superficial ways, the military spectacle can even be thought of as a kind of carnival. There were "costumes"—in the form of uniforms, which in the case of the Swiss troopers were derived from a harlequin-type carnival costume. There was "dance," or at least musically driven motion—in the form of the march—and to this day the overlap between marching and dancing is exemplified, in the United States, by drill and drill-dance teams that perform at special events, as well as by the African American collegiate practice of "stepping." But the military spectacle represents an oddly inverted form of carnival: While carnival aims to mock all customary kinds of social hierarchy, the military spectacle aims only to reinforce them.

Governance by Spectacle

As young men, both Hitler and Mussolini had been well prepared for the task of perfecting the late-eighteenth- and nineteenth-century nationalist spectacle. Not only had each served in World War I and been thoroughly impressed with the galvanizing power of military spectacles and parades, they were also familiar with Le Bon's theories. Whether they had been alarmed, as dictators-to-be, by Le Bon's ideas about the madness and unpredictability of crowds, we do not know, but both happily appropriated his thoughts on "the leaders of crowds and their means of persuasion."[41] The very irrationality of the crowd, Le Bon had asserted, rendered it putty in the hands of "the strong-willed man, who knows how to impose himself upon it."[42] Through simple demagogic tricks—such as constant repetition of simplified ideas—the leader could mold large numbers of people to his will. Ignoring, as usual, the fact that the crowds of the French Revolution, his primary example of collective insanity, fought for their liberty, Le Bon insisted that "it is the need not of liberty but of servitude that is always predominant in the soul of crowds. They are so bent on obedience that they instinctively submit to whoever declares himself their master."[43] This must have been excellent news for a dictator-in-training, so long as he skipped the passage where Le Bon observed that the men who seized power by manipulating what he saw as the rabble were likely to be "morbidly nervous, excitable, half-deranged persons who are bordering on madness."[44]

Actually, neither Hitler nor Mussolini achieved power through the kind of mob action that concerned Le Bon—another argument against those who see an inevitable connection between collective excitement and fascist evil. Violent "mobs" of the *menu peuple* had played a decisive role in the French Revolution. But to the extent that violence played a role in the rise of twentieth-century fascism, it was the violence exerted by organized fascist paramilitary forces—the *Freikorps* and brownshirts in Germany, the *arditi* and black-shirted *squadristi* in Italy—who crushed the socialist opposition and intimidated the general population in their respective nations. Opposition leaders were beaten or assassinated, their offices bombed, their demonstrations attacked by organized ruffians.

For Hitler and Mussolini, mass rallies were not only a means of mobilizing the population for the war effort but a means of governing it. There was of course no semblance of democracy in totalitarian Germany or Italy; but this did not mean that either dictator could afford to completely ignore his people—as, for example, the Bourbon kings had before the revolutionary year of 1789, running France as if it were their private estate. If the French Revolution offered one great lesson to all future regimes, it was that "the people" had to be encouraged to identify with the state, even in the case of a state they had no way of influencing. The new media—radio and film—helped propagate the fascist message, but they could not give people a sense of direct and personal involvement. That was the function of the mass rallies: to create a kind of ersatz participation. Soldiers would march, demonstrating the power of the state; the dictator would speak, perhaps announcing new policies; and the assembled people would cheer, thus registering their approval without anything as cumbersome and potentially divisive as a vote.

Hence the need for regular and frequent mass rallies, scheduled according to a new calendar of nationalist holidays. No one, so far as I can tell, has totaled up the cost of these rallies, but it must have been enormous, beginning with the expense involved in giving the majority of the population a day off from work. As for their frequency, Lindholm comments that Hitler strove to "turn all of Germany into a gigantic and permanent mass meeting, awaiting his galvanizing appearance."[45] In the same vein, a contemporary observer described Mussolini's mass rallies as "the chief industry of Fascist Italy."[46] The piazzas of Italian towns and the central squares of German cities—once the sites of lively festivities on religious holidays—became the settings for the new nationalist spectacles, with ancient Roman ruins (in Italy) and newly built nationalist monuments (in both countries) providing an imposing backdrop.

As in the case of the Jacobins, the Nazis and fascists frowned on alternative forms of celebration and entertainment. The Nazis famously banned swing music and fretted about what constituted a racially acceptable rhythm.

> On no account will Negroid excesses in tempo (so-called hot jazz) or in solo performances (so-called breaks) be tolerated; so-called jazz compositions may contain at most 10 percent syncopation; the remainder must consist of a natural legato movement devoid of the hysterical rhythmic reverses characteristic of the music of the barbarian races and conducive to dark instincts alien to the German people (so-called riffs).[47]

Traditional, Christian-based entertainments presented them with a more difficult problem, since these could be seen as a legitimate part of the Aryan heritage. A 1939 article in the Nazi party journal agonized over Christmas.

> Both according to popular custom and popular view, the Christmas holiday can justifiably be seen as a festival of the homeland . . . But if we do this, we must realize that the Christmas holiday or Christmas festival is more than a date on the calendar suitable for cheap entertainment events. We cannot meet our goals in the style of pre-war clubs with their "variety evenings," raffles or the ever so popular military farce. Not even if "Bananini the Magician" or "Bear Mouth the Sword Swallower" make a guest appearance.[48]

While the official Nazi attitude toward traditional holidays was one of toleration, the party covertly sought to discourage them. As Michael Burleigh writes, "Feast days, pilgrimages and religious processions were [a] . . . flashpoint between the faithful and the Nazis, especially in Catholic regions."[49] The Nazis would, somewhat spitefully, schedule compulsory Hitler Youth activities on the same days as church events, or make attendance difficult by canceling round-trip train service to the site of a religious festivity.

Not having gone through the Reformation, Italy had a more robust tradition of festivities for the fascists to worry about. In 1926, Mussolini declared that "it's time to put a stop to such ceremonies, assemblies, and festivals," citing their lack of "seriousness." A year later, he officially banned "any ceremony, demonstration, celebration, anniversary, centenary great or small, as well as speeches of any sort," other than his own, of course.[50] Apparently these prohibitions were not entirely effective, because in 1932 we find the Fascist party secretary Achille Starace banning "gala shows" and New Year's Eve parties, which not only lacked seriousness but snubbed the official fascist year-end date of October 29. Echoing the seventeenth-century Calvinists, he warned against participation in banquets and prohibited people's attempts to humanize the mass rallies by using them, or their aftermath, as an occasion for dancing: there would be no dancing at fascist events.[51] Some traditional rural festivals were permitted, so long as they were conducted in a somber, "healthy" fashion and "permeated with Fascist symbolism."[52] The wine harvest celebration, for example, was to be "very similar to that of the Romans, who"—the fascist youth newspaper averred—"did not admit barbarian influences in their rituals and did not want orgiastic contamination of the joyful festival of the wine harvest."[53]

Mussolini's ostensible concern was that festivities other than official mass rallies would both take too much time and "satiate" the public.[54] And why, a good fascist might wonder, should the public require any source of collective excitement beyond what the state provided? Both Hitler and Mussolini held rather grandiose views about the psychological impact of their spectacles, which they believed to be on a par with religious epiphany. Ideally, the individual spectator should experience complete self-loss and submergence in the larger collective—the *volk*, or the nation. In Italy, the Fascist party leadership sought to forge the masses into "an organic whole," which, in their rhetoric, more resembled a homogeneous substance than a collection of individual people.[55] Hitler was equally explicit about the need to meld the public into a single unit, and the agreeable effect this transformation would have on the individual: "There will be no license, no free space, in which the individual belongs to himself . . . The day of individual happiness has passed. Can there be any greater happiness than a National Socialist meeting in which speakers and audience feel as one?"[56]

But the alleged delights of the mass rallies did not mean that the spectators and marchers could be trusted to follow their impulses in the slightest degree. The rallies were heavily policed and scripted in every detail; attendance was often compulsory: "No citizen must be allowed to stay at home," insisted a Nazi official in Northeim.[57] Hitler's biographer John Toland reports that the party members who participated in the 1934 Nuremberg rally had been "carefully selected months in advance, each had a number, a designated truck, a designated seat in the truck, and a designated cot in the vast tent city near Nuremberg. By the time the ceremonies began on Sept 4, the thousands of party members had been rehearsed to perfection."[58] At pre-Nazi May Day celebrations, the crowds had been disorderly, "roaming around, singing or speech-making," but at the Nazis' 1933 May Day event the working-class participants "observed exemplary shopfloor discipline, arranging themselves into teams, lines, and squares, following directions, signals, and cordons: I, II, III, IV, . . ."[59] In Italy, "order and punctuality dominated the events, which were structured around Mussolini's arrival and departure from the train stations."[60] Even the clothing of spectators was specified: no "festive dress" and, for men anyway, the emblematic fascist black shirt was recommended. Furthermore, the Fascist party ruled that all ceremonies should be "marked by the greatest possible austerity and sobriety. To this end, banquets and lavish receptions are prohibited."[61]

It's not easy to gauge the subjective impact of the Nazi and Italian fascist rallies. For one thing, memoirs are unreliable, in part because in the aftermath of fascism witnesses of the rallies were likely to downplay whatever thrills they may have experienced. But contemporary accounts from the state-dominated media are no better, since these no doubt erred in the other direction, by exaggerating the enthusiasm and size of the crowds. The newspaper *Il Popolo d'Italia*, for example, offered a typically breathless account of a fascist rally in 1932.

> Squadrons of airplanes fly in ever-tighter circles overhead, as if to crown this splendid assembly.
>
> The crowd never tires of following their maneuvers, and the thunder of their engines mixes with the peals of the fanfares and the songs of the Fascists. Meanwhile, Piazza Venezia has reached its flood point. The clamor of the music and the constant *alala* [the fascist chant, which had no meaning] deafens all. The people are carried away by the huge roar calling for the Duce . . .
>
> The crowd continues to swell. The square is thronged. Fifty thousand are there waiting for Mussolini, fifty thousand shout his name . . .
>
> The bands break into "Giovinezza." The flags are raised high. Mussolini! . . . "Duce! Duce!" The cry is infinitely multiplied over the clanging of the music.[62]

Nor can we trust the highly edited *Triumph of the Will* to provide a representative sample of images from the 1934 Nuremberg rally. Riefenstahl shows only upraised faces, smiling in exaltation—no sullen children or foot-sore spectators.

There is scattered evidence that, especially as the novelty of the rallies wore off, many of the spectators and even participants may have been dragging their feet. On the basis of her study of railroad receipts, one historian, for example, makes a case that the crowds that watched Italian fascist rallies did not assemble spontaneously but were rounded up by train and transported to the rally sites "to give the appearance of volume."[63] Another historian observes of the Italian scene that "the unremitting mobilization on behalf of the collective rituals could indeed give rise to feelings of satiety and impatience in some."[64] Certainly the much-heralded 1934 "18BL" mass performance in Florence—featuring an air squadron, brigades from various branches of the military, and fifty of the new Fiat 18BL trucks—was a flop, with a contemporary reviewer fretting that its main result would be to create "a certain aversion on the part of the masses towards this sort of spectacle."[65] Meanwhile, in Germany, at the Nazis' 1933 May Day rally,

> only a thinning line of bystanders stretched along parts of the parade route. On this May Day at least, the theaterical nature of Nazi political production was too apparent. For many observers, it was obvious that the streets were but stage scenery, the blue smocks simply costumes, the gestures and speeches awkwardly followed scripts, and the audience insufficiently animated.[66]

The historian Peter Fritschze quotes a worker who was required to march in this event: "As the parade passed a pissoir, I said to myself 'in you go . . .' As I stepped out of line, the guy next to me followed, and when we were done, we ran home."[67]

As for the great Nuremberg rallies: In recent years, German historians have emphasized their "tedium and banality" as well as their manipulative intent. The official Documentation Center opened at the rally site in 2001 shows a side of the events either unglimpsed by Riefenstahl or carefully edited out: the influx of prostitutes that accompanied the rallies, along with soaring rates of venereal disease; the shortage of public toilets, and the "filthy" conditions of the few that were available.[68] And if the show itself was endless and dull, there seems to have been plenty of beer drinking on its margins. The police reported the arrest of drunken "political leaders" caught vandalizing a fountain—perhaps by putting it to use as a toilet.[69] After 1935, even the Nazi party began to lose interest in the rallies, which were not only expensive but unreliably productive of the proper "mystic" effects: "So many ingredients were needed to create the right atmosphere for a mass celebration: a starlit summer sky . . . a receptive audience, a well-rehearsed mass choir or a choreographed march past [*sic*]—and then a shower of rain could ruin everything."[70]

We can conclude, then, with some confidence, that the nationalist spectacles of the modern era—from the official festivals of the French Revolution to the fascist mass rallies of the 1920s and '30s—were a sorry substitute for the traditional festive gatherings they replaced. This failure had nothing to do with ideological content, which ranged from radically left-wing during the French Revolution to viciously reactionary in the fascist states of the twentieth century. It was the medium that failed: the endless parades, the reviews of the troops, the exhortatory speeches. One could argue that this medium necessarily contains its own message—about power, militarism, the need for the individual to be subsumed by the collective—and that the message itself had grown tiresome over time.

But judged simply as a species of entertainment, the nationalist spectacles seem to have fallen rather short of the mark. They were, for one thing, utterly solemn events. The traditional carnival had been an occasion for subversive humor, in which customary forms of authority could be inverted and the mighty safely mocked, for a few days at least. But the nationalist events we have surveyed in this chapter featured no parodies of the puritanical Robespierre, for example, and certainly no one playing the part of Hitler as a "king of fools," riding backward on a donkey through the streets. Where the carnival had been joyously irreverent, the nationalist rallies, and especially the fascist ones, were celebrations of state authority, designed to instill citizenly virtue or at least inspire awe.

Could better nationalist spectacles have been devised, with perhaps more color, less speechifying, and some comic relief? Yes, certainly, and Queen Elizabeth's jubilee celebration in 2002 provides an example of what can be done with the spectacular medium: There were the usual military touches—flyovers by fighter jets, for example—but also a veritable variety show featuring pop music, extravagantly dressed dancers, and humanizing glimpses of the royals. But a spectacle, by its nature, offers an inherently more limited experience than a participatory event. In a late medieval carnival, for example, everyone had a role to play and a chance to distinguish themselves individually by the brilliance of their costumes, the wittiness of their jokes, or their talents as dancers or athletes. You went to be seen, as well as to see. At an event organized entirely as a spectacle, though, all creativity is invested in the spectacle itself, and none is demanded of the spectators. They are not there to be seen, except as part of an inert mass. All attention focuses on a central point: the parade, the speaker, or the hoopla that showcases the arrival of the head of state.

But we do not have to confine ourselves to inferences about the limits and frustrations of spectatorship relative to more physical forms of participation: Within a generation after the mass rallies of the 1930s and '40s, young people in the heart of the postfestive Western world would rebel against the immobility required of the "audience" and, against all expectation, begin to revive the ancient tradition of ecstatic festivity.

10

The Rock Rebellion

What has been repressed, no matter how forcibly and thoroughly, often finds a way of resurfacing. In the late 1950s and early 1960s, Anglo-American culture was struck by an outbreak of "hysteria" or "mania" described by alarmed observers as obscene, disruptive, and even criminal. Neither the United States nor England was, in the mid-twentieth century, a likely site for such unrestrained behavior. Both societies were heavily burdened by the puritanical legacy of the sixteenth century; each had contributed to the suppression of festive and ecstatic traditions among colonized—or, in the case of the Americans, enslaved—peoples. But it may be that their very success in expunging "foreign" ecstatic traditions heightened their vulnerability to the call, when it came, to get up and move and dance and shout.

From the beginning, the rock rebellion manifested itself as a simple refusal to sit still or to respect anyone who insisted that one do so. Wherever the "new" music was performed—and it was new at least to most white people—kids jumped out of their seats and began to chant, scream, and otherwise behave in ways that the authorities usually interpreted as "rioting." Most of these incidents, according to Linda Martin and Kerry Segrave in their book *Anti-Rock: The Opposition to Rock 'n' Roll*, "just involved kids dancing in the aisles at theaters; jiving in their seats; and stomping, clapping, and yelling a lot—having a good time, in short. The authorities thought an audience should sit quietly and sedately, perhaps clapping a little at the end of the performance."[1] In 1956, performances by Bill Haley and His Comets, who were at the moment the most popular rock group in the world, provoked "a national outbreak of dancing in the aisles, chanting in the streets, and deliberate rudeness toward assorted figures of authority."[2] In both England and the United States, managers of the theaters and concert halls where rock groups performed responded by enlisting the police to control the "rioters," so that early rock concerts evolved into a kind of slapstick ritual: Kids would stand up and begin dancing in the aisles; the police would chase them and stuff them back into their seats; the kids would get up again.

Throughout the 1960s as well, rock concerts were routine settings for confrontations between young fans and the police. Members of the Jefferson Airplane complained that "as soon as kids got up to dance in the aisles the cops would disconnect the amps."[3] Rolling Stones concerts almost invariably led to "riots," with the Vancouver chief of police, for example, complaining that one of the group's concerts provided the "most prolonged demand of physical endurance I have ever seen police confronted with during my 33 years of service." In Vancouver, as in other cities, the police began to demand and get complete control of the curtains, lighting, and sound systems for rock concerts.[4] Audiences responded with still more "riotous" behavior, such as rushing the stage or counterattacking the police with fire extinguishers and missiles. Jim Morrison of the Doors blamed the cops: "If there were no cops there, would anybody try to get onstage? . . . The only incentive to charge the stage is because there's a barrier."[5] Barriers of any kind only served as a provocation to the fans, who sought a freedom of motion and physical self-expression horrifying to the adult world—a chance to mingle with one another, to move to the music, and later to assert themselves in the streets outside the concert venues.

Of course the rock performers had to take some of the blame for their fans' unruly behavior, if only because they too moved—dancing and jiving to their own music in ways that shocked and offended adult viewers. Pop singers like Eddie Fisher had moved too, but only from one conventional, operatic gesture to another—clasping their hands together on their chests or stretching their arms out, palms up. A good part of the frisson of early rock lay in the rhythmic and often sexually suggestive movements of the performers—grinding their hips, thrusting their pelvises, rolling their shoulders, leaping and falling on the floor—"rocking," in short, as a way of announcing that the "new" music was inseparable from creative, free-form, beat-driven motion.

Among white performers, Elvis Presley pioneered the new physical expressiveness, requiring the family-oriented *Ed Sullivan Show* to censor out his lower body from the TV screen. Bo Diddley, a black performer, was not so lucky. His contract for a 1958 nationwide TV booking stipulated that he had to perform without moving, in order to "preserve decency." Once on air, he forgot this rule or, more likely, simply found it impossible to hold his body separate from the music, and was docked his entire fee.[6] Little Richard probably got away with jumping, prancing, and climbing on his piano only because of his over-the-top, manic, seemingly asexual persona.

But it was, again and again, the audience that stole the show, often to the consternation of the performers. The rock historian James Miller reports that the better Elvis Presley got at performing, "the less he got to do it. The problem was the tumult he now routinely provoked." Describing a 1957 concert, the *St. Louis Post-Dispatch* reported that "Presley clung to the microphone standard and staggered about in a distinctive, distraught manner, waiting for the noise to subside a bit."[7] A few years later, Beatlemaniacs—the just-pubescent followers of the Beatles—effectively silenced their heroes with their frenzied screams. At no time during their U.S. tours was the group audible above the shrieking, which forced the band to abandon the concert stage in 1966, only two years after their first American appearances.

By the late 1960s, rock performers were negotiating their own security arrangements with the managers of concert venues, partly out of fear that they would be crushed by their fans, should the latter succeed in actually conquering the stage. Even the gentle, cerebral Grateful Dead eventually got "sick of out-of-control fan behavior" and distributed a flyer to concertgoers forbidding gate-crashing, bottle throwing, kicking down fences, and "miracling," or begging for free tickets outside the venue.[8] When the content of the spectacle was rock music, young people were no longer willing to accept the spectacle form, with its requirement that large numbers of people sit still and in silence while a talented few perform.

The Revolt of the Audience

The rock rebellion can be interpreted in all kinds of ways. It was an uprising of the postwar generation, bored by affluence and stifled by the prevailing demands for conformity in lifestyle, opinion, and appearance. It was a challenge to the racial segregation that divided not only communities but music, which could be "pop" (for whites) or "race music" (for everyone else). And as the 1960s wore on, it fed into a widespread counterculture, which in turn helped animate a political movement countering war and domestic injustice.

But the rock rebellion was also something simpler and ostensibly less "political"—a rebellion against the role of the *audience*. In the history of festivities, the great innovation of the modern era had been the replacement of older, more participatory forms of festivity with spectacles in which the crowd serves merely as an audience. In the two centuries leading up to the twentieth, even audiences had been successfully tamed. If you went back to seventeenth- and early-eighteenth-century France or England, you would have found theater audiences, for example, that were disruptively rowdy, interrupting the actors with their own comments, milling around during the performance, or actually sitting on the stage in the midst of the action. By the end of the eighteenth century, aristocratic ideas of decorum—along with the innovation of reserved seating—brought, according to sociologist Richard Sennett, "a certain deadness into the theater. There were no more shouts from the back of the hall, no more people eating food while they stood watching the play. Silence in the theater seemed to diminish the enjoyment of watching the play."[9]

Utterly missing from the audience's new role was any kind of muscular involvement beyond the occasional applause, and this prohibition extended to musical performances as well as the theater. From the nineteenth century on, all forms of Western music were being consumed by immobile audiences. At a military parade, for example, the martial music might be stirring and the marching soldiers might themselves be caught up in the pleasures of rhythmic synchrony, but the good spectator—as opposed to the occasional exhibitionist—stood perfectly still and, except when straining to see better, remained as unobtrusive as possible. Concerts had become the most common setting for musical performances, and at these the role of the audience was to sit quietly and refrain from any motion at all. Even the most covert forms of dancing—foot tapping and head nodding—could disturb one's fellow listeners; audience members had learned how to hold themselves in a state of frozen attention.

The motionless perception required of an audience takes effort, especially when the performance involves the rhythmic motions of others. As we saw in chapter 1, recent research in neuroscience suggests that the neuronal mechanisms underlying the perception of motion by another person are closely linked to the *execution* of that motion by the perceiver.[10] To see a man marching or dancing, swaying as he plays the saxophone, or simply waving his arms to draw melodies from an orchestra is to ready oneself internally to join in the marching, dancing, swaying, or arm waving. Infants automatically imitate the actions of others; with age, they acquire the ability to inhibit the imitative impulse. So the well-behaved audience member—who does not snap her fingers or nod her head in time to the music—is not really at rest; she is performing a kind of work—the silent, internal work of muscular inhibition.

It is *sexual* inhibition that rock is usually credited—or blamed—for challenging, as in one writer's explanation of rock as "the unleashing of generations of repressed sexuality,"[11] with the music serving only to convey a less inhibited, African American sexual sensibility to the repressed white middle-class "mainstream." No doubt mid-twentieth-century Anglo-American culture was sexually repressive—homophobic and skittish about heterosexual sex as well. There's no doubt, too, that sex had a lot to do with the rock rebellion, if only because of the irresistible appeal, at least from a female point of view, of stars like the "sleazy," working-class Elvis or the witty and vaguely androgynous Beatles: They represented romantic possibilities that went well beyond necking in a car with the khaki-clad, buttoned-down, young white men of the time. But there is more to the story than sexual repressiveness and the perhaps inevitable revolt against it. Mainstream mid-twentieth-century culture was deeply restrictive of physical motion in general, whether or not it had anything to do with sex.

Entertainment, for example, meant sitting and watching TV or movies. There were still "carnivals," but these no longer involved dancing or sports other than, say, throwing objects at a target. At a mid-twentieth-century carnival or fair, machines did the moving for you; all the carnival-goers had to do was sit in a seat and let the roller coaster or Ferris wheel propel their bodies along a preexisting path. Religious worship was, in the dominant Protestant tradition, equally sedentary, allowing participation only in the form of hymn singing. There was dancing too, of course, but before rock's emergence into white culture, this typically meant ballroom dancing—decorously choreographed fox-trots and waltzes that allowed for little group interaction or individual variation. Even walking had been made largely obsolete by suburbanization and the automobile culture it spawned. At the time, of course, no one reckoned the eventual price of all this routine immobilization in the form of obesity and other health problems.

In the mid-1950s, sports still offered an opportunity for physical expression, primarily for the athletes and cheerleaders. Most people, though, were merely spectators, encouraged at high school pep rallies to stand up in the bleachers and cheer for an occasional good play, but otherwise to remain motionless. The restrictions against physical motion weighed particularly heavy on girls: Not only were there no school sports for girls, but those sports that were open to girls, usually under the sponsorship of YWCAs and churches, had been redesigned to limit the amount of motion involved. In the official girls' version of basketball, for example, players were allowed only two dribbles in succession and were prohibited from crossing the center line. For females, even sex was meant to be motionless and passive. The leading marital advice book of mid-twentieth-century America warned against female "*movements*" during sex—the idea being disturbing enough to merit italics.[12] Insofar as sexual activity was described at all, it was in terms of static "positions."

Hence, in no small part, the particular appeal of rock mania to teenage girls. Elvis and especially the Beatles inspired a kind of mass hysteria among crowds of young white women, who jumped up and down, screamed, cried, fainted, and sometimes wet their pants in the presence of their idols. To adult commentators, Beatlemania was pathological—an "epidemic" set off by the Beatles as carriers or "foreign germs." In a particularly ingenious, partly tongue-in-cheek explanation offered by the *New York Times Magazine* in 1964, the girls were merely "conforming" and "expressing their desire to obey." They wanted to be subsumed into the mass, which, in the author's view, was the same as being "transformed into an insect." After all, he observed triumphantly, there had been an

earlier craze of "jitter*bugs*,"* and "Beatles, too, are a type of bug."[13]
But former Beatlemaniacs report that the experience was empowering and freeing. Brought together in a crowd, girls who individually
might have been timid and obedient broke through police lines,
rushed stages, and, of course, through their actions, determined
that the Fab Four would be the most successful and best-known
band in world history.

Rock struck with such force, in the 1950s and early 1960s, because the white world it entered was frozen over and brittle—not
only physically immobilizing but emotionally restrained. In pre-
rock middle-class teenage culture, for example, the requisite
stance was *cool*, with the word connoting not just generic approval,
as it does today, but a kind of aloofness, emotional affectlessness,
and sense of superiority. Rock, with its demands for immediate
and unguarded physical participation, thawed the coolness, summoned the body into action, and blasted the mind out of the isolation and guardedness that had come to define the Western
personality. To the Black Panther leader Eldridge Cleaver, white
rock fans were simply trying to reclaim "their Bodies again after
generations of alienation and disembodied existence."

> They were swinging and gyrating and shaking their dead little asses
> like petrified zombies trying to regain the warmth of life, rekindle
> the dead limbs, the cold ass, the stone heart, the stiff, mechanical,
> disused joints with the spark of life.[14]

Rock and the African Ecstatic Tradition

Possibly there would have been a youth revolt in the mid- to late
twentieth century without rock and roll. As Daniel Bell observed in

---

*Jitterbugs, devotees of the Lindy in the late 1920s and early 1930s, had come in for much
of the same kind of criticism. According to Katherine Stern, "the jitterbugs carried away
with them . . . an encounter with black power, with black victory, or jubilation, the implications of which made them 'jitter,' and made the media in turn splutter over the jitterbugs, calling them 'poison,' 'a plague,' or the 'victims' of some perilous infection."
(Personal communication with the author, February 3, 2006.)

the 1950s, mainstream American culture stood poised unstab tween its puritanical legacy and the hedonism encouraged l expanding consumer culture. People were enjoined to work hard and save, even as advertising conveyed the steady exhortation to spend and indulge oneself in the here and now. Similarly, their premarital sexual explorations were supposed to proceed no lower than the neck, despite the fact that the commercial culture was already heavily—although by today's standards, somewhat coyly—sexualized. These contradictions, or examples of gross societal hypocrisy, might eventually have touched off a widespread cultural revolt on their own.

Rock's contribution was to weigh in decisively on the side of hedonism and against the old puritanical theme of "deferred gratification." First, because it was a kind of music—rhythmic and heavy on the percussion—that almost *demanded* an immediate muscular response. And second, because the kind of dancing evoked by rock—unlike such European varieties as polkas or waltzes—bore traces of a centuries-old ecstatic religious tradition. At first, in the 1950s and early 1960s, people danced to rock music in couples—a form of dancing that originated in Europe in the nineteenth century and served largely as a courtship ritual. As rock evolved, people began to move to it more freely, dancing individually or in lines and circles. A person might get up and start dancing alone, another might follow, women might dance with women, men with men, couples might dissolve and re-form—until the entire gathering was swept up by the rhythm.

There is no doubt, among scholars, that such distinctively African American contributions as jazz, gospel, the blues, and rhythm and blues all have roots in indigenous African music. The common characteristics of African, African American, and much Caribbean music—polyrhythms, antiphonal responses, and a capacity for both repetition and creative variation—delineate a singularly hardy musical tradition, one that had endured the Middle Passage and centuries of enslavement. Even particular stylistic themes—like the famous "Bo Diddley beat"—which inspired white performers including Elvis Presley, Buddy Holly, Mick Jagger, and Bruce Springsteen—can be traced to West Africa via, in this case, Cuba.[15]

And as we saw in chapter 8, one hallmark of African-derived musical traditions is their intimate connection to dance. Within the western and central African societies that supplied the Americas with slave laborers, music was performed to be danced to, not just listened to, and the performers themselves often danced as they played their instruments. So inseparable were African music and dance that many African languages lack distinct words for the two activities, although they possess "rich vocabularies for forms, styles, and techniques."[16] As the cops who attempted to maintain order at early rock concerts perhaps should have realized, rock and roll is part of a family of music that it is almost impossible *not* to respond to with dance or some other form of rhythmic involvement.

In the Caribbean and in Brazil, African traditions of music and dance had found a home in new religions, like Vodou and Candomblé, that mixed elements of both European Christian and African theologies. In North America, however, the same traditions were preserved within the unlikely environment of Christian theology, which slaves embraced in part because Christian worship was the only form of communal activity they were allowed, outside of laboring together in the fields.[17] Segregated from white worshippers and for the most part ignored by them, black Christians developed their own distinctive forms of worship based on African religious traditions of music and dance. One of these was the *holy dance*, or *ring-shout*, involving "hand clapping, foot stamping, and leaping"—and dating from at least the early-nineteenth-century revivals in Virginia.[18] A black plantation preacher wrote that "the way in which we worshipped was almost indescribable. The singing was accompanied by a certain ecstasy of motion, clapping of hands, tossing of heads."[19]

Nothing like this had occurred in the context of Christian worship since dance was prohibited in European Catholic churches in the thirteenth century. Other accounts make it clear that the ring-shout involved not only an "ecstasy of motion" but an ecstasy of the spirit, as in West African pagan rituals. The historian Albert Raboteau reported that the ring-shout would typically proceed to the point where "the individual shouter stood outside himself, literally in ecstasy, transcending time and place as the rhythms of the chorus were repeatedly beat out with hands, feet, and body in the constant shuffle of the ring."[20] A nineteenth-century white observer offered this description of a ring-shout performed by African slaves:

> One by one of the congregation slipped out into the center of the floor and began to "shout"—(that is whirl around and sing and clap hands, and so round and round in circles). After a time as this went on, the enthusiasm became a frenzy and only the able bodied men and women remained—the weak dropping out one by one, returning to the "sidelines" to clap and urge the "shouters" on.[21]

Toward the end of the nineteenth century, many newly freed African Americans had sought respectability by toning down their religious services—"banning the shout, discouraging enthusiastic religion, and adopting more sedate hymns."[22] But as mainstream black religion became more staid, "Holiness" sects sprang up to celebrate the old ecstatic forms of worship, featuring "healing, gifts of prophecy, speaking in tongues, spirit possession, and religious dance."[23] The Holiness churches, which gave birth to interracial Pentecostalism in the early twentieth century, took the added step of bringing more secular black sounds back into church—ragtime, jazz, and blues—along with drums, tambourines, saxophones, and guitars.

Gospel music, arising in the 1930s, was smoother and more professional than the old spirituals, but still invited physical participation by congregations and performers alike. "Don't let the movement go out of the music," warned gospel bandleader Thomas

A. Dorsey. "Black music calls for movement!"[24] Mahalia Jackson wrote, "I want my hands . . . my feet . . . my whole body to say all that is in me. I say 'Don't let the devil steal the beat from the Lord!' The Lord doesn't like us to act dead. If you feel it, tap your feet a little—dance to the glory of the Lord!"[25] By the 1950s, when the civil rights movement began to break through segregation, and on the very eve of rock and roll's emergence into white culture, African American intellectuals had claimed the African-derived tradition of religious music and responsive motion as a means not only of artistic expression but of collective survival. In *Juneteenth*, for example, Ralph Ellison has his hero, Reverend Hickman, tell a crowd: "Keep to the rhythm and you'll keep to life . . . Keep, keep, keep to the rhythm and you won't get weary. Keep to the rhythm and you won't get lost . . . They couldn't divide us now [thanks to our music]. Because anywhere they dragged us we throbbed in time together."[26] In a musical tradition featuring rhythmic participation by the congregation, it almost goes without saying that the "audience" is no longer confined to spectatorship. As one scholar observes, the "Western barrier between performer and audience" had been breached, making way for "an inclusive, communal, communicative event."[27]

This was rock and roll's heritage: a participatory experience, rooted in an ecstatic religious tradition. Black rock, or "rhythm and blues," performers of the 1950s and '60s—including such stars as Little Richard, Ray Charles, Aretha Franklin, and many others—acknowledged their obvious debt to black church music, often moving effortlessly from religious to secular songs and back again. Except for Elvis Presley, who was devoted to gospel music, white performers were not always so gracious, often simply stealing their songs from black performers, unaware of their religious origins. But one way or another the chain was completed—from pre-Christian African ecstatic rituals, through African American Christian forms of worship, to African American secular rhythm and blues, and finally to the mostly white rockers who inspired white kids to "riot." The early rock audiences who stomped and jumped out of their seats to dance were announcing, whether they knew it or not, the rebirth of an ecstatic tradition that been repressed and marginalized by Europeans and Euro-Americans for centuries.

Opposition, Triumph, and Decline

The establishment reaction to rock and roll was swift and almost universal. "No other form of culture . . . " the rock historians Martin and Segrave claim, unaware of the Europeans' suppression of indigenous cultures in the eighteenth and nineteenth centuries, "has met with such extensive hostility."[28] With the passage of decades, the late 1950s and early 1960s opposition to rock has acquired a quaint comicality, but at the time it was daunting to the music's purveyors, if not to the performers and fans. Clergymen joined psychiatrists in calling for bans of the "obscene" and disruptive new music. Disk jockeys vowed never to play the stuff, sometimes burning stacks of the offending 45s to advertise their commitment to "good" music, as opposed to the faddish new "junk." Cities, as we have seen, mobilized their police forces against the fans, and some did their best to discourage visits by rock musicians. Civic leaders denounced rock as an incitement to juvenile delinquency, violence, and sex. No wonder, then, that most of the major record companies initially eschewed rock and roll, leaving it to smaller, independent companies to test the new music's profitability.

Unnoted at the time was the way antirock commentary almost precisely echoed the language that eighteenth- and nineteenth-century Europeans had used to denounce the "native" ecstatic rituals they encountered during their phase of imperialist expansion. Aware only of its black roots, the enemies of rock attacked it as "jungle music," "tribal music," and even, weirdly, "cannibalistic."[29] The conductor of the BBC symphony orchestra opined that rock wasn't really new, because it "had been played in the jungle for

centuries"—never mind the later centuries of African American innovation, carried out in the fields of the American South. Similar
references to "jungles" and "savages" peppered antirock rhetoric,
with the industry publication *Music Journal* editorializing that
teenage rock fans were "definitely influenced in their lawlessness by
this throwback to jungle rhythms. Either it actually stirs them to
orgies of sex and violence (as its model did for the savages themselves), or they use it as an excuse for the removal of all inhibitions
and the complete disregard of the conventions of decency."[30] Images of undisciplined "savages" losing control under the influence
of a compelling rhythm reinforced the idea of rock and roll as a
threat not just to public order but to civilization itself. To complete
the historical parallel, some clergymen raised the possibility that
rock and roll would "turn young people into devil worshippers."[31]

In one way, the critics were right: Rock was much more than a
musical genre; it was becoming, by the mid-1960s, the rallying
point of an alternative culture utterly estranged from the dominant
"structures," as the anthropologist Victor Turner would term them,
of Government, Corporations, Church, and Family. Spilling out of
theaters, rock drew the fans to more expansive and congenial
venues—"psychedelic ballrooms" lit by mind-dissolving strobe
lights, and the outdoor sites of rock festivals from Monterey to
Woodstock. In these settings, young people began to assemble all
the ancient ingredients of carnival: They "costumed" in torn jeans,
tie-dyed T-shirts, granny dresses, feathers, and billowing scarves.
They painted their faces and perfumed themselves with patchouli.
They shared beer, wine, vegetarian snacks. They passed around
joints. Young antiwar activists, like myself, could take a holiday
from our usual work of persuasion and organizing, because peace
was already in the air.

The hippie rock fans had re-created carnival—and more. To
most participants rock festivals were something beyond temporary
interruptions in otherwise dull and hardworking lives. These events
were the beachheads of a new, ecstatic culture meant to replace the

old repressive one—or, as Jim Miller puts it, "a bucolic and cosmo-politan utopia, a world of benign liberty, happy nonconformity, and miraculously nonpossessive individualism, an egalitarian city-state where the dancers with the face paint freaking freely in the crowd were now as much the stars as anyone's music up on the stage."[32]

One way to expand the festival into an ongoing community was to take to the road and go from one concert or festival to another. "Deadheads," fans of the Grateful Dead, formed a floating commu-nity that followed the band from city to city in "elderly bread vans and decommissioned school buses painted with rust primer and furnished with curtains and the kind of mattresses that are chucked under lampposts at 3 A.M. On their windows were stickers showing skulls or tap-dancing skeletons, talismanic to the Dead."[33] A former Deadhead writes of his fellow fans:

> I would see them again at the Meadowlands, at Madison Square Garden and up in Boston, all the way across the country to San Francisco and back east again. I would find things to love in the parking lots, and in the hallways of the arenas. Strange, clumpy pyr-amids of naked deadheads writhed intertwined in asexual hallucino-genic ecstasy. Angel boys stood wide-eyed and grinning on the same square of asphalt for hours. Angel girls spun in the same tight circle all night, bells jangling on their ankles . . . Food and drink were shared freely, drugs and even tickets too. You could count on run-ning into the same people from city to city, grubby nomads who would find you among thousands of unknowns and greet you with unfeigned warmth.[34]

The counterculture's dream of an ongoing ecstatic community incensed Victor Turner. He could see the parallel between rock fes-tivities and the ecstatic rituals of small-scale societies; he understood rock's challenge to the dominant society, stating, somewhat wood-enly, that "rock is clearly a cultural expression and instrumentality of that style of communitas which has arisen as the antithesis of the 'square,' 'organization man' type of bureaucratic social structure of mid-twentieth-century America."[35] But, as we saw earlier, Turner rejected the rock culture's aspiration to replace "square" culture with a permanently festive way of life. Communal ecstasy, or *communitas*, as he put it, could only be "liminal," or marginal and occasional. Any attempt to make it a daily experience would be destructive of structure and hence of civilization. Quite possibly, this distaste for the hippie counterculture helped shape his anthropological theories, or at least his insistence that collective ecstasy be consumed only in measured and scheduled doses.

Opposition to rock persists into our own time, only in less egregiously racist and sometimes more historically sophisticated forms. Political conservatives tend to categorize it as a manifestation of the "permissiveness" of the "toxic 1960s," during which "traditional values" were supposedly undermined by hedonism and self-indulgence. On the occasion of Jerry Garcia's death, for example, the right-wing *Washington Times* dismissed rock as "merely the sounds they [the Grateful Dead] made in worshipping an infantile hedonism that infests the culture yet," and went on to sound the "jungle" theme: Rock is a reminder of "how fragile civilization always is, how close the darkness of the forest surrounds."[36] Or we find on the Web site of Pastor David L. Brown today an attack on rock for its "sexuality" and "lawlessness," followed breathlessly by: "But that is not the only problem! The beat of rock is nothing new. Pagan, animistic tribes had the 'rock beat' long before it came to America. They use the driving beat to get 'high' and bring them into an altered state of consciousness . . . You see, the beat 'is a vehicle for demon infestation.' "[37]

Rock, of course, survived to see its early enemies eat their words. Most important, it proved to be a moneymaking commodity, capable of enriching recording companies and performers, while its live audiences, no longer containable in theaters, moved on to fill football stadiums and even larger venues in what were often truly ecstatic events. The market had spoken: By the late 1960s the no-longer-new music not only rocked but ruled. Having become a successful commodity itself, rock was quickly enlisted to market other commodities, from cars to financial services. Rock was, by the 1980s, almost inescapable—offered around the clock on thousands of radio stations, sampled in commercials, bowdlerized as Muzac, or deployed in its original form to provide shopping-friendly background music at stores like Kmart, the Gap, and Express. At the same time it was evolving into so many diverse forms—acid, disco, punk, heavy metal, alternative, house, techno, et cetera—that "rock and roll" became an almost impossibly large and blurry target. Rock and rock-derived music was everywhere, from sports events to churches; in fact, the above statement by Pastor Brown was actually directed at "*Christian* rock."

Certainly commercialization had a debilitating effect on rock. The defiant self-assertion of a song like "I Can't Get No Satisfaction" is lost, for example, when that song becomes part of the background noise in a shopping mall. Worse still, businesses sought to appropriate the defiance itself, as when, in the 1990s, "new economy" companies used it in commercials to project their newness, coolness, and all-around impatience with the old. There is no better way to subvert a revolution than to enlist it in the service of moneymaking.

Quite apart from its employment as a marketing tool, rock's sheer ubiquity may have had an even greater taming effect simply by severing its life-giving connection to physical participation and collective pleasure. Rock that can be heard everywhere is rock that can be heard largely in places where a physical response is impossible. What better way to desensitize people to a beat than to force them to hear it in scores of settings, like shopping malls, where no response is acceptable or permitted? Since you can't start dancing to the tunes pumped into a RadioShack or Winn-Dixie—at least not without risking the interference of a security guard—you learn to sever the neural connections linking the perception of rhythm to its expression through muscular motion. This lesson is repeated in our lives every day: Resist the rhythmic provocation. No matter how tempting the beat, you must stand still or remain in your seat.

But *something* happened in the rock rebellion, traces of which persist not only in today's club scene but in the most banal settings for rock, like shoe stores and supermarkets. Rock and roll reopened the possibility of ecstasy, or at least a joy beyond anything else the consumer culture could offer. Drugs, particularly marijuana and LSD, contributed to the revival of the ecstatic possibility; so did the sexual revolution, which meant, in the 1960s and '70s, not just male exploitativeness but women's demand for female orgasms too. People of course continue to seek pleasure through shopping, drinking, and forms of prepackaged entertainment that are mildly engaging at best. But the news is out, and has been at least since the 1960s: We are capable of so much more.

Rock and roll no doubt encouraged indulgence in drugs and sex, but it hardly needed them as accompaniments, speaking as it did from ancient traditions of collective ecstasy achieved solely through rhythmic participation. As no less an expert than Joseph Campbell remarked of a Grateful Dead concert he attended— rather soberly we must imagine, since he was a conservative and already elderly man at the time: "That was a real Dionysian festival."[38] Dionysus had briefly deigned to visit the cultures of his historic enemies, and, every so often, when an otherwise dreary "classic rock" station lets loose with Derek and the Dominos' "Layla" or Junior Walker and the All Stars' "(I'm a) Roadrunner," it is possible to imagine that he will come again.

11

Carnivalizing Sports

For most people in the world today, the experience of collective ecstasy is likely to be found, if it is found at all, not in a church or at a
concert or rally but at a sports event. Football, baseball, basketball,
and hockey in the United States; soccer worldwide: These games
now provide what the sports sociologist Allen Guttmann calls
"Saturnalia-like occasions for the uninhibited expression of emotions which are tightly controlled in our ordinary lives."[1] In a stadium or at an arena, the audience has been expected for decades to
leap up from their seats, shout, wave, and jump up and down with
the vicissitudes of the game. This relative freedom of motion, combined with the crowding in the bleachers, creates what another
sports scholar, drawing on the language Durkheim used to describe
ecstatic religious rituals, considers "an in-group effervescence that
generates a communal solidarity."[2] A Mexican soccer fan reports on
his own experience of self-loss in the crowd: "At some point you
get the feeling that you don't care what happens to you . . . If
something were to trigger a riot, I would want to participate . . .
Everyone is one unit, you don't have any responsibility."[3] And on a
Web site offering information on Korean tourism, the emotional

transports of local fans are offered as one of the country's selling points.

> There is no denying the awe-inspiring chill of the solidarity reflected in the Korean street cheerers. Brought together by a game, the Koreans still show us what it's like to want to be a part of something larger than yourself, even if you can't quite put your finger on what the larger meaning of screaming and crying in front of a stadium screen with thousands of other people really means.[4]

Meaning may be the wrong thing to ask for in a setting where powerful collective emotions are controlled by the motions of a ball or puck. One reason sports events generate so much collective excitement is simply because we expect them to, and we know that the physical expression of this excitement—the shouting, jumping up and down, et cetera—is not only permitted but expected as well. Sports events can be thought of, quite apart from the game, as a medium for generating collective thrills—a not entirely reliable one, since some games are dull and one team must always lose anyway, but in at least one way more effective than many rock concerts. At a concert held in a theater, everyone faces toward the stage and sees little of the other concertgoers except for the backs of their heads. Sports stadiums, however, are round, so "the spectator confronts the emotion apparent on the faces of other spectators."[5] People may say they are going to see the Browns or the A's or Manchester, but they are also going to see one another, and to become part of a mass in which excitement builds by bouncing across the playing field, from one part of the stadium to the other.

There were, in the early twentieth century, few other settings in which to find the communal élan offered by sports—only marginal ecstatic religious sects, at least in the industrialized countries, and little by way of exuberant public festivity to compete with the drama of the moving ball. As the century wore on, sports expanded and tightened their grip on the public imagination, calling forth elaborately organized networks of fans in the United Kingdom and South America, encroaching on and altering the celebration of traditional holidays, like Thanksgiving in the United States. As early as the 1920s, the journalist Frederick Lewis Allen could reasonably describe American sport as a national "obsession."[6]

By the latter part of the century, the increasing commercialization of sports fueled another growth spurt, perhaps most dramatically in the United States: Televised sports moved into prime time and, beginning in the 1980s, required dozens of cable channels to carry twenty-four-hour coverage of games and commentary. At the same time, the possibility of viewing live games in person began to grow along with the nation's stadium seating capacity. A hundred and one stadiums were built between the years 1980 and 2003,[7] each with a capacity of about seventy thousand. The ancient Romans had centered their civic life on the arena, building one for every city they conquered or created; Americans seem determined to do no less, often giving a higher priority to stadium construction than to routine expenditures for public services such as education, including school sports.[8]

But a spectacle, even one at which a certain amount of rowdiness is tolerated, has its limits. In the 1950s, American commentators often rued the disappearance of neighborhood baseball games as more people came to the sport vicariously, as spectators rather than as players and "stars" themselves. Whether the fans eventually grew impatient with their relatively passive role is hard to say; we have few firsthand accounts of the fan experience other than those provided by sports journalists, whose profession places them squarely within the sports industry. But beginning in the 1960s in the United Kingdom and somewhat later in the United States, sports audiences were carving out new and often creative forms of participation—much as rock audiences were refusing to sit quietly through performances. Spectators began "carnivalizing" sports events, coming in costume, engaging in collective rhythmic activities that went well beyond chants, adding their own music, dance,

and feasting to the game. The parallel to rock audiences is not incidental; part of what brought sports audiences to life in the late
twentieth century was rock 'n' roll itself.

A Brief History of Western Sports

It is this little-noted "revolt" of sports fans that concerns us in this
chapter, but first we need a bit of historical perspective on just
whose sports we are talking about. For activities with no intrinsic
meaning beyond the prowess of the players—no obvious ideology
or transcendent vision—sports have a history of surprisingly intense conflict over who can play, who can watch, and whether there
will even be a game at all. In recent decades, the most visible clashes
have had to do with race and gender: whether blacks could play
American Major League Baseball, for example, or whether women
can be allowed to compete with men at golf. But for centuries the
tensions over sports ran along lines of class. The upper classes had
their sports, such as hunting; the lower classes had archery compe-
titions and various "folk sports" in which there was little distinction
between players and spectators. Early football, for example, often
pitted whole villages against each other—men, women, and children battling over the pig's bladder that served as a ball. There were
footraces for women as well as men and, in some cases, competi-
tions pitting one sex against the other, with a dance or a kiss as a
prize.

Early modern European sports typically occurred in the context
of festivities like carnival or, in England, at parish holidays and
fairs, and when those festivities came under fire from "reformers"
from the sixteenth century on, so did the sports. Disorderly folk
sports, like the original form of football, particularly outraged the
authorities, who repeatedly tried to ban them. The court records of
Middlesex, England, in 1576 mention the prosecution of seven men
who "with unknown malefactors to the number of one hundred assembled themselves unlawfully and played a certain unlawful game

called football, by means of which there was amongst them a great affray, likely to result in homicides and serious accident."[9] When industrialization left working-class people with only Sunday for sports, the strict Sabbatarians moved quickly to ban any activity other than worship on that day. Sports were condemned as a waste of time better spent at work or in contemplation of the status of one's soul. In the puritan New England colonies, sports were never legal, with the law banning even "unnecessary and unseasonable walking" on the Lord's Day.[10]

Like so many of the festivities that they had once been a part of, sports were, by the late nineteenth century, transformed into spectacles. These were not, originally, spectacles organized from on high, but rather grudgingly permitted by elites. Baseball, for example, which began as a thoroughly working-class sport in the United States, met elite opposition ostensibly directed at "the crowd behavior: the drunks, the gamblers, the pickpockets, the mashers who bothered the women; the fans who yelled obscenities and threatened the umpire," according to the sports historian Ted Vincent. As he goes on to comment, the real source of the opposition to baseball was the middle-class fear of working-class crowds: "It seemed that certain people didn't like certain other people gathering in big crowds, a situation that gave those attending late-nineteenth-century spectator sports something in common with the defiant long-haired youth at rock concerts of the late 1960s."[11]

Soccer, which ultimately derived from folk football, had been reformulated in mid-nineteenth-century England as an elite sport meant to inculcate "the virtues of hard work, discipline, and self-control."[12] Within a couple of decades, the ball, so to speak, passed once again to the working class, who learned the game from clergymen and factory owners interested in instilling the same virtues in the workforce. The professionalization of soccer from the 1880s on drove out the upper-class amateurs, who were replaced by professional players drawn from the working class, eventually leaving both the playing field and the bleachers to blue-collar men and, in much smaller numbers, women. In South America, local people learned the sport by watching amateur English players—sailors and the officials of British-owned businesses. Brazilian soccer had passed through three constituencies by 1915: from the British to the local elite and finally to the working class. "The fashionable ladies in the stands went home when the working class took over the game," the sportswriter Janet Lever reports of the game in Brazil.[13] Spectator sports became, by the early twentieth century, what Eric Hobsbawm called "a mass proletarian cult."[14]

What finally made spectator sports acceptable to the elites who at first disdained these unruly gatherings was the use of sports events, in Hobsbawm's words, as "a medium for national identification and factitious community."[15] If the upper classes could not be present in person, at least sporting events could feature the flags and anthems that symbolized the supposed harmony of rich and poor under the aegis of the nation. With encouragement from teams' businessmen backers, sporting events in the United States came to involve, by World War I, "elaborate pageantry, ceremony, politicians, military bands, and national anthems."[16] The bands and—in the United States—precision drill teams performing during halftime or other breaks gave sporting events a resemblance to the military reviews that had delighted nineteenth-century British crowds; the flags, ceremonies, and anthem singing foreshadowed the nationalist rallies staged by Hitler and Mussolini in the 1920s and '30s. One might say that Hitler's big mistake, in the design of events like the Nuremberg rallies, was to leave out the game.

So either way—whether through the proletarianization of formerly elite sports or the increasing respectability of proletarian ones—sporting events evolved into a socially acceptable gathering space for working-class people, especially working-class men. They gathered also in factories and other workplaces, but the stadium or arena was uniquely theirs—a place to meet with friends, drink, and cheer, all with minimal interference from representatives of the elites. The working class, or at least the male half of it, had reclaimed a vestige of the lost tradition of carnival. Very soon, they would want the whole thing.

The Carnivalization of Sports

The first sign of a new assertiveness on the part of sports fans—and the only one ever noticed by most sports sociologists and journalists—was the emergence of hooliganism among English spectators in the early 1960s. Young male soccer "supporters," as the fans are known in the United Kingdom, seemed to be taking the game too seriously—instigating riots in the stadiums and, more commonly, engaging in postgame street battles with the supporters of the "enemy" team. Many observers recognized that the violence had something to do with class and class resentment, since the hooligans were typically to be found occupying the cheapest seats or standing, seatless, throughout the game in the "terraces," as they are called in Britain, of a stadium. About a decade later, hooliganism began showing up on the Continent, probably spread by traveling English fans following their teams as well as by television reports on English hooliganism at home. Noting the geographic distribution of soccer violence, a Belgian psychologist suggested that

> the violence is a symptom of societal problems, not soccer problems. In Belgium and France, there are relatively few problems. But in much of Latin America, in Britain and Italy, where the gaps between rich and poor are growing, there are more problems. Soccer is a poor-man's game as much as any sport, and a lot of unhappy people are rebelling against their surroundings.[17]

Whatever the hooligans' motivations, they succeeded, in many instances, in stealing the show. Just as reports of rock and roll "riots" often eclipsed reviews of the music in the early 1960s, news stories on fan violence could easily overshadow accounts of the game.

Engrossed by the violence, few observers noted a far more

widespread and appealing change in fan behavior. Beginning in the 1970s, or at least first reported at that time, fans of soccer worldwide and various sports (football, basketball, baseball, and hockey) in the United States were unmistakably treating sports events as occasions for traditional carnival-like activities: costuming, masking, singing, and indulging in rhythmically synchronous behavior, if not actually dancing.

Writing in 1983, when the trend was well under way, the sociologist Louis Kutcher observed that American sports "have long had some elements of carnival—feasting, masquerading, merrymaking and rule and role suspension."[18] Masquerading, at an American game, traditionally meant wearing team colors.* The sports version of carnival's king of fools was the team mascot—a person dressed as something like a chicken or a pirate and displaying a comic lack of athletic skill or even basic coordination. As for feasting, it involved, at the very least, peanuts, hot dogs, and Cracker Jacks, washed down with the requisite quantities of beer. More elaborately, American fans had, by the 1950s, started the day hours before the game with tailgate parties in the arena parking lots, usually featuring grilled meats or regional specialties. Although each group or family brought its own picnic meal, sharing with strangers, especially those with a beer to exchange for some food, was common, as in the feasts that so often accompanied traditional festivities.

But by the last three decades of the twentieth century, the carnivalization of sports events was moving well beyond the hot dog and team colors stage. In one of the very few studies of festive fan behavior, the anthropologist Desmond Morris found English soccer fans in the 1970s wearing huge top hats or giant Afro wigs, as well as scarves and trouser bows in team colors. "Many of the costumes are

---

*The custom of dressing for games in team colors may have been started in Brazil, the land of *carnaval*, by a fan named Jayme de Carvalho. Alex Bellos reports that "Jayme was a low-level state functionary, a job as anonymous as it was possible to get. Yet on the terraces he was a celebrity . . . He dressed up in club colours and brought flags and banners." Since club color clothes were not commercially available at the time, he relied on his wife to sew his costumes. (Bellos, p. 126.)

obviously home-made," he observed, making it clear that "many days of planning and preparation have gone into the build-up to the great event."[19] In the United States, a single exhibitionist fan—Rollen ("Rock 'n' Rollen") Stewart—probably deserves some of the credit for popularizing the wearing of outlandish outfits to games. He traveled from game to game—football, baseball, and even golf matches—trying to attract the TV cameras to his outsized rainbow-colored Afro wig, which he abandoned only after a "born again" religious experience in 1980.[20]

Another American innovator, a particularly fervent Cleveland Browns fan nicknamed "Big Dawg," found a dog costume in a store in 1984, started wearing it to games, and thus helped set the trend toward team-related gear such as the foam-rubber Cheeseheads now routinely worn by Green Bay Packers fans, the Viking helmets of Minnesota Vikings fans, and the pig snouts assumed by Washington Redskins fans. By the late 1980s, as commercial enterprises moved in on the growing demand for team-related costumes, far less innovation was required on the part of individual fans. They could simply buy ready-made team T-shirts, sweatshirts, characteristic head gear, and, for the ever-growing number of female fans, earrings and dresses.*

Costuming serves different, even opposite, functions for different people. For most, the wearing of team colors allows a fan to blend in with the mass of other similarly clad fans; it would be unwise to flout the color coding by inadvertently wearing the opponent's colors while sitting in a section of the bleachers occupied by home team fans. But for others, costuming—and in some cases, uncostuming, as with the Yalies who run naked through the stadium at the annual Harvard–Yale game—is a vivid, some might say exhibitionist, bid for attention, as in the case of an unnamed Oakland A's fan observed by a local journalist.

---

*According to *USA Today* (August 28, 1997), 44 percent of the National Football League's fan base were women, up from 33 percent in 1990. The "feminization" of sports fandom deserves investigation in its own right, but I haven't found a satisfactory account.

There's something poetic and beautiful about watching a middle-aged fan dressed from head-to-toe in A's garb, brandishing a baseball glove, proudly sporting an American flag fanny pack, waving a giant Bob Marley flag in the air, punctuating his bursts of obscenities by pounding on a conga drum, and loudly commanding visiting Yankees fans of Japanese descent to go back to Iraq.[21]

Sports fans seldom wear masks to accompany their costumes; instead, they paint their faces in team colors. The origins of this practice are as murky as those of costuming. The British soccer journalist Simon Kuper referred to it as a European custom, Morris noted it among English fans in the 1970s, and some Americans insist it began in their country outside of the sports context, at hippie gatherings and rock concerts in the 1960s. Another theory is that it began among the habitually more expressive South American fans and spread northward as North Americans gained a taste for soccer. An account of the 1994 World Cup held in Palo Alto, California, for example, describes the carnivalistic, and no doubt contagious, behavior of fans who had followed their team from Brazil.

It was a party. A horde of Brazilians marched down El Camino to the stadium, dancing as a band played "Brazil." Countless Brazilian flags were waved from cars and worn as capes or shawls or wraparound skirts. Fans painted their faces to resemble the Brazilian flag, including a blue nose signifying the night sky and Southern Cross that is at the center of the flag.[22]

Wherever face painting began, though, television quickly spread the fad worldwide. Mentions of face painting in the United States go back at least to the 1980 Super Bowl, but not until the mid-1990s did the custom become firmly enough entrenched to merit commercial exploitation within the United States. As late as 1996, American fans were using Magic Markers or even house paint to give their allegiances epidermal expression. Now there are at least a half dozen (and possibly many more) purveyors of skin-compatible colored makeup, and spokespersons for these companies, interviewed in 2000, described the business as "really surprising"[23] and "huge."[24] A similar industry has sprung up in South Korea, where "the popularity of the World Cup has created a secondary craze in the form of face painting. The popularity of game day face paint continues to grow producing long lines at shopping centers in Myeong-dong where the face painters ply their trade."[25]

But a sports event is hardly a party without some sort of rhythmic participation by the fans. The earliest form was chanting, often of derisive lines directed at the opponents, such as, in the United States, "Nah nah nah nah, hey hey hey, go-ood-bye." As in the case of costuming and face painting, more elaborate songs arose spontaneously from within the ranks of fans themselves, most strikingly in the case of soccer. The *Washington Post* observed in 1994 that "soccer songs are traditionally born in the cheap-ticket sections . . . of league club stadiums, where working-class fans, often forced to stand throughout the game, compose sarcastic, musical epithets directed at their opponents."[26] One of the rare academic studies of nonviolent fan behavior found Germans fairly quiet and "unimaginative" in the 1960s, except to celebrate victory with the traditional carnival song "What a Day, What a Wonderful Day Today." By the mid-1990s, however, German fans had created and memorized thirty to fifty songs of their own devising, some blending rock and roll with familiar soccer chants—the traditional "Olé," for example, sung to the tune of a Pet Shop Boys song.[27]

There are more energetic forms of rhythmic participation. South American fans often dance in the bleachers to the beat of drums they carry to the stadium. The Hawks of the Faithful, an organization of fans of São Paulo's Corinthians soccer team, sing a song called "Fly, Hawk" while stretching out their arms and turning from side to side to imitate the bird in flight.[28] In England in the 1970s, Morris observed soccer fans "Pogo jumping," or jumping vertically "until a whole section of the crowd appears to be heaving and swelling like a rough sea"[29]—a practice that may have originated at punk rock concerts. English fans also invented "synchroclapping," in which they clap rhythmically with their hands held over their heads. A psychologist who studied this activity marveled at the degree of synchrony a soccer crowd could achieve without the slightest central coordination: "How this remarkable precision is achieved, within what most people would see as a disorderly rabble, is a mystery . . . it is orderly to an almost absurd extent."[30]

But by far the most widespread form of rhythmic participation is "the wave," in which fans in one section of the stadium stand and raise their arms, then sit down while fans in an adjacent section follow suit, so that the motion appears to roll around the bleachers, "creating what many fans consider an exhilarating and visually stunning experience."[31] Who invented it is, again, unclear. The Europeans call it "the Mexican wave," but Americans are sure it was an American who invented it in 1981; they're just not sure who or where: "Crazy George" Henderson, a professional cheerleader for the Oakland A's games, claims to be the wave's inventor; others insist it was first performed by the fans at a University of Washington, or possibly at a University of Michigan, football game.

Although fans may think exuberant behavior like the wave somehow aids their team, coaches and players initially objected to it as distracting, with the *New York Times* sportswriter George Vecsey going so far as to condemn it as a "plague": "like acid rain defoliating the countryside or a new strain of virus or killer bees mercilessly working their way up the Americas."[32] But the wave proved to be unstoppable, spreading to baseball in 1984 and to soccer by 1992 and sweeping up such notable soccer spectators as Fidel Castro, King Juan Carlos of Spain, and François Mitterrand. As the sociologist Michael Givant observed in 1984: "It's a way of not being passive . . . They want to participate. If everybody is a celebrity these days, they ask, 'Why can't I be involved?' "[33]

So by the close of the twentieth century, the clash of the athletes on the field was only one part, and for many only a minor part, of the activities and events that made up a game. People went to the stadium for the opportunity to dress up and paint their faces, to see and be seen, to eat and drink immoderately, to shout and sing and engage in the sports fan's equivalent of dancing. The games on the playing field had changed very little since the early part of the century; it was the behavior of the fans that would have seemed ludicrous and disruptive by the standards of, say, the 1920s. Why this global carnivalization of sports in the final decades of the last century? Or, given what is perhaps a natural human tendency to liven up spectacles with drink and fancy dress and dance, we might ask why the carnivalization of sports has accelerated so spectacularly since the 1970s.

The Revolt of the Fans

The British sociologist Ernest Cashmore suggests that the festive behavior was encouraged by elites—stadium and team owners—as a peaceable alternative to hooliganism. "They were pacified," he says of the hooligans, "by replica shirts, videos, logo-plastered bedsheets, face painting and a miscellany of commodities derived from a sport that realized that the only way to prosper was to re-invent itself."[34] Whether they did so to "pacify" the fans or not, the stadium owners quickly seized on and amplified many of the new forms of fan behavior: In the United States, they installed "Cheer Meters" in the stadiums so that the fans could measure the noise they contributed, along with message boards on video screens to exhort the fans to cheer louder or commence the wave. They added fireworks, sexily clad cheerleaders, more kinds of mascots, loud recorded music, and live music from pipe organs.[35] They encouraged costuming, "often asking the fans to wear a certain color. Indeed, the sale of such items is an important part of total revenue."[36] A woman attending a 1999 game reported, with some relief, that American football had at last become entertaining.

I came prepared to hate the game—but turns out it was really just a flashy, well-staged show. Football was kinda the extra added attraction. There were fantastic scoreboards at each end of the field with slick video productions, rock music, and a light screen that told the crowd when to do the wave—football fans not being smart enough to figure it out on their own.[37]

But the commercial exploitation of various forms of fan behavior—by face paint purveyors or by team owners trying to attract demographic groups, like women, who had not previously been fans—tells us nothing about the initial urge to paint and costume and sing and do the wave. "These ritual displays are impressive," Morris observed of English soccer-fan behavior in the 1970s, "because they have grown naturally from within the ranks of the fans themselves."[38] A few individual innovators deserve some credit: There is Claudio Ribeiro, or "Cotton Bud," in São Paulo, a veteran of brutal poverty, who made a name for himself as "the hyperactive, drumming lunatic with the ever-expanding Afro that TV pictures always hone in on during Brazil's World Cup games."[39] There is Edward Anzalone, a New York City firefighter, who rides into games on his brother's shoulders, wearing a green and white fire helmet and leading a Jets chant.[40] Or we might consider Josh Rosenberg, the founder of the Oakland A's Drummers, a group of five young men who drum loudly, if somewhat chaotically, from their favorite spot in the left-field bleachers.[41]

One might, rather innocently, hypothesize that festive forms of fan behavior simply represent an intensified loyalty to the sports teams, but it is hard to see why such loyalty should have been increasing at a time when the teams were showing less and less loyalty to their fans. In the United States anyway, the late twentieth century saw a fairly heartless degree of commercialization, with whole teams being sold off to distant cities at their owners' whims. As *Sports Illustrated* observed, with some perplexity, in 1992:

Sports have become so desentimentalized that it's hard to believe anyone can even root for the same team from one year to the next. Neither players nor owners seem to acknowledge the fans' loyalty, much less repay it. And yet every time you walk into a ballpark or flip on ESPN, there seem to be more and more superfans, megafans, *uber*fans: fans who yell louder, dress louder, spend more, suffer more, exult more and even seem to *care* more.[42]

Besides, fan loyalty could be expressed in many less festive ways—with closer attention to the game itself, for example, rather than with actions like the wave that are known to annoy the players.

Whatever their degree of team loyalty, the fact is that the fans were choosing to express it in ways that drew attention away from the game and to themselves. As Susan Faludi observes of the Cleveland Browns' blue-collar fans, the "Dawgs": "Rabid fans increasingly became focused not on helping the players perform but on cultivating their own performances. The show in the stands began to conflict with, even undermine, the drama on the gridiron."[43] Or as the reporter—and ardent soccer fan—Alex Bellos reflects on the São Paulo fan organization called the Hawks of the Faithful: "It strikes me that the football experience has come full circle. With the Hawks, the football [soccer] fan is no longer a spectator. He is the spectacle. The Hawks are the football fans that have their own fans."[44]

At least part of the explanation for the fans' new insistence on being part of the show must be television. Sports had been televised almost since the invention of the medium, but in the United States it was only in the 1970s that they broke into prime time—with ABC's *Monday Night Football* leading the way. One of the immediate effects of television, as Guttmann notes, was to change the demographics of the crowd in the stadium. Since older fans could now enjoy the game at home, without the discomforts of hard seats and inclement weather, the stadium crowds got younger.[45] We might generalize, and speculate that television allowed the elimination, from the stadium, of any fan who did not seek the stadium experience; if it was only the game that interested you, you could watch it at home or in a bar. So by a process of natural selection, the people who actually attended the games tended to be those who sought the thrill of the crowd.

There is no doubt that television encourages exhibitionist fan behavior, in at least two ways. First, it offers some of the more exuberant fans—those willing, for example, to dress and paint themselves outlandishly or strip to the waist in freezing weather—the chance to achieve a tiny measure of fame. "Rock 'n' Rollen" Stewart, for example, eagerly sought the cameras' attention and was finally rewarded with a part in a Budweiser commercial. In her analysis of Cleveland Browns fans, Faludi observes: "The battle now, the one that fans and players alike were caught up in, was really for the camera's attention. The show of hard hats, of dog suits, of toughing it out in the rain and the snow, in the end, became exactly that—a show, a beauty contest of sorts, where the object was to attract the camera with bizarre caricatures of working stiffs."[46] The second, and more significant, effect of television is of course to spread exhibitionist—or perhaps we should say, less judgmentally, spectacular—forms of fan behavior from country to country and sport to sport. If it's almost impossible to pin down the origins of particular kinds of behavior, like face painting or doing the wave, this is because they are picked up by fans in other places almost as soon as they are invented.

Another outside force affecting fan behavior starting in the 1970s was rock 'n' roll. South Americans had long enjoyed danceable music at their soccer matches, generally provided by drumming fans and accompanied by dancing in the bleachers. In the United States, games had traditionally been fairly music-free except for the singing of the national anthem and the marching music provided by drill teams during halftime or other breaks. The exception, until the 1950s, were the games of segregated, all-black sports leagues, which were enlivened by blues or jazz bands and much dancing in the stands. Only in the 1970s did rock 'n' roll find a place in the pageantry of major league American sports, bringing with it some of rock's rebellious spirit, or at least a desire to get up out of the seats and become part of the show.

American sports and rock music did not at first seem to be likely partners. "The '60s were about youth culture, and sports weren't peddled as part of that culture," according to a *Rolling Stone* editor in 1999. "Rock-and-roll sort of defined itself in opposition to the NFL."[47] Or as Bob Weir, who had played football in high school before becoming a member of the Grateful Dead, put it: "In the '60s, music and sports were worlds apart. People who were into sports were generally a little more accepting of a regimented life and basically lived like soldiers . . . Musicians—if something didn't suit us, we'd make a little stink or just not obey orders."[48]

But by the early 1970s, some of the college marching bands that played at breaks were abandoning military music for rock tunes, perhaps in response to the antiwar mood on campuses. Recorded rock music began showing up at professional games in the latter part of the decade, a development that *Time* attributes to the emergence of a newly hip mood among America's corporate executives, the group that supplies most team owners: "Corporate America shed its square image and began incorporating antiestablishment themes into advertising,"[49] and from that it was apparently a short step to incorporating rock into sports events. But the innovation would never have survived if the fans had rejected it, and, increasingly, sports fans themselves were likely to be veterans of rock concerts, perhaps held in the same stadium as the game, and brought with them a certain impatience with the spectator's appointed role as a seat warmer. Besides, if rock could be found in commercials, in elevator Muzac, at weddings—why not at the big game?

However unlikely their original union, rock and American sports were soon as tightly mated as baseball and beer. By 1994, commentators were even talking about a potential merger of sports and rock music: "The distinctions between the two industries [sports and music] are fading, becoming just another facet of the mammoth entertainment industry."[50] Stadium managers now employ music staffs of up to ten people to determine the playlist that will go with the game; music companies have come to view professional sports franchises as an outlet on the same scale as radio stations.[51]

The result is a kind of event that a blind person, wandering into the stadium, would have difficulty distinguishing from a rock concert, with music at breaks, after significant plays, when a new player comes up to bat, and to celebrate victory at the end. Not any song will do; a special genre of rock—"jock rock"—has been adapted to service the sports industry, including generally well-known hits such as Sister Sledge's "We Are Family," as well as songs, like the Baha Men's "Who Let the Dogs Out," made famous largely through sports venues. Jock rock, collections of which can be purchased on CDs, leans heavily toward anthemic, pump-it-up tunes like Queen's "We Will Rock You" and the Village People's "YMCA," but stadiums' playlists include more varied fare too, including songs by Santana, Eminem, the Clash, and the Red Hot Chili Peppers. Halftime at the 2006 Super Bowl featured the Rolling Stones, with the fans swaying and holding up lighters, exactly as they would do at a concert.

No one, to my knowledge, has studied the impact of rock on any aspect of sports, from ticket sales to the athletes' performance. It is unlikely to improve the latter, judging from players' complaints about the noise, which can reach a decibel level approaching that of rock concerts.[52] But for the fans, the effect of rock music at sporting events is probably much the same as its effect at concerts: It makes people want to jump up and dance. No doubt this exuberance is carefully contained at stadiums, just as it is limited to scheduled times—halftime and other kinds of breaks—but the experience of dancing in the bleachers with fifty thousand other people has to be compelling. One fan describes outbreaks of dancing at Yankee Stadium, "where male members of the grounds crew lip-synch and dance to 'YMCA' as they sweep the infield during the fifth inning break, and are joined in performance by the ballpark crowd en masse."[53] A commentator writes of the effect of Gary Glitter's song "Rock and Roll Part 2," to which the fans shout "Hey!": "I first heard it in Denver at a Steelers-Broncos game, and the faithful there, who are as committed a group of fans as any I've ever seen, literally would rock Mile High Stadium. The stands would actually shake and sway when they bounced up and down and reached a Rocky Mountain 'Hey!'"[54] Rock ramps up the party atmosphere—the mood of excess and self-abandonment—which in turn encourages the more extravagant forms of costuming, face painting, and stadium-wide synchronized motions. Decades earlier, in the middle of the century, sports events in America had been fairly disciplined, thoroughly masculine gatherings, heavy on the marching music and other militaristic flourishes. Rock entered this unlikely setting and carved out a space for Dionysian pleasure.

While Americans were acquiring the habit of dancing at games, global soccer culture was encouraging the notion of the game as an occasion for festivity, regardless of its outcome. An American reporter observed in 1994 that

> some Americans like to party before games. Some like to party afterward. Some do both. Brazil and Holland say: Why let the game interrupt a good party? . . . At World Cup, which is held every four years, the fans feel they are part of the game. And your team doesn't even have to be here. Take those five guys dressed in green and gold, including one dressed as a banana. They're from Tokyo. Spent about $4,000 each to jet in for the Brazil game.[55]

Nationalism remains a potent force motivating soccer fans at international matches, but some fans transcend it to celebrate any team's performance. At the England–Denmark game at the 2002 World Cup, for example, the Japanese spectators, who made up half of the stadium crowd, wore red and white in support of England, even though there was still a possibility that Japan might face England in the semifinals.[56] Most fans, of course, retain an intense loyalty to their teams and interest in the technical aspect of the games, but there seems to be a kind of hollowing out of sports events going on, as the game diminishes in comparison to the pageantry and the collective high induced by tens of thousands of people singing, chanting, and dancing in unison.

But if the carnivalization of sports represents a kind of victory for the fans—a chance to party and break free of the traditional passivity of the spectator role—it was not a victory for the same *kind* of fans who created modern spectator sports in the first place. Obviously, few working-class fans can afford to travel to soccer matches in distant countries, and the price of a ticket to a home game rose precipitously in the 1990s, thanks to fancy new stadiums and skyrocketing salaries for the players. In 1996, a sports sociologist noted that, with the price of a ticket for American hockey, football, and basketball games approaching fifty dollars, "the high cost of going to sporting events has denied the underclass and even the lower-middle class from attending them."[57] In the United Kingdom, new "all seater" stadiums not only inflated the price of tickets but eliminated the terraces in which working-class fans once stood as a mass to sing and clap in synchrony. Working-class fans have been "cut out of the loop," according to Faludi: "Fans of value were the rich and corporate who could afford the luxury boxes and personal seat licenses, the latter costing as much as $5,000 in some cities. Watching a football game in person . . . was like buying a car now; it required a down payment."[58]

Whether the festive atmosphere of the games will survive this demographic change remains to be seen. In the last few years, the wealthiest fans have signaled their distaste for the ongoing carnival by withdrawing into their own closed-in skyboxes or luxury suites built into the stadium, where executives can pursue business deals over cocktails and buffet meals while keeping an eye on the game.

An article in *American Way* magazine explains the need for the growing separation of the classes.

> If a CEO is forking over a cool million a year [in fees for his luxury suite at the stadium] to wheel and deal new clients, he or she isn't the least bit interested in bumping elbows with bleacher-seat fans. The last person these people would want in their private room is a fanatic who paints his face and hollers obscenities at the officials. (Ironically, a team's most loyal fans are often those least likely to be able to afford such luxurious accommodations.)[59]

As for the working-class fans who have been priced out of their erstwhile gathering place: Maybe they will be able to keep the tradition of festive fandom alive within the sports bars, which have proliferated within the United States to the point where it is hard to find a bar *without* team paraphernalia and multiple large-screen TVs permanently tuned to the sports channels. Or maybe, like the folk football and footraces of centuries ago, the colorful traditions of late-twentieth-century sports fandom will be lost forever—at least to the class of people who invented them.

Conclusion:
The Possibility of Revival

As we saw at the beginning of this book, nineteenth-century Protestant reformers sometimes sought to shame European carnival-goers by imagining the reaction of a converted "Hottentot" to such unseemly goings-on. The converted "savage" would, in these fanciful accounts, be disgusted to find supposedly civilized Christians dancing, masking, and cavorting in public exactly like his unconverted brethren at home. But the more interesting case would be that of an *un*converted "savage" plopped down in the modern urban world—say, an eighteenth-century indigenous Australian, Plains Indian, or resident of New Guinea—transported into midtown Manhattan just as the lunch-hour crowds are hitting the street.

He will necessarily be dumbfounded by flashing lights, automobiles, and the near-complete replacement of trees and grass by a built environment. But leaving aside the technological future-shock, with all its comic possibilities, what will amaze him most is the size of the crowd he finds himself in: as many people, within a block or so, as he has ever seen together in his life, and then only at the annual gatherings of his tribe, where several hundred people might come together at a time, for days of dancing, feasting, and other carnival-like activities.

In his experience, a crowd is the raw material for festivity, and a large crowd is the making of more intense and creative festivity than anything that can be generated in his own band of a few dozen people. For a moment, the prevalence of face paint on the New Yorkers and—from our "savage's" point of view—their universal "costuming" may fool him into thinking he has emerged into a similar kind of festivity, but the facial expressions of the people around him will immediately belie this supposition. The faces are closed, unsmiling, intent on unknown missions, wary of eye contact. Whatever these people are doing, they are not celebrating. And this will be the biggest shock to him: their refusal, or inability, to put this abundant convergence of humanity to use for some kind of celebration.

In the at least three-thousand-year-old struggle between Pentheus and Dionysus—between popes and dancing peasants, between Puritans and carnival-goers, between missionaries and the practitioners of indigenous ecstatic danced religions—Pentheus and his allies seem to have finally prevailed. Not only has the possibility of collective joy been largely marginalized to the storefront churches of the poor and the darkened clubs frequented by the young, but the very source of this joy—other people, including strangers—no longer holds much appeal. In today's world, other people have become an obstacle to our individual pursuits. They impede our progress on urban streets and highways; they compete for parking spots and jobs; they drive up the price of housing and "ruin" our favorite vacation spots with their crass enjoyments and noisy presence; they may even be criminals or terrorists. We have evolved to be highly social animals and, more so than any other primate, capable of pleasurable bonding with people unrelated to ourselves. But on a planet populated by more than 6 billion of our fellow humans, all ultimately competing for the same dwindling supplies of land and oil and water, this innate sociality seems out of place, naive, and anachronistic.

There is no powerful faction in our divided world committed to upholding the glories of the feast and dance. The Protestant fundamentalism of the United States and the Islamic radicalism of the Middle and Far East are both profoundly hostile to the ecstatic undertaking. Radical Islam cut its teeth on the suppression of ecstatic Sufism; it opposes music, dancing, and the public mixing of the sexes. American evangelical Protestantism may have its "born-again" moments of individual religious revelation, but it is, by and large, a cold and Calvinist business—urging hard work, sobriety, and meager forms of charity. As for the secular viewpoint represented by the scholars and intellectuals of the West, we have encountered their visceral disdain for the "primitive" excitement of the crowd throughout this book. Even communism, which might have been expected to celebrate human sociality, turned out—with the arguable exception of Cuba—to be a drab and joyless state of affairs, in which, as in the capitalist West, mass spectacles and military parades replaced long-standing festive traditions.

It can be argued—as the enemies of festivity have done for centuries—that festivities and ecstatic rituals are incompatible with civilization, at least in its modern form. Even scholars who are relatively sympathetic to the festive tradition have tended to see it as an archaic remnant, unsuited to survive "as society becomes more complex and differentiated within classes and professions," in the words of the anthropologist Alfred Métraux.[1] Or as the French sociologist Jean Duvignaud put it, "Market economies and increasing industrialization are crystallizing the social conditions for eliminating such manifestations [festivities]."[2] The incompatibility of festivity with industrialization, market economies, and a complex division of labor is simply assumed, just as Freud assumed—or posited—the incompatibility of civilization and unbridled sexual activity. If you want antibiotics and heated buildings and air travel, these scholars seem to be saying, you must abstain from taking hold of the hands of strangers and dancing in the streets.

The presumed incompatibility of civilization and collective

ecstatic traditions presents a kind of paradox: Civilization is good—right?—and builds on many fine human traits such as intelligence, self-sacrifice, and technological craftiness. But ecstatic rituals are also good, and expressive of our artistic temperament and spiritual yearnings as well as our solidarity. So how can civilization be regarded as a form of progress if it precludes something as distinctively human, and deeply satisfying, as the collective joy of festivities and ecstatic rituals? In a remarkable essay titled "The Decline of the Choral Dance," Paul Halmos wrote in 1952 that the ancient and universal tradition of the choral dance—meaning the group dance, as opposed to the relatively recent, European-derived practice of dancing in couples—was an expression of our "group-ward drives" and "biological sociality." Hence its disappearance within complex societies, and especially within industrial civilization, can only represent a "decline of our biosocial life"—a painfully disturbing conclusion.[3]

Perhaps the problem with civilization is simply a matter of scale: Ecstatic rituals and festivities seem to have evolved to bind people in groups of a few hundred at a time—a group size at which it is possible for each participant to hear the same (unamplified) music and see all the other participants at once. Civilizations, however, tend to involve many thousands—or in our time, millions—of people bound by economic interdependencies, military exigency, and law. In a large society, ancient or modern, an emotional sense of bonding is usually found in mass spectacles that can be witnessed by thousands or—with television, even billions—of people at a time.

Ours is what the French theorist Guy Debord called the "society of the spectacle," which he described as occurring in "an epoch without festivals."[4] Instead of generating their own collective pleasures, people absorb, or consume, the spectacles of commercial entertainment, nationalist rituals, and the consumer culture, with its endless advertisements for the pleasure of individual ownership. Debord bemoaned the passivity engendered by constant spectatorship, announcing that "the spectacle is the nightmare of imprisoned modern society which ultimately expresses nothing more than its desire to sleep."[5]

But there is no obvious reason why festivities and ecstatic rituals cannot survive within large-scale societies. Whole cities were swept up in the French Revolution's Festival of Federation in 1790, with lines of dancers extending from the streets and out into the countryside. Rock events have sometimes drawn tens of thousands for days of peaceful dancing and socializing. Modern Brazil still celebrates *carnaval;* Trinidad preserves its carnival. Today's nonviolent uprisings, like Ukraine's Orange Revolution, invariably feature rock or rap music, dancing in the streets, and "costuming" in the revolution-appropriate color. There is no apparent limit on the number of people who can celebrate together.

Nor can the growing size of human societies explain the long hostility of elites to their people's festivities and ecstatic rituals—a hostility that goes back at least to the city-states of ancient Greece, which contained only a few tens of thousands of people each. It was not a concern about crowd size that led to Pentheus's crackdown on the maenads or Rome's massacre of its Dionysian cult. No, the repression of festivities and ecstatic rituals over the centuries was the conscious work of men, and occasionally women too, who saw in them a real and urgent threat. The aspect of "civilization" that is most hostile to festivity is not capitalism or industrialism—both of which are fairly recent innovations—but social hierarchy, which is far more ancient. When one class, or ethnic group or gender, rules over a population of subordinates, it comes to fear the empowering rituals of the subordinates as a threat to civil order.

We saw how this worked in late medieval Europe, and later the Caribbean: First the elite withdraws from the festivities, whether out of fear or in an effort to maintain its dignity and distance from the hoi polloi. The festivities continue for a while without them and continue to serve their ancient function of building group unity among the participants. But since the participants are now solely, or almost solely, members of the subordinate group or groups, their unity inevitably presents a challenge to the ruling parties, a challenge that may be articulated in carnival rituals that mock the king and Church. In much of the world, it was the conquering elite of European colonizers that imposed itself on native cultures and saw their rituals as "savage" and menacing from the start. This is the real bone of contention between civilization and collective ecstasy: Ecstatic rituals still build group cohesion, but when they build it among subordinates—peasants, slaves, women, colonized people—the elite calls out its troops.

In one way, the musically driven celebrations of subordinates may be more threatening to elites than overt political threats from below. Even kings and colonizers can feel the invitational power of the music. Pentheus could not resist; he finally put on women's clothing and joined the maenads—only to die hideously, torn limb from limb by his own mother. And why did nineteenth-century European colonizers so often describe the dancing natives as "out of control"? The ritual participants hadn't lost control of their actions and were in fact usually performing carefully rehearsed rituals. The "loss of control" is what the colonizers feared would happen to themselves. In some cases, the temptation might be projected onto others, especially the young. The Romans feared the effect of Bacchic worship on their young men. In the fairy tale, the Pied Piper used his pipe to lure away the children from a German town. Rock 'n' roll might have been more acceptable to adults in the 1950s if it could have been contained within the black population, instead of percolating out to a generation of young whites.

But elite hostility to Dionysian festivities goes beyond pragmatic concerns about the possibility of uprisings or the seduction of the young. Philosophically, too, elites cringe from the spectacle of disorderly public joy. Hierarchy, by its nature, establishes boundaries between people—who can go where, who can approach whom, who is welcome, and who is not. Festivity breaks the boundaries down. The classicist Charles Segal put it this way: "As Apollo imposes limits and reinforces boundaries, Dionysus, his opposite and complement, dissolves them."[6]

While hierarchy is about exclusion, festivity generates inclusiveness. The music invites everyone to the dance; shared food briefly undermines the privilege of class. As for masks: They may serve symbolic, ritual functions, but, to the extent that they conceal identity, they also dissolve the difference between stranger and neighbor, making the neighbor temporarily strange and the stranger no more foreign than anyone else. No source of human difference or identity is immune to the carnival challenge; cross-dressers defy gender just as those who costume as priests and kings mock power and rank. At the height of the festivity, we step out of our assigned roles and statuses—of gender, ethnicity, tribe, and rank—and into a brief utopia defined by egalitarianism, creativity, and mutual love. This is how danced rituals and festivities served to bind prehistoric human groups, and this is what still beckons us today.

So civilization, as humans have known it for thousands of years, has this fundamental flaw: It tends to be hierarchical, with some class or group wielding power over the majority,* and hierarchy is antagonistic to the festive and ecstatic tradition. This leaves hierarchical societies with no means of holding people together except for mass spectacles—and force. Contemporary civilization, which—for all its democratic pretensions—is egregiously hierarchical along lines of class and race and gender, may unite millions in economic interdependency, but it "unites" them with no strong affective ties. We who inhabit the wealthier parts of the world may be aware of our dependence on Chinese factory workers, Indian tech

---

*Whether this is an inherent feature of civilization, we do not know, though advocates of genuine democracy can only hope that this is not the case. Contemporary anarchists and socialists differ on this point, with some proposing complex methods of grassroots democratic planning that would presumably abolish hierarchy of all kinds while preserving modern means of production. For an example of such a proposed system, see Michael Albert's book *Parecon* (London: Verso, 2003). Others, most notably the anarchist thinker John Zerzan, argue that the problem goes much deeper, and that we cannot achieve true democracy without eliminating industrialization and possibly the entire division of labor.

workers, and immigrant janitors, but we do not know these people or, for the most part, have any interest in them. We barely know our neighbors and, all too often, see our fellow workers as competitors. If civilization offers few forms of communal emotional connection other than those provided by the occasional televised war or celebrity funeral, it would seem to be a rather hollow business.

We pay a high price for this emotional emptiness. Individually, we suffer from social isolation and depression, which, while usually not fatal on their own, are risk factors for cardiovascular and a host of other diseases. Collectively, we seem to have trouble coming to terms with our situation, which grows more ominous every day. Half the world's people live in debilitating poverty. Epidemics devastate whole nations. The ice caps melt, and natural disasters multiply. But we remain for the most part paralyzed, lacking the means or will to organize for our survival. In fact the very notion of the "collective," of the common good, has been eroded by the self-serving agendas of the powerful—their greed and hunger for still more power. Throughout the world (capitalist and postcommunist), decades of conservative social policy have undermined any sense of mutual responsibility and placed the burden of risk squarely on the individual or the family.

The family is all we need, America's ostensibly Christian evangelicists tell us—a fit container for all our social loyalties and yearnings. But if anything represents a kind of evolutionary regression, it is this. Insofar as we compress our sociality into the limits of the family, we do not so much resemble our Paleolithic human ancestors as we do those far earlier prehuman primates who had not yet discovered the danced ritual as a "biotechnology" for the formation of larger groups. Humans had the wit and generosity to reach out to unrelated others; hominids huddled with their kin.

Our civilization has its compensatory pleasures of course. Most often cited is the consumer culture, which encourages us to deflect our desires into the acquisition and display of *things:* the new car, or shoes, or face-lift, which will enhance our status and make us less lonely, or so we are promised. The mall may be a dreary place compared to a late medieval English fair, but it offers goods undreamed of in that humbler setting—conveniences and temptations from around the globe. We have "entertainment" too, in the form of movies; ever-available, iPod-delivered music for solitary enjoyment; computer games; and, possibly, coming soon, experiences in virtual reality. And we have drugs, both legal and illegal, to lift the depression, calm the anxiety, and bolster our self-confidence. It is a measure of our general deprivation that the most common referent for *ecstasy* in usage today is not an experience but a drug, MDMA, that offers fleeting feelings of euphoria and connectedness.

But these compensatory pleasures do not satisfy our longings. Anyone who can resist addiction to the consumer culture, the entertainments, and the drugs arrives sooner or later at the conclusion that "something's missing." What that might be is hard to pin down and finds expression in vague formulations such as "spirituality" or "community." Intellectuals regularly issue thoughtful screeds on the missing glue in our society, the absence of strong bonds connecting us to those outside our families. In 1985, Robert Bellah et alia's book *Habits of the Heart: Individuals and Commitment in American Life* found Americans caught up in their personal ambitions, unable to imagine any larger sense of community. In 2000, Robert D. Putnam published *Bowling Alone: The Collapse and Revival of American Community*, in which he reported a decline not just in civic participation but in any kind of group activity. There is even an intellectual current called *communitarianism*, which aims to somehow restore the social cohesion characteristic of smaller, less divided societies, and its adherents have included such notables as Bill and Hillary Clinton.

For most people, though, the "something" that's missing is most readily replaced by religion. Far from withering away, as Marx predicted, religion has undergone a spectacular revival, especially in the largely Christian United States and the Muslim parts of the world.

People find many things in their religions—a sense of purpose and metaphysical explanations for human suffering, for example. They may also find a sense of community—the *umma* of Islam or the neighborliness of a small-town church. The anthropomorphized God of Christianity, in particular, is himself a kind of substitute for human solidarity, an invisible loving companion who counsels and consoles. Like a genuinely caring community, he is said to be a cure for depression, alienation, loneliness, and even mundane, all-too-common addictions to alcohol and drugs.

But compared to the danced religions of the past, today's "faiths" are often pallid affairs—if only by virtue of the very fact that they *are* "faiths," dependent on, and requiring, belief as opposed to direct knowledge. The prehistoric ritual dancer, the maenad or practitioner of Vodou, did not *believe* in her god or gods; she *knew* them, because, at the height of group ecstasy, they filled her with their presence. Modern Christians may have similar experiences, but the primary requirement of their religion is *belief*, meaning an effort of the imagination. Dionysus, in contrast, did not ask his followers for their belief or faith; he called on them to apprehend him directly, to let him enter, in all his madness and glory, their bodies and their minds.

For all kinds of reasons, then, our imaginary "unconverted savage" might despair over what civilization has wrought. He would bemoan the absence of the gods, which is manifested by the new requirement that they be summoned by the imagination, through interior faith rather than through shared ritual. He would be baffled by the fact that our great reproductive achievement as a species—the huge population, even overpopulation, of the earth—routinely leads to frustration and hostility, rather than to an enrichment of individual experience. He would cringe from the misery around him—the poverty and disease that our technological cunning has proved incapable of relieving. Above all, he would be stricken to find his species on what may be the verge of extinction—through pandemics, global warming, the nuclear threat, and the exhaustion of resources—yet too isolated from one another to stand together, as early *Homo sapiens* once learned to do, and mount any sort of mutual defense.

We try, of course. Many millions of people around the world are engaged in movements for economic justice, peace, equality, and environmental reclamation, and these movements are often incubators for the solidarity and celebration so missing in our usual state of passive acquiescence. Yet there appears to be no constituency today for collective joy itself. In fact, the very term *collective joy* is largely unfamiliar and exotic.

The silence demands some sort of explanation, so let us give the enemies of festivity—or at least the revolutionaries among them, like Robespierre and Lenin—their due. What is lost is not that important, they would argue, should they be good-humored enough to even entertain the argument. And indeed you would have to be a fool, or a drug-addled hippie, to imagine that a restoration of festivity and ecstatic ritual would get us out of our current crisis, or even to imagine that such activities *could* be restored in our world today, with anything like their original warmth and meaningfulness. No amount of hand-holding or choral dancing will bring world peace and environmental healing. In fact, festivities have served at times to befuddle or becalm their celebrants. European carnival coexisted with tyranny for centuries, hence the common "safety valve" theory of their social function. Native American Ghost Dancers could not reverse genocide with their ecstatic rituals; nor could colonized Africans render themselves bulletproof by dancing into a trance. In the face of desperately serious threats to group survival, the ecstatic ritual can be a waste of energy—or worse. The Haitian dictator "Papa Doc" Duvalier actually encouraged Vodou as a means of strengthening his grip on the population.

My own Calvinist impulses—inherited in part from those of my ancestors who were genuine Calvinists, Presbyterian Scots—tell me insistently to get the work done, save the world, and then maybe there'll be time for celebration. In the face of poverty, misery, and possible extinction, there is no time, or justification, for the contemplation of pleasure of any kind, these inner voices say. Close your ears to the ever-fainter sound of drums or pipes; the wild carnival and danced ritual belong to a distant time. The maenads are long dead, a curiosity for the classicists; the global "natives" have been subdued. Forget the past, which is half imagined anyway, and get to work.

And yet . . . It does not go away, this ecstatic possibility. Despite centuries of repression, despite the competing allure of spectacles, festivity keeps bubbling up, and in the most unlikely places. The rock rebellion broke through the anxious conformity of postwar America and generated an entire counterculture. Then, at the other end of the cultural spectrum, where the spectacle of athleticism merged with nationalism, people undertook to carnivalize sports events, reclaiming them as occasions for individual creativity and collective joy. Religions, too, still generate ecstatic undertakings, like the annual Hasidic pilgrimage to the Ukrainian town of Uman, which has sprung up just since the fall of communism and features thousands of Hasidic men, dressed entirely in white, dancing and singing in the streets in honor of their dead rebbe. The impulse to public celebration lives on, seizing its opportunities as they come. When Iran, which is surely one of the world's more repressive states, qualified for the World Cup in 1997, "celebrations paralyzed Tehran," according to *Newsweek*. "Women ripped off their government-mandated veils; men gave out paper cups of strictly forbidden vodka as teenagers danced in the streets."[7]

There are also cases of people coming together and creating festivity out of nothing, or at least without the excuse of a commercial concert or athletic event. Thousands of women gather every summer for the Michigan Womyn's Music Festival, described on its Web site as "the best party on the planet." Gay male culture features "circuit parties," involving dancing and sometimes costuming, and, with some help from chemical stimulants, these can go on for days. It was gay culture, too, that first appropriated Halloween as an adult holiday, now celebrated with parades of costumed people of all sexual inclinations. The historian Nicholas Rogers summarizes recent observances of the holiday.

> In San Francisco, alongside huge gay promenades at Castro and Polk, the Trocadero Transfer Club ran a three-day bash on the theme of the Australian cult movie *The Road Warrior* [*sic*]. At Salem, Massachusetts, witchery generated forty events for some 50,000 visitors. Even in Salt Lake City, where the Mormons frowned on public profanity and excess, private clubs promoted Halloween parties with gusto. One observer remembered pregnant nuns and lewd priests cavorting on the dance floor, and three gold-painted angels mimicking the figure atop the city's Mormon temple.[8]

We might also note such recently invented festivities as the Berlin Love parade, an outdoor dance party that has attracted over a million people at a time, or the annual Burning Man event in the Black Rock Desert in Nevada, where thousands of people of all ages gather annually to create art, dance, and paint and costume themselves.

And whatever its shortcomings as a means to social change, protest movements keep reinventing carnival. Almost every demonstration I have been to over the years—antiwar, feminist, or for economic justice—has featured some element of the carnivalesque: costumes, music, impromptu dancing, the sharing of food and drink. The media often deride the carnival spirit of such protests, as if it were a self-indulgent distraction from the serious political point. But seasoned organizers know that gratification cannot be deferred until after "the revolution." The Texas populist Jim Hightower, for example, launched a series of "Rolling Thunder" events around the country in the early 2000s, offering music, food, and plenty of conviviality, and with the stated aim of "putting the party back in politics." People must find, in their movement, the immediate joy of solidarity, if only because, in the face of overwhelming state and corporate power, solidarity is their sole source of strength.

In fact, there has been, in the last few years, a growing carnival-ization of protest demonstrations, perhaps especially among young "antiglobalization" activists in Europe, Latin America, Canada, and the United States. They wear costumes—most famously, the turtle suits symbolizing environmental concerns at the huge Seattle protest of 1999. They put on masks or paint their faces; they bring drums to their demonstrations and sometimes dance through the streets; they send up the authorities with street theater and effigies. A Seattle newspaper reported of the 1999 demonstrations: "The scene . . . resembled a New Year's Eve party: People banged on drums, blew horns and tossed flying discs through the air. One landed at the foot of a police officer, who threw it back to the crowd amid cheers."[9] The urge to transform one's appearance, to dance outdoors, to mock the powerful and embrace perfect strangers is not easy to suppress.

And why, in the end, would anyone want to? The capacity for collective joy is encoded into us almost as deeply as the capacity for the erotic love of one human for another. We can live without it, as most of us do, but only at the risk of succumbing to the solitary nightmare of depression. Why not reclaim our distinctively human heritage as creatures who can generate their own ecstatic pleasures out of music, color, feasting, and dance?

A couple of years ago, on the stunning Copacabana beach in Rio de Janeiro, where the mountains march right down into the water, my companion and I were drawn by the sound of drumming. Walking north along the beach, we came to a phalanx of samba dancers, about ten people abreast and at least a block long—members of a samba school practicing for *carnaval*, we were told. There were people of all ages, from tots of four or five up to octogenarians, men and women, some gorgeously costumed and some in the tank tops and shorts that constitute Rio street clothes. To a nineteenth-century missionary or even a twenty-first-century religious puritan,

their movements might well have seemed lewd or at least suggestive. Certainly the conquest of the streets by a crowd of brown-
skinned people would have been distressing in itself.

But the samba school danced down to the sand in perfect dignity, wrapped in their own rhythm, their faces both exhausted and
shining with an almost religious kind of exaltation. One thin latte-
colored young man dancing just behind the musicians set the pace.
What was he in real life—a bank clerk, a busboy? But here, in his
brilliant feathered costume, he was a prince, a mythological figure,
maybe even a god. Here, for a moment, there were no divisions
among people except for the playful ones created by *carnaval* itself.

As they reached the boardwalk, bystanders started falling into
the rhythm too, and, without any invitation or announcements,
without embarrassment or even alcohol to dissolve the normal con-
straints of urban life, the samba school turned into a crowd and the
crowd turned into a momentary festival. There was no "point" to
it—no religious overtones, ideological message, or money to be
made—just the chance, which we need much more of on this
crowded planet, to acknowledge the miracle of our simultaneous
existence with some sort of celebration.

NOTES

INTRODUCTION: INVITATION TO THE DANCE

1. Quoted in Oesterley, p. 2.
2. Quoted in Moorehead, p. 30.
3. Quoted in ibid., p. 94.
4. Quoted in ibid., pp. 128–29.
5. Quoted in Durkheim, *The Elementary Forms of the Religious Life*, p. 249.
6. Frey and Wood, p. 147.
7. Quoted in ibid., p. 59.
8. Quoted in Cowley, pp. 40–41.
9. Quoted in Raboteau, p. 62.
10. Quoted in Murphy, p. 149.
11. Quoted in Oesterreich, pp. 140–41.
12. Quoted in Frey and Wood, p. 25.
13. Buchan, p. 83.
14. Hambly, pp. 16–17.
15. Cheeseman, p. 124.
16. Quoted in Oesterreich, pp. 285–86.
17. Goodman, p. 36. See also Platvoet.
18. Quoted in Oesterreich, p. 286.
19. Michael Taussig, *Mimesis and Alterity: A Particular History of the Senses* (New York: London: Routledge, 1993), p. 241.
20. Conrad, p. 32.

21. Oesterreich, p. 237.
22. Street, p. 62.
23. Davenport, p. 243.
24. Ibid., p. 306.
25. Kreiser, pp. 257–58.
26. Oesterreich, p. 237.
27. Weidkuhn.
28. Stoler, p. 125.
29. Quoted in Kupperman, p. 107.
30. Quoted in Stoler, p. 124.
31. Crapanzano, p. xiii.
32. Turner, *The Ritual Process*, p. 7.
33. Ibid., p. 129.
34. Ibid., pp. 138–39.
35. Ibid.
36. Crapanzano, p. 234.
37. Quoted in Castillo.
38. Quoted in ibid.
39. Sass, p. 362.
40. Trish Hall, "Seeking a Focus on Joy in the Field of Psychology," *New York Times*, April 28, 1998.
41. Quoted in Stallybrass and White, p. 190.
42. Lindholm, pp. 57–58.
43. Freud, *Civilization and Its Discontents*, p. 64.
44. Suryani and Jensen, p. 173.
45. http://www.psychnet-uk.com/dsm_iv/depersonalization_disorder.htm.
46. Lindholm, p. 66.
47. Ibid., p. 70.
48. Lofland.
49. Turner, *Celebration*, p. 12.
50. See, for example, Beverly J. Stoeltje, "Festival," in Bauman, pp. 264–66.
51. Ibid., p. 262.
52. Quoted in Raboteau, p. 223.

1. THE ARCHAIC ROOTS OF ECSTASY

1. Garfinkel, p. 11.
2. John Pickrell, "Unprecedented Ice Age Cave Art Discovered in U.K.," *National Geographic News*, August 18, 2004.
3. Dunbar, pp. 147–48.

4. Freeman, p. 129.
5. McNeill, *Keeping Together in Time*, p. 2.
6. D'Aquili, p. 22.
7. Sandra Blakeslee, "Cells That Read Minds," *New York Times*, January 10, 2006.
8. Marcel Kinsbourne, "The Role of Imitation in Body Ownership and Mental Growth," in Meltzoff and Prinz, pp. 312–30.
9. Lewis, pp. 35–36.
10. Heather Pringle, "Ice Age Communities May Be Earliest Known Net Hunters," *Discover*, August 29, 1997.
11. Granet, p. 168.
12. André Gunnel, "Ecstatic Prophesy in the Old Testament," in Holm, pp. 187–200.
13. Garfinkel, pp. 61–62.
14. Gunnel, p. 34.
15. Patai, p. 242.
16. See Lawler, pp. 238–39.
17. Sachs, pp. 238–39.
18. Ibid., p. 237.
19. Quoted in ibid., p. 238.
20. Quoted in Dodds, *The Greeks and the Irrational*, p. 271.
21. Lawler, p. 92.
22. Evans, p. 52.
23. Nietzsche, p. 23.
24. Ibid., p. 102.
25. Obbink, pp. 65–86.
26. Dodds, Introduction to Euripides, *The Bacchae*, p. xiv.
27. Evans, p. 140.
28. Calasso, p. 78.
29. Daniélou, p. 39.
30. Turner, *The Ritual Process*, p. 156.
31. Ibid., p. 160.
32. Ibid.
33. Dodds, Introduction to Euripides, *The Bacchae*, p. xiv.
34. Joyce, pp. 33–34.
35. Euripides, *The Bacchae*, p. 202.
36. Joyce, p. 43.
37. Portefaix, p. 205.
38. Vellacott, p. 25.

39. Otto, p. 136.
40. Euripides, *The Bacchae*, pp. 194–95.
41. Evans, p. 19.
42. Jameson, p. 44.
43. Ibid., p. 47.
44. Durkheim, *The Elementary Forms of the Religious Life*, p. 250.
45. Dodds, *The Greeks and the Irrational*, p. 272.
46. Lawler, p. 50.
47. Burkert, *Ancient Mystery Cults*, p. 31.
48. Backman, p. 5.
49. Burkert, "Bacchic *Teletai* in the Hellenistic Age."
50. Jameson, p. 63.

2. CIVILIZATION AND BACKLASH

1. Euripides, *The Bacchae*, p. 205.
2. Joyce Marcus and Kent V. Flannery, "The Co-Evolution of Ritual and Society: New C-14 Dates from Ancient Mexico," *Proceedings of the National Academy of Sciences* 1, no. 52 (2004): 18257–18261.
3. For more on the shaping of early societies by war, see my book *Blood Rites*, chapter 9.
4. Quoted in Patai, p. 230.
5. Armstrong, p. 24.
6. Quoted in Evans, p. 149.
7. Lawler, p. 95.
8. Burkert, *Ancient Mystery Cults*, p. 97.
9. Quoted in ibid., p. 90.
10. Max Weber, *The Sociology of Religion*, p. 180.
11. Sachs, p. 248.
12. Weber, *The Sociology of Religion*, p. 180.
13. Quoted in Balsdon, p. 274.
14. The historian Richard Gordon, quoted in Sawyer, p. 122.
15. Sachs, p. 246.
16. Balsdon, p. 275.
17. Juvenal, p. 44.
18. Cumont, p. 29.
19. Gordon Richard, "From Republic to Principate: Priesthood, Religion and Ideology," in Beard and North, pp. 179–98.
20. Beard, p. 165.
21. Gordon, p. 122.

22. Quoted in ibid., p. 123.
23. Juvenal, p. 50.
24. Quoted in Livy, p. 409.
25. Quoted in Wilken, p. 12.
26. *Oxford Classical Dictionary*, 3rd ed., edited by Simon Hornblower and Anthony Spawforth (Oxford: Oxford University Press, 1996), p. 229.
27. Livy, pp. 401–2.
28. Ibid., pp. 406–7.
29. Ibid., p. 402.
30. Ibid., p. 409.
31. Quoted in ibid., p. 410.
32. Balsdon, p. 247.

3. JESUS AND DIONYSUS

1. George Steiner, lecture at Boston University, 1999, reported at www.bu.edu/bridge/archive/1999/features2.html.
2. Timothy Freke and Peter Gandy, *The Jesus Mysteries: Was the "Original Jesus" a Pagan God?* (New York: Three Rivers Press, 1999), p. 5.
3. See Morton Smith, *Jesus the Magician*.
4. Euripides, *The Bacchae*, p. 194.
5. See Chance.
6. Burkert, "Bacchic *Teletai* in the Hellenistic Age," p. 21.
7. Kerényi, p. 387.
8. Momigliano, p. 197.
9. Morton Smith, *Studies in the Cult of Yahweh*, vol 1.
10. Ibid., p. 233.
11. Price.
12. Kerényi, p. 257.
13. Morton Smith, *Jesus the Magician*, p. 158.
14. Freke and Gandy, p. 52.
15. Cumont, p. 65.
16. "Mystery religions," *Encyclopedia Britannica 2006*, Encyclopedia Britannica Premium Service, May 30, 2006, http://www.britannica.com/eb/article-15867.
17. Quoted in Wilken, p. 96.
18. Quoted in ibid., p. 19.
19. Ibid.
20. Armstrong, p. 87. See also Meeks, pp. 140–63.
21. Robert Jewett, "Are There Allusions to the Love Feast in Romans

13.8–10?" in Julian V. Hills et al., eds., *Common Life in the Early Church* (Harrisburg, PA: Trinity Press International, 1998), pp. 265–78.

22. Stephen G. Wilson, "Early Christian Music," in Hills, pp. 390–401. See also Meeks, pp. 144–45.

23. Quoted in Backman, p. 21.

24. Ibid., pp. 21–22.

25. Quoted in Sawyer, p. 104.

26. Quoted in Knox, p. 28.

27. Quoted in Dodds, *The Greeks and the Irrational*, p. 274.

28. Quoted in Boles, p. 68.

29. H. Wayne House, "Tongues and Mystery Religions of Corinth," *Bibliotheca Sacra* 140, no. 558 (April 1983): 134.

30. William Samarin, telephone interview with the author, June 30, 1999.

31. See, for example, Morton T. Kelsey, *Tongue Speaking: An Experiment in Spiritual Experience* (Garden City, NY: Doubleday, 1964).

32. Quoted by Janet MacIntosh, personal communication with the author, May 5, 2003.

33. "Speaking in Tongues—Believers Relish the Experience," *Los Angeles Times*, September 19, 1987.

34. Mary Smalara Collins, "I May Speak in the Tongue of Angels," *U.S. Catholic*, March 1994, p. 25.

35. Meeks, p. 149.

36. James Hastings, ed., *Encyclopedia of Religion and Ethics*, vol. 3 (New York: Scribner's, no date), p. 371.

37. Meeks, p. 121.

38. Knox, pp. 27–29; Walker, pp. 55–56.

39. Burkert, *Ancient Mystery Cults*, p. 43.

40. Brown, p. 147.

41. Quoted in ibid., p. 140.

42. Walker, p. 47.

43. Quoted in Backman, p. 25.

44. Quoted in ibid., pp. 30–31.

45. Quoted in ibid., p. 32.

46. Quoted in Evans, p. 20.

47. Lewis, p. 34.

48. Ibid., p. 132.

49. Weber, *The Sociology of Religion*, p. 161.

50. Ibid., p. 160.

51. Ibid., p. 178.

4. FROM THE CHURCHES TO THE STREETS: THE CREATION OF CARNIVAL

1. Gurevich, p. 180.
2. Hutton, p. 65.
3. Delumeau, pp. 73–74.
4. Chambers, p. 161.
5. Lonsdale, *Animals and the Origins of Dance*, p. 29.
6. Backman, p. 157.
7. Cambrensis, p. 92.
8. Backman, p. 51.
9. Ibid., p. 91.
10. Doob, p. 125.
11. Cohn, pp. 136–41.
12. Hecker, p. 8.
13. Ibid., p. 2.
14. Ibid.
15. Ibid., p. 12.
16. Donaldson, Cavanagh, and Rankin, pp. 201–4.
17. Hecker, p. 21.
18. Ibid., p. 2.
19. Ibid., p. 21.
20. Davis, *Society and Culture in Early Modern France*, p. 137.
21. Quoted in Orloff, p. 178.
22. Quoted in ibid., p. 187.
23. Chambers, p. 325.
24. Quoted in ibid., p. 294.
25. Ibid., p. 292.
26. Ibid., p. 332.
27. Ibid., p. 98.
28. Thompson, *Customs in Common*, p. 51.
29. William Shakespeare, *The Merchant of Venice*, act 2, scene 5, lines 876–81.
30. Goethe, p. 390.

5. KILLING CARNIVAL: REFORMATION AND REPRESSION

1. Scribner, pp. 303–29.
2. Desplat.
3. Chouraqui.
4. Hoffman, pp. 46–54.
5. Hill, p. 154.

6. Quoted in Thompson, *Customs in Common*, p. 54.
7. Quoted in Elias and Dunning, p. 178.
8. Hill, p. 59.
9. Stallybrass and White, p. 176.
10. Quoted in Hoffman, p. 52.
11. Quoted in Malcolmson, p. 105.
12. Hill, p. 121.
13. Weber, *The Protestant Ethic*, p. 168.
14. Quoted in Humphrey, p. 33.
15. Quoted in Stallybrass and White, p. 13.
16. Quoted in Bakhtin, p. 75.
17. Quoted in Thompson, *Customs in Common*, p. 47.
18. Ladurie, *The French Peasantry*, p. 367.
19. Quoted in Ladurie, *Carnival in Romans*, p. 100.
20. Jan Darby, "Robin Hood: The Lord of Misrule," *Renaissance* 9, no. 3 (2004): 41–46.
21. Muir, p. 106.
22. Davis, *Society and Culture in Early Modern France*, p. 119.
23. Weidkuhn, p. 39.
24. Ladurie, *Carnival in Romans*, pp. 178–80.
25. Thompson, *Customs in Common*, p. 68.
26. Quoted in ibid., p. 234.
27. Stallybrass and White, p. 14.
28. Quoted in Burke, p. 217.
29. Ibid.
30. Scribner, p. 317.
31. Burke, p. 217.
32. Quoted in Tripp, p. 136.
33. Scribner, p. 309.
34. Weidkuhn, p. 42.
35. Scribner, p. 321.
36. Weidkuhn, p. 40.
37. Walzer, p. 45.
38. Ladurie, *Carnival in Romans*, p. 42.
39. Ibid., p. 96.
40. Ibid., p. 101.
41. Ingram, p. 82. See also Underdown, p. 58.
42. Ozouf, p. 238.
43. Ibid., p. 239.
44. Ibid., p. 241.

45. Ibid.
46. Ibid., p. 89.
47. Quoted in ibid., p. 236.
48. Ruiz, p. 311.
49. Twycross, p. 20.
50. Nijsten.
51. Ruiz, p. 311.
52. Ladurie, *Carnival in Romans*, p. 313.
53. Chouraqui.
54. Spencer, p. 369.
55. Quoted in Thompson, *Customs in Common*, pp. 56–57.
56. Muir, p. 37.
57. Quoted in Darnton, *The Great Cat Massacre*, p. 133.
58. Ibid., p. 133.
59. Malcolmson, p. 165.
60. Elias, *Power and Civility*, pp. 236–37.
61. Ibid., p. 271.
62. Quoted in ibid., pp. 65–66.
63. Ibid., p. 69.
64. Castiglione, p. 75.
65. Greenblatt, p. 103.

6. A NOTE ON PURITANISM AND MILITARY REFORM

1. Huntington, p. 111.
2. Vasil'ev, p. 78.
3. Hakima, p. 35. (I am grateful to Elizabeth Thompson for finding and translating this passage.)
4. Geoffrey Parker, pp. 20–21.
5. McNeill, *The Pursuit of Power*, pp. 129–30.
6. Feld, p. 422.
7. Walzer, p. 278.
8. Quoted in ibid., p. 287.
9. Corancez, p. 8.
10. Gilsenan.
11. Weber, *The Religion of China*, pp. 27–28.
12. Ibid., pp. 145–46.

7. AN EPIDEMIC OF MELANCHOLY

1. Quoted in Doughty, p. 259.
2. Quoted in Oppenheim, p. 14.

3. Boswell, p. 44.
4. Quoted in Jamison, p. 232.
5. Solomon, p. 299.
6. Quoted in Sánchez, p. 157.
7. Trossbach, p. 5.
8. Goldstein, p. 97.
9. Klerman and Weissman.
10. "Mental Disorders, Depression Set to Rise, UN Says," Reuters, January 11, 2001.
11. Boswell, p. 152.
12. Quoted in Porter, p. 84.
13. Quoted in ibid., p. 96.
14. Quoted in Solomon, p. 300.
15. Quoted in Wolpert, p. 7.
16. Quoted in Julius H. Rubin, p. 8.
17. Burton, p. 16.
18. Porter, pp. 82, 87.
19. Kinsman, p. 275.
20. Burton, p. 346.
21. Boswell, p. 127.
22. Quoted in Newton, p. 99.
23. Quoted in James, p. 136.
24. Styron, p. 45.
25. James, p. 132.
26. Quoted in Coffin, p. 270.
27. Quoted in Newton, p. 100.
28. Trilling, p. 19.
29. Sass, p. 2.
30. See Hsia, Tuan, and Sass.
31. Davis, *The Return of Martin Guerre*, p. 40.
32. Burton, p. 53.
33. Trilling, p. 19.
34. Tuan, p. 139.
35. Ibid.
36. Klerman and Weissman. See also Baumeister and Leary.
37. Durkheim, *Suicide*, p. 336.
38. Oppenheim, p. 7.
39. Quoted in Brann, p. 70.
40. Weber, *The Protestant Ethic and the Spirit of Capitalism*, p. 106.

41. Bunyan, *Pilgrim's Progress*, p. 15.
42. Bunyan, *Grace Abounding*, p. 24.
43. Weber, *The Protestant Ethic*, p. 104.
44. Ibid., p. 119.
45. William Buchan, quoted in Jackson, p. 37.
46. Bunyan, *Grace Abounding*, p. 14.
47. Quoted in Mazlish, p. 68.
48. Quoted in ibid., p. 69.
49. Quoted in Mitzman, p. 48.
50. Quoted in ibid., pp. 49–50.
51. Ibid.
52. Durkheim, *Suicide*, p. 154.
53. Hsia, pp. 162–65.
54. Quoted in Ozouf, p. 15.
55. Quoted in Stallybrass and White, p. 182.
56. Ibid., p. 171.
57. Ibid., p. 176.
58. Burton, p. 482.
59. Ibid., p. 451.
60. Ibid., p. 89.
61. Quoted in Kinsman, p. 291.
62. Browne, p. 55.
63. Ibid., p. 16.
64. Ibid., p. 65.
65. Quoted in Malcolmson, p. 71.
66. Quoted in Burkert, *Ancient Mystery Cults*, p. 113.
67. Solomon, p. 296.
68. Katz, p. 54.
69. Crapanzano, pp. 4–5.
70. "Global Youth," *For di People* (Freetown, Sierra Leone), April 28, 2001.
71. Hecker, p. 20.
72. Ibid., p. 31.
73. Lewis, pp. 76–77.
74. Nietzsche, p. 102.
75. Ibid., pp. 23–24.

8. GUNS AGAINST DRUMS: IMPERIALISM ENCOUNTERS ECSTASY

1. Howarth, p. 162.
2. Davenport, p. 323.

3. Quoted in Harris, p. 55.
4. MacDonald, p. 58.
5. Comaroff, p. 151.
6. Janzen, p. 164.
7. Comaroff, p. 151.
8. Quoted in *The Drums of Winter* (a documentary film by Sarah Elder and Leonard Kamerling), University of Alaska Museum, Fairbanks, Alaska, 1988.
9. Kirby, p. 60.
10. Stoeltje, "Festival," in Bauman, p. 262.
11. Quoted in Dougherty, p. 60.
12. Quoted in ibid., p. 62.
13. Kirby, p. 61.
14. Quoted in Frey and Wood, p. 25.
15. Quoted in ibid., p. 26.
16. Murphy, p. 118.
17. Quoted in Ward, p. 211.
18. Comaroff, p. 151.
19. Quoted in ibid.
20. Quoted in Oesterley, p. 80.
21. Thorsley, p. 288.
22. Quoted in ibid., p. 289.
23. MacDonald, p. 60.
24. Quoted in Harris, p. 24.
25. Quoted in Comaroff and Comaroff, p. 101.
26. Quoted in Tom Englehardt, "The Cartography of Death," *Nation* 271, no. 12 (October 23, 2000): 25.
27. Quoted in Cocker, p. 136.
28. Englehardt.
29. Cocker, p. 6.
30. Raboteau, pp. 214–15.
31. Quoted in MacRobert, p. 16.
32. Voeks, p. 156; Fenn.
33. Hiney, pp. 212–13.
34. "Most missionaries considered the colonial administration as allies in the essential task of destroying existing [native] structures." Kirby, p. 61.
35. MacDonald, p. 57.
36. Comaroff, p. 151.

37. Quoted in Ward, p. 210.
38. Quoted in Fenn, p. 127.
39. Quoted in ibid., p. 138.
40. A major source on Trinidadian carnival, which I rely on extensively here, is John Cowley's *Carnival, Canboulay and Calypso: Traditions in the Making.*
41. Quoted in ibid., pp. 20–21.
42. Ibid., p. 22.
43. Ibid., p. 21.
44. Quoted in ibid., p. 27.
45. Chasteen.
46. Quoted in Cowley, p. 69.
47. Quoted in ibid., p. 73.
48. Campbell, p. 14.
49. Fenn, pp. 141, 135.
50. Quoted in Cowley, p. 13.
51. Bettelheim.
52. Quoted in Fenn, p. 141.
53. Cowley, pp. 102–4.
54. Quoted in Olmos and Paravisini-Gebert, introduction, p. 7.
55. Métraux, p. 89.
56. Joan Dayan, "Vodoun, or the Voice of the Gods," in Olmos and Paravisini-Gebert, p. 19.
57. Raboteau, p. 64; Simpson, p. 17.
58. Voeks, p. 38.
59. Omari, p. 148.
60. Quoted in Murphy, p. 47.
61. Ibid.; Laguerre, p. 14.
62. Laguerre, p. 14.
63. Ibid., pp. 63–64.
64. Ward, p. 223.
65. Lanternari, p. 143.
66. Ibid., p. 153.
67. Ibid., p. 251.
68. Ibid., p. 252.
69. See Karen E. Fields, *Revival and Rebellion in Colonial Central Africa*, for an excellent discussion of the anthropological aversion to the "irrational."
70. Ibid., p. 21.

71. Lanternari, p. 315.
72. Wilson, p. 19.
73. Quoted in Mazlish, p. 90.
74. Quoted in Ozouf, p. 282.
75. Quoted in Walzer, pp. 313–14.
76. Ibid., p. 310.
77. Ward, p. 202.
78. Fields, pp. 140–41.
79. Campbell, p. 7.
80. Laguerre, p. 59.
81. Murphy, p. 47.
82. Mooney, pp. 782–83.
83. Quoted in Juneja, p. 91.
84. Quoted in Cowley, p. 100.
85. Benítez, p. 199.
86. Lewis, p. 116.
87. Comaroff, p. 233.
88. Howarth, p. 124.
89. Ibid., p. 172.
90. Moorehead, pp. 83–85.
91. Cocker, p. 263.

9. FASCIST SPECTACLES

1. Shirer, p. 15.
2. Toland, p. 492.
3. Shirer, p. 18.
4. Ibid., p. 16.
5. François-Poncet, p. 209.
6. Lindholm, p. 156.
7. McNeill, *Keeping Together in Time*, p. 151.
8. S. Alexander Haslam and Stephen D. Reicher, "The Psychology of Tyranny," *Scientific American Mind*, October 2005: 44.
9. Quoted in Laura Flanders, "Come Together!" *Common Dreams News Center*, April 18, 2002.
10. Dave Martin, quoted by Kevin Connolly, "Dying with Dignity," *Eye-Comedy*, February 24, 2000.
11. Quoted in Martin and Segrave, p. 123.
12. Leslie Epstein, "The Roar of the Crowd," *The American Prospect*, May 8, 2000, http://www.prospect.org/web/page.ww?section=root&name=ViewPrint&articleId=4408.

13. Le Bon, p. 11.
14. Ibid., p. 33.
15. Ibid., p. xvi.
16. Quoted in Turner and Killian, p. 2.
17. Mosse, *Masses and Man*, p. 111.
18. Louis-Sébastien Mercier, quoted in Gutwirth, pp. 243–44.
19. Quoted in Ozouf, p. 22.
20. Quoted in Blum, p. 212.
21. Ozouf, pp. 3.
22. Hibbert, p. 182.
23. Quoted in Gutwirth, p. 308.
24. Ozouf, p. 29.
25. Quoted in ibid., p. 229.
26. Gutwirth, p. 308.
27. Quoted in Hibbert, p. 110.
28. Carlyle, p. 360.
29. Michelet, p. 445.
30. Ibid., p. 448.
31. Ozouf, p. 111.
32. McNeill, *Keeping Together in Time*, p. 134.
33. Ozouf, p. 6.
34. Myerly, p. 142.
35. Ibid., p. 139.
36. Ibid., p. 39.
37. Quoted in ibid., pp. 140–41.
38. Quoted in ibid., p. 140.
39. Quoted in ibid., p. 142.
40. Quoted in ibid., p. 161.
41. Le Bon, p. 112.
42. Ibid., p. 114.
43. Ibid., p. 117.
44. Ibid., p. 113.
45. Lindholm, p. 111.
46. Quoted in Gentile, p. 88.
47. Quoted in Michael Golston, " 'Im Anfang War der Rhythmus': Rhythmic Incubations in Discourses of Mind, Body, and Race from 1850–1944," *SEHR*, vol. 5, supplement: Cultural and Technological Incubations of Fascism, 1996.
48. Kremer.
49. Burleigh, pp. 262–63.

50. Quoted in Gentile, p. 51.
51. Falasca-Zamponi, p. 104.
52. Gentile, pp. 90–91.
53. Ibid., p. 91.
54. Quoted in ibid., p. 52.
55. Falasca-Zamponi, p. 25.
56. Quoted in Lindholm, p. 112.
57. Quoted in Fritzsche, p. 221.
58. Toland, p. 494.
59. Fritzsche, p. 219.
60. Berezin, p. 89.
61. Quoted in Gentile, p. 88.
62. Quoted in ibid., p. 145.
63. Berezin, p. 85.
64. Gentile, p. 98.
65. Quoted in Schnapp, p. 79.
66. Fritzsche, p. 218.
67. Quoted in ibid., p. 220.
68. "Nazism Punctured: Nuremberg Rallies Turned Inside Out," *Guardian*, November 6, 2001.
69. "Showing Off for the Party People," *Financial Times*, November 10, 2001.
70. Peukert, p. 188.

10. THE ROCK REBELLION

1. Martin and Segrave, p. 8.
2. Miller, p. 94.
3. Martin and Segrave, p. 134.
4. Ibid., p. 133.
5. Quoted in ibid., p. 136.
6. Ibid., p. 42.
7. Miller, p. 152.
8. David Gates, "Requiem for the Dead," *Newsweek*, August 21, 1995.
9. Sennett, p. 74.
10. See Meltzoff and Prinz.
11. Pratt, p. 140.
12. Van de Velde, p. 235.
13. Quoted in Barbara Ehrenreich, Elizabeth Hess, and Gloria Jacobs, *Remaking Love: The Feminization of Sex* (New York: Anchor Press, 1986), p. 16.

14. Quoted in Miller, p. 148.
15. Bernard Weinraub, "Pioneer of a Beat Is Still Riffing for His Due," *New York Times*, February 16, 2003.
16. Small, p. 116.
17. Frey and Wood, p. 118.
18. Ibid., p. 145.
19. Quoted in Malone, p. 227.
20. Raboteau, p. 246.
21. Quoted in Frey and Wood, p. 147.
22. Levine, pp. 179–80.
23. Ibid., p. 180.
24. Quoted in Malone, p. 228.
25. Quoted in ibid., p. 228.
26. Quoted in ibid., p. 234.
27. Ashe, p. 278.
28. Martin and Segrave, p. 3.
29. Ibid., pp. 48–51.
30. Quoted in ibid., p. 53.
31. Quoted in ibid., p. 49.
32. Miller, p. 265.
33. John Skow, "In California, the Dead Live On," *Time*, February 11, 1985.
34. Ben Ehrenreich, "Burying the Dead," *Topic*, 2003, http://www.webdel sol.com/Topic/articles/04/ehrenreich.html#top.
35. Quoted in Chidester.
36. Woody West, "A Farewell to the Dead," *Washington Times*, September 11, 1995.
37. http://www.logosresourcepages.org/rock.html#bottom.
38. Quoted in McNally, p. 387.

11. CARNIVALIZING SPORTS

1. Guttmann, 156.
2. Lipksy, p. 20.
3. Quoted in Goodman, p. 163.
4. http://www.koreainfogate.com/2002worldcup/news.asp?column=97.
5. Lever, p. 16.
6. Quoted in Mark Dyreson, "The Emergence of Consumer Culture and the Transformation of Physical Culture: American Sport in the 1920s," in Wiggins, pp. 207–24.
7. Robert A. Baade, "Evaluating Subsidies for Professional Sports in the

United States and Europe: A Public Sector Primer," *Oxford Review of Economic Policy* 19, no. 4 (2003): 587–93.

8. Steve Lopez, "Money for Stadiums, But Not for Schools," *Time*, June 4, 1999.

9. Holt, p. 36.

10. Rader, p. 7.

11. Vincent, pp. 28–29.

12. Lever, p. 36.

13. Ibid., p. 41.

14. Hobsbawm, "Mass Producing Traditions," pp. 288–89.

15. Ibid., p. 300.

16. Pope, p. 328.

17. Norman Chad, "World Cup Soccer Stirs Emotions That Few Americans Can Understand," *Los Angeles Times*, June 15, 1986.

18. Louis Kutcher, "The American Sports Event as Carnival: An Emergent Norm Approach to Crowd Behavior," *Journal of Popular Culture* 16, no. 4 (Spring 1983): 34–41.

19. Morris, p. 248.

20. See http://www.straightdope.com/classics/a2_186.html.

21. Bob Harvilla, "Thumping for Tejada," *East Bay Express*, May 2, 2003, p. 58.

22. Mark Simon, "A Little Bit of Brazil in Palo Alto," *San Francisco Chronicle*, June 21, 1993.

23. May Colleen, the Airbrush Shoppe, phone interview with the author.

24. Bobbi Weiner, phone interview with the author.

25. http://www.koreainfogate.com/2002worldcup/news.asp?column=97.

26. "Soccer Crowds Sing, Sing, Sing for the Homeland Team," *Washington Post*, July 16, 1994.

27. Klaus Hansen, review of *Soccer Fan Singing: A FANomenology*, by Reinhard Kopiez and Guido Brink, *RPM*, no. 26, Summer 1998.

28. Bellos, p. 140.

29. Morris, p. 258.

30. Quoted in ibid., p. 258.

31. Mark Trumbull, "How 'the Wave' Swept the Nation," *Christian Science Monitor*, January 29, 1993.

32. George Vecsey, "Help Stop the Wave," *New York Times*, June 25, 1984.

33. "Sports of the Times: Permanent Wave in Motown," *New York Times*, October 6, 1984.

34. Cashmore, p. 182.

35. Wann et al., p. 128.
36. Kutcher, p. 39.
37. Sheila Moss, http://www.humorcolumnist.com/football.htm.
38. Morris, p. 252.
39. Bellos, p. 128.
40. "It Isn't Just a Game: Clues to Avid Rooting," *New York Times*, August 11, 2000.
41. Harvilla, "Thumping for Tejada."
42. Franz Lidz, "Out of Bounds," *Sports Illustrated*, November 30, 1992.
43. Faludi, pp. 205–6.
44. Bellos, p. 140.
45. Guttmann, p. 145.
46. Faludi, p. 204.
47. Quoted in Michael Silver, "Rock 'n' Roll Is Here to Play," *Time*, May 24, 1999.
48. Quoted in ibid.
49. Ibid.
50. Damian Dobrosielski and Deepika Reddy, "The Art of Sports," http://www.collegian.psu/hppt//www.collegian.psu.edu/07-05-94index.asp-news07-05-94index.asp-news.
51. Catherine Applefeld Olson, "Pro Sports Marketing Pitches for Athletic Events," *Billboard*, September 8, 2002.
52. Sean Jensen, "Bring Down the Noise," *Pioneer Press*, March 20, 2002.
53. Tara Rodgers, "Take Me 'Out' to the Ballgame: Interventions into the Transformation of the Village People's 'YMCA' from Disco Anthem to Ballpark Fun," Pinknoises.com, http://www.pinknoises.com/ymca.shtml.
54. Stan Savran, "Stadium Music Has Gone to Dogs," http://www.post-gazette.com/sports/columnist/20001022stan.asp.
55. David Jackson, "Passion Fuels Soccer's Biggest Party," *Dallas Morning News*, July 10, 1994.
56. Masakazu Yamazaki, "A Parody of Nationalism: Soccer and the Japanese," *Correspondence* [Council on Foreign Relations], Winter 2002–3: 30.
57. D. S. Eitzen, quoted in Wann et al., p. 197.
58. Faludi, p. 211.
59. Jack Boulware, "Plush Rush," *American Way*, September 1, 1997, p. 51.

CONCLUSION: THE POSSIBILITY OF REVIVAL

1. Métraux, p. 9.
2. Duvignaud, p. 16.

3. Paul Halmos, "The Decline of the Choral Dance," in Josephson and Josephson, pp. 172–79.

4. Debord, paragraph 154.

5. Ibid., paragraph 20.

6. Quoted in Roth, p. 38.

7. Christopher Dickey, "Iran's Soccer Diplomacy," *Newsweek*, April 27, 1998.

8. Nicholas Rogers, p. 126.

9. "Party Time for the Protesters," *Seattle Post-Intelligencer*, December 4, 1999.

BIBLIOGRAPHY

Abrahams, Roger D. "The Language of Festivals: Celebrating the Economy." In Turner (1982), pp. 161–77.

Anderson, Benedict. *Imagined Communities: Reflections on the Origins and Spread of Nationalism.* London: Verso Books, 1991.

Armstrong, Karen. *A History of God: The 4,000-Year Quest of Judaism, Christianity and Islam.* New York: Knopf, 1994.

Ashe, Bertram D. "On the Jazz Musician's Love/Hate Relationship with the Audience." In Caponi, pp. 277–92.

Babb, Lawrence. *The Elizabethan Malady: A Study of Melancholia in English Literature from 1580 to 1642.* East Lansing: Michigan University Press, 1951.

Backman, E. Louis. *Religious Dances in the Christian Church and in Popular Medicine.* Translated by E. Classen. London: Allen and Unwin, 1952.

Bakhtin, Mikhail. *Rabelais and His World.* Translated by Helene Iswolsky. Boston: MIT Press, 1968.

Balsdon, J. P. V. D. *Roman Women: Their History and Habits.* New York: Barnes and Noble Books, 1983.

Bauman, Richard, ed. *Folklore, Cultural Performances, and Popular Entertainments.* New York: Oxford University Press, 1992.

Baumeister, Roy F., and Mark R. Leary. "The Need to Belong: Desire for Interpersonal Attachments as a Fundamental Human Motivation." *Psychological Bulletin* 117, no. 3 (1995): 497–520.

Beard, Mary. "The Roman and the Foreign: The Cult of the 'Great Mother' in Imperial Rome." In *Shamanism, History, and the State*, ed. Nicholas Thomas and Caroline Humphrey, pp. 164–90. Ann Arbor: University of Michigan Press, 1994.

Beard, Mary, and John North, eds. *Pagan Priests: Religion and Power in the Ancient World*. Ithaca, NY: Cornell University Press, 1990.

Bell, Daniel. *The Cultural Contradictions of Capitalism*. New York: Basic Books, 1996.

Bellos, Alex. *Futebol: Soccer, the Brazilian Way*. New York: Bloomsbury, 2002.

Benítez, Antonia Rojo. "The Role of Music in Afro-Cuban Culture." Translated by James Maraniss. In *The African Diaspora: African Origins and New World Identities*, ed. Isidore Okpewho, Carole Boyce Davies, and Ali A. Mazrui, pp. 197–203. Bloomington, IN: Indiana University Press, 1999.

Bercé, Yves-Marie. *History of Peasant Revolts: The Social Origins of Rebellion in Early Modern France*. Translated by Amanda Whitmore. Ithaca, NY: Cornell University Press, 1990.

Berezin, Mabel. *Making the Fascist Self: The Political Culture of Interwar Italy*. Ithaca, NY: Cornell University Press, 1997.

Bertaud, Jean-Paul. *The Army of the French Revolution: From Citizen-Soldiers to Instrument of Power*. Translated by R. R. Palmer. Princeton, NJ: Princeton University Press, 1988.

Bettelheim, Judith. "Negotiations of Power in Carnaval Culture in Santiago de Cuba." *African Arts* 24, no. 2 (1991): 66–75.

Blakely, Thomas E., W. E. A. van Beek, and D. L. Thomson, eds. *Religion in Africa*. London and Portsmouth, NH: Heinemann-James Currey, 1994.

Bloch, Maurice. *From Blessing to Violence: History and Ideology in the Circumcision Ritual of the Merina of Madagascar*. Cambridge: Cambridge University Press, 1986.

Blum, Carol. *Rousseau and the Republic of Virtue: The Language of Politics in the French Revolution*. Ithaca, NY: Cornell University Press, 1986.

Boles, John B. *The Great Revival, 1787–1805*. Lexington, KY: University Press of Kentucky, 1972.

Boswell, James. *The Life of Samuel Johnson*. London: Penguin Books, 1986.

Boyle, Raymond, and Richard Haynes. *Power Play: Sport, the Media and Popular Culture*. London: Longman, 1999.

Brann, Noel L. "The Problem of Distinguishing Religious Guilt from

Religious Melancholy in the English Renaissance." *Journal of the Rocky Mountain Medieval and Renaissance Association* 1 (1980): 63–72.

Brown, Peter R. *The Body and Society: Men, Women, and Sexual Renunciation in Early Christianity.* New York: Columbia University Press, 1988.

Browne, Richard. *Medicina Musica or, A Mechanical Essay on the Effects of Singing, Music, and Dancing, on Human Bodies.* London: J. and J. Knapton, 1729.

Buchan, John. *Prester John.* New York: Doran, 1910.

Bunyan, John. *Grace Abounding to the Chief of Sinners.* London: Penguin Books, 1987.

———. *Pilgrim's Progress.* Mineola, NY: Dover, 2003.

Burke, Peter. *Popular Culture in Early Modern Europe.* New York: Harper Torchbooks, 1978.

Burkert, Walter. *Ancient Mystery Cults.* Cambridge, MA: Harvard University Press, 1987.

———. "Bacchic *Teletai* in the Hellenistic Age." In Carpenter and Faraone, pp. 259–75.

Burleigh, Michael. *The Third Reich: A New History.* New York: Hill and Wang, 2000.

Burton, Robert. *The Anatomy of Melancholy.* Vol. 1. Whitefish, MT: Kessinger, no date.

Caillois, Roger. *Man and the Sacred.* Translated by Meyer Barash. Glencoe, IL: Free Press, 1959.

Calasso, Roberto. *Ka: Stories of the Mind and Gods of India.* Translated by Tim Parks. New York: Knopf, 1998.

Caldwell, Sarah. "Bhagavati: Ball of Fire." In *Devi: Goddesses of India*, ed. John S. Hawley and Donna S. Wulff, pp. 195–226. Berkeley: University of California Press, 1996.

Cambrensis, Giraldis. *The Journey Through Wales and the Description of Wales.* London: Penguin Classics, 1978.

Campbell, Susan. "Carnival, Calypso, and Class Struggle in Nineteenth-Century Trinidad." *History Workshop* 26 (1988): 1–27.

Caponi, Gena Dagel, ed. *Signifyin[g], Sanctifyin' & Slam Dunking: A Reader in African American Expressive Culture.* Amherst: University of Massachusetts Press, 1999.

Carlyle, Thomas. *The French Revolution.* Edited by K. J. Fielding and David Sorensen. Oxford: Oxford University Press, 1989.

Carpenter, Thomas H., and Christopher A. Faraone, eds. *Masks of Dionysus.* Ithaca, NY: Cornell University Press, 1993.

Case, Shirley Jackson. *The Evolution of Early Christianity: A Genetic Study of First-Century Christianity in Relation to Its Religious Environment.* Chicago: University of Chicago Press, 1914.

Cashmore, Ernest. *Sports Culture.* London: Routledge, 2000.

Castiglione, Baldesar. *The Book of the Courtier.* Edited by Daniel Javitch. New York: Norton, 2002.

Castillo, Richard J. "Spirit Possession in South Asia: Dissociation or Hysteria?" *Culture, Medicine and Psychiatry* 18, no. 1 (1994): 1–21.

Chambers, E. K. *The Mediaeval Stage.* Vol. 1. London: Oxford University Press, 1903.

Chance, M. R. A. "Biological Systems Synthesis of Mentality and the Nature of the Two Modes of Mental Operation: Hedonic and Agonic." *Man-Environment Systems* 14, no. 4 (July 1984): 143–57.

Chasteen, John Charles. "The Prehistory of Samba: Carnival Dancing in Rio de Janeiro, 1840–1917." *Journal of Latin American Studies* 28 (1996): 29–47.

Cheeseman, Evelyn. *Backwaters of the Savage South Seas.* London: Jarrolds, 1933.

Chidester, David. "The Church of Baseball, the Fetish of Coca-Cola, and the Potlatch of Rock 'n' Roll." *Journal of the American Academy of Religion* 64, no. 4 (Winter 1994): 743–66.

Chouraqui, J.-M. "Le combat de Carnval et de Carême en Provence, XVIe–XIXe siècle." *Révue d'histoire moderne et contemporaine* 32 (January–March 1985): 114–24.

Clopper, Lawrence M. *Drama, Play, and Game: English Festive Culture in the Medieval and Early Modern Period.* Chicago: University of Chicago Press, 2001.

Cocker, Mark. *Rivers of Blood, Rivers of Gold: Europe's Conquest of Indigenous Peoples.* New York: Grove Press, 1998.

Coffin, Charles Monroe. *John Donne and the New Philosophy.* New York: Humanities Press, 1958.

Cohn, Norman. *The Pursuit of the Millennium: Revolutionary Millenarians and Mystical Anarchists of the Middle Ages.* New York: Oxford University Press, 1970.

Comaroff, Jean. *Body of Power, Spirit of Resistance: The Culture and History of a South African People.* Chicago: University of Chicago Press, 1985.

Comaroff, Jean, and John Comaroff. *Of Revelation and Revolution: Christianity, Colonialism and Consciousness in South Africa.* Vol. 1. Chicago: University of Chicago Press, 1991.

Conrad, Joseph. *Heart of Darkness.* New York: Dover, 1990.

Cook, Michael. "On the Origins of Wahhabism." *Journal of the Royal Asiatic Society,* 3rd ser., vol. 2, no. 2 (1992): 191–202.

Corancez, Louis Alexandre Olivier de. *A History of the Wahhabis.* Reading, UK: Garnet, 1995.

Cowley, John. *Carnival, Canbouley and Calypso: Traditions in the Making.* Cambridge: Cambridge University Press, 1996.

Cox, Harvey. *The Feast of Fools: A Theological Essay on Fantasy and Festival.* Cambridge, MA: Harvard University Press, 1969.

Crapanzano, Vincent. *The Hamadsha: A Study in Moroccan Ethnopsychiatry.* Berkeley: University of California Press, 1973.

Crapanzano, Vincent, and Vivian Garrison, eds. *Case Studies in Spirit Possession.* New York: Wiley, 1977.

Cumont, Franz. *The Oriental Religions in Roman Paganism.* New York: Dover, 1956.

Daniélou, Alain. *Shiva and Dionysus: The Religion of Nature and Eros.* Translated by K. F. Hurry. New York: Inner Traditions International, 1984.

D'Aquili, Eugene G. "Human Ceremonial Ritual and Modulation of Aggression." *Zygon* 20, no. 1 (1985): 21–30.

D'Aquili, Eugene G., and Charles D. Laughlin, Jr. "The Neurobiology of Myth and Ritual." In *The Spectrum of Ritual: A Biogenetic Structural Analysis,* ed. Charles D. Laughlin, John McManus, Eugene G. D'Aquili, et al., pp. 152–81. New York: Columbia University Press, 1982.

Darnton, Robert. *The Great Cat Massacre and Other Episodes in French Cultural History.* New York: Basic Books, 1999.

———. *Mesmerism and the End of the Enlightenment in France.* Cambridge, MA: Harvard University Press, 1968.

Davenport, Frederick Morgan. *Primitive Traits in Religious Revivals: A Study in Mental and Social Evolution.* New York: Macmillan, 1906.

Davis, Natalie Zemon. *The Return of Martin Guerre.* Cambridge, MA: Harvard University Press, 1983.

———. *Society and Culture in Early Modern France.* Stanford, CA: Stanford University Press, 1975.

Debord, Guy. *Society of the Spectacle.* Detroit: Black and Red, 1977.

Delumeau, Jean. *Sin and Fear: The Emergence of a Western Guilt Culture, 13th–18th Centuries.* Translated by Eric Nicholson. New York: St. Martin's Press, 1990.

Desplat, Christian. "Réforme et culture populaire en Béarn du XVI siècle au XVIII siècle." *Histoire, Economie et Société* 3, no. 2 (1984): 183–202.

Dodds, E. R. *The Greeks and the Irrational*. Berkeley: University of California Press, 1951.

Donaldson, L. J., J. Cavanaugh, and J. Rankin. "The Dancing Plague: A Public Health Conundrum." *Public Health* 111, no. 4 (1997): 201–4.

Donne, T. E. *The Maori Past and Present*. London: Seeley Service, 1927.

Doob, Penelope Reed. *The Idea of the Labyrinth: From Classical Antiquity Through the Middle Ages*. Ithaca, NY: Cornell University Press, 1990.

Dougherty, Michael. *To Steal a Kingdom: Probing Hawaiian History*. Waimanalo, HA: Island Style Press, 1992.

Doughty, Oswald. "The English Malady of the Eighteenth Century." *Review of English Studies* 2, no. 7 (1926): 257–69.

Dowd, David Lloyd. *Pageant-Master of the Republic: Jean-Louis David and the French Revolution*. University of Nebraska Studies, new series no. 3, 1948.

Dunbar, Robin. *Grooming, Gossip, and the Evolution of Language*. Cambridge, MA: Harvard University Press, 1996.

Dunning, Eric, Patrick Murphy, Tim Newburn, and Ivan Waddington. "Violent Disorders in Twentieth-Century Britain." In *The Crowd in Contemporary Britain*, ed. George Gaskell and Robert Benewick, pp. 19–75. London: Sage, 1987.

Durkheim, Emile. *The Elementary Forms of the Religious Life*. New York: Free Press, 1915.

———. *Suicide: A Study in Sociology*. New York: Free Press, 1951.

Duvignaud, Jean. "Festivals: A Sociological Approach." *Cultures* 3, no. 1 (1976): 13–25.

Ehrenreich, Barbara. *Blood Rites: Origins and History of the Passions of War*. New York: Metropolitan Books, 1998.

Elbourne, Elizabeth. "Word Made Flesh: Christianity, Modernity and Cultural Colonialism in the Work of John and Jean Comaroff." *American Historical Review* 108, no. 2 (2003): 435–59.

Elias, Norbert. *The Civilizing Process: The Development of Manners*. Translated by Edmund Jephcott. New York: Urizen Books, 1978.

———. "An Essay on Sport and Violence." In Elias and Dunning, pp. 150–74.

———. *Power and Civility: The Civilizing Process*. Vol. 2. Translated by Edmund Jephcott. New York: Pantheon Books, 1982.

Elias, Norbert, and Eric Dunning. *Quest for Excitement: Sport and Leisure in the Civilizing Process*. Oxford: Blackwell, 1986.

Ellwood, Robert S., Jr. *One Way: The Jesus Movement and Its Meaning*. Englewood Cliffs, NJ: Prentice Hall, 1973.

Erikson, Erik H. *Young Man Luther: A Study in Psychoanalysis and History.* New York: Norton, 1958.

Euripides, *The Bacchae.* Edited by E. R. Dodds. Oxford: Clarenden Press, 1960.

Evans, Arthur. *The God of Ecstasy: Sex Roles and the Madness of Dionysos.* New York: St. Martin's Press, 1988.

Falasca-Zamponi, Simonetta. *Fascist Spectacle: The Aesthetics of Power in Mussolini's Italy.* Berkeley: University of California Press, 2000.

Faludi, Susan. *Stiffed: The Betrayal of the American Man.* New York: Morrow, 1999.

Feld, M. D. "Middle-Class Society and the Rise of Military Professionalism." *Armed Forces and Society* 1, no. 4 (1975): 419–42.

Fenn, Eliabeth A. " 'A Perfect Equality Seemed to Reign': Slave Society and Jonkonnu." *North Carolina Historical Review* 65, no. 2 (1988): 127–53.

Fields, Karen E. *Revival and Rebellion in Colonial Central Africa.* Princeton, NJ: Princeton University Press, 1985.

Flanigan, C. Clifford. "Liminality, Carnival, and Social Structure: The Case of Late Medieval Biblical Drama." In *Victor Turner and the Construction of Cultural Criticism: Between Literature and Anthropology,* ed. Kathleen M. Ashley, pp. 42–63. Bloomington: Indiana University Press, 1990.

Flynn, Maureen. "The Spectacle of Suffering in Spanish Streets." In Hanawalt and Reyerson, pp. 153–61.

François-Poncet, André. *The Fateful Years: Memoirs of a French Ambassador in Berlin, 1931–1938.* Translated by Jacque LeClerq. New York: Harcourt, Brace, 1949.

Freeman, Walter J. *Societies of Brains: A Study in the Neuroscience of Love and Hate.* Hillsdale, NJ: Erlbaum, 1995.

Freud, Sigmund. *Civilization and Its Discontents.* Translated and edited by James Strachey. New York: Norton, 1961.

———. *The Standard Edition of the Complete Psychological Works of Sigmund Freud.* Vol. 18. Translated by James Strachey. London: Hogarth Press and the Institute of Psycho-Analysis, 1937.

Frey, Sylvia R., and Betty Wood. *Come Shouting to Zion: African American Protestantism in the American South and British Caribbean to 1830.* Chapel Hill: University of North Carolina Press, 1998.

Fritzsche, Peter. *Germans into Nazis.* Cambridge, MA: Harvard University Press, 1998.

Garfinkel, Yosef. *Dancing at the Dawn of Agriculture.* Austin: University of Texas Press, 2003.

Gentile, Emilio. *The Sacralization of Politics in Fascist Italy.* Translated by Keith Botsford. Cambridge, MA: Harvard University Press, 1996.

Gilbert, Paul. *Depression: The Evolution of Powerlessness.* New York: Guilford Press, 1991.

Gilsenan, Michael. "Signs of Truth: Enchantment, Modernity, and the Dreams of Peasant Woman." *Journal of the Royal Anthropological Society* 6, no. 4 (2000): 597–615.

Ginzburg, Carlo. *Ecstasies: Deciphering the Witches' Sabbath.* Translated by Raymond Rosenthal. New York: Penguin Books, 1991.

Glassman, Jonathan. *Feasts and Riot: Revelry, Rebellion and Popular Consciousness on the Swahili Coast, 1856–1988.* Portsmouth, NH: Heinemann, 1995.

Goethe, Johann Wolfgang von. *Italian Journey.* New York: Suhrkamp, 1989.

Goldstein, Jan. *Console and Classify: The French Psychiatric Profession in the Nineteenth Century.* Cambridge: Cambridge University Press, 1987.

Goodman, Felicitas. *Speaking in Tongues: A Cross-Cultural Study of Glossolalia.* Chicago: University of Chicago Press, 1972.

Goody, Jack. *Technology, Tradition, and the State in Africa.* London: Oxford University Press, 1971.

Gordon, Richard. "From Republic to Principate: Priesthood, Religion and Ideology." In Beard and North, pp. 179–98.

Granet, Marcel. *Chinese Civilization.* New York: Barnes and Noble, 1957.

Greenblatt, Stephen J. *Learning to Curse: Essays in Early Modern Culture.* New York, London: Routledge, 1990.

Gurevich, Aron. *Medieval Popular Culture: Problems of Belief and Perception.* Translated by János M. Bale and Paula A. Hollingsworth. Cambridge: Cambridge University Press, 1988.

Guttmann, Allen. *Sports Spectators.* New York: Columbia University Press, 1986.

Gutwirth, Madelyn. *The Twilight of the Goddesses: Women and Representation in the French Revolutionary Era.* New Brunswick, NJ: Rutgers University Press, 1992.

Hakima, Ahmad Mustafa Abu. *Kitab Lam' al-Shihab fi Sirat Muhammad ibn 'Abd al-Wahhab.* Beirut: Dar al-Thaqafa, 1967.

Hambly, W. D. *Tribal Dancing and Social Development.* London: H. F. and G. Witherby, 1926.

Hanawalt, Barbara A., and Kathryn L. Reyerson, eds. *City and Spectacle in Medieval Europe.* Minneapolis: University of Minneapolis Press, 1994.

Harris, John. *One Blood: 200 Years of Aboriginal Encounter with Christianity: A Story of Hope.* Claremont, CA: Albatross, 1990.

Harvey, Graham, ed. *Indigenous Religions: A Companion.* London and New York: Cassell, 2000.

Hastings, Adrian, ed. *A World History of Christianity.* Grand Rapids, MI: Eerdmans, 1999.

Heaton, John Wesley. *Mob Violence in the Late Roman Republic, 133–49 BC.* Illinois Studies in the Social Sciences, vol. 23, no. 4. Urbana: University of Illinois Press, 1939.

Hecker, J. F. C., M.D. *The Dancing Mania of the Middle Ages.* Translated by B. G. Babington, M.D. New York: Franklin, 1970.

Hibbert, Christopher. *The Days of the French Revolution.* New York: Morrow Quill Paperbacks, 1981.

Hill, Christopher. *Society and Puritanism in Pre-Revolutionary England.* New York: St. Martin's Press, 1997.

Hiney, Tom. *On the Missionary Trail.* New York: Atlantic Monthly Press, 2000.

Hobsbawm, Eric. *The Age of Revolution, 1789–1848.* Cleveland and New York: World, 1962.

———. "Mass Producing Traditions: Europe, 1870–1914." In *The Invention of Tradition,* ed. Eric Hobsbawm and Terence Ranger, pp. 263–307. Cambridge: Cambridge University Press, 1983.

Hoffman, Philip T. "The Church and the Rural Community in the 16th and 17th Centuries." *Proceedings of the Annual Meeting of the Western Society for French History* 6 (1978): 46–54.

Holm, Nils G. *Religious Ecstasy.* Stockholm: Almqvist and Wiksell, 1982.

Holt, Richard. *Sport and the British: A Modern History.* Oxford: Oxford University Press, 1990.

Horne, Alistair. *The Fall of Paris: The Seige and the Commune, 1870–71.* New York: St. Martin's Press, 1965.

Howarth, David. *Tahiti: A Paradise Lost.* New York: Viking Press, 1984.

Hsia, Po-Chia R. *Social Discipline in the Reformation: Central Europe, 1550–1750.* London and New York: Routledge, 1989.

Humphrey, Chris. *The Politics of Carnival: Festive Misrule in Medieval England.* Manchester: Manchester University Press, 2001.

Huntington, Samuel P. *The Clash of Civilizations and the Remaking of World Order.* New York: Simon and Schuster, 1996.

Hutton, Ronald. *The Rise and Fall of Merry England: The Ritual Year, 1400–1700.* Oxford: Oxford University Press, 1994.

Ingram, Martin. "Ridings, Rough Music and the 'Reform of Popular Culture' in Early Modern England." *Past and Present,* no. 105 (1984): 77–113.

Jackson, Stanley W. *Melancholia and Depression: From Hippocratic Times to Modern Times.* New Haven, CT: Yale University Press, 1986.

James, William. *The Varieties of Religious Experience.* New York: Macmillan, 1961.

Jameson, Michael. "The Asexuality of Dionysus." In Carpenter and Faraone, pp. 44–64.

Jamison, Kay Redfield. *Touched with Fire: Manic-Depressive Illness and the Artistic Temperament.* New York: Free Press, 1993.

Janzen, John M. *Ngoma: Discourses of Healing in Central and Southern Africa.* Berkeley: University of California Press, 1992.

Josephson, Eric, and Mary Josephson, eds. *Man Alone: Alienation in Modern Society.* New York: Dell, 1962.

Joyce, Lillian Bridges. "Maenads and Bacchantes: Images of Female Ecstasy in Greek and Roman Art." Ph.D. diss., University of California, Los Angeles, 1997.

Juneja, Renu. "The Trinidad Carnival: Ritual, Performance, Spectacle, and Symbol." *Journal of Popular Culture* 21, no. 1 (Spring 1988): 87–99.

Juvenal. *The Sixteen Satires.* Translated by Peter Green. London and New York: Penguin, 2004.

Katz, Richard. *Boiling Energy: Community Healing Among the Kalahari Kung.* Cambridge, MA: Harvard University Press, 1982.

Kerényi, Carl. *Dionysus: Archetypal Image of Indestructible Life.* Translated by Ralph Manheim. Princeton, NJ: Princeton University Press, 1976.

Kinsman, Robert S. "Folly, Melancholy, and Madness: A Study in Shifting Styles of Medical Analysis and Treatment, 1450–1675." In *The Darker Vision of the Renaissance*, ed. Robert S. Kinsman, pp. 273–320. Berkeley: University of California Press, 1974.

Kirby, Jon P. "Cultural Change and Religious Conversion in West Africa." In Blakely et al., pp. 57–71.

Klerman, Gerald L., and Myrna M. Weissman. "Increasing Rates of Depression." *JAMA* 261, no. 15 (1989): 2229–35.

Knox, Ronald A. *Enthusiasm: A Chapter in the History of Religion.* Notre Dame, IN: University of Notre Dame Press, 1950.

Kraemer, Ross S., ed. *Maenads, Martyrs, Matrons, Monastics.* Philadelphia: Fortress Press, 1988.

Kreiser, B. Robert. *Miracles, Convulsions, and Ecclesiastical Politics in Early Eighteenth-Century Paris.* Princeton, NJ: Princeton University Press, 1978.

Kremer, Hannes. "Neuwertung 'überlieferter' Brauchformen?" *Die neue Gemeinschaft* 3 (1937): 3005 a–c, translation at http://www.calvin.edu/ academic/cas/gpa/feier37.htm.

Kupperman, Karen Ordahl. *Settling with the Indians: The Meeting of English and Indian Cultures in America, 1580–1640.* Totowa, NJ: Rowman and Littlefield, 1980.

Kutcher, Louis. "The American Sports Event as Carnival: An Emergent Norm Approach to Crowd Behavior." *Journal of Popular Culture* 16, no. 4 (Spring 1983): 34–41.

Kyle, Donald G. *Spectacles of Death in Ancient Rome.* London: Routledge, 1998.

Ladurie, Emmanuel Le Roy. *Carnival in Romans.* Translated by Mary Feeney. New York: George Braziller, 1979.

———. *The French Peasantry, 1450–1660.* Translated by Alan Sheridan. Berkeley: University of California Press, 1987.

Laguerre, Michel S. *Voodoo and Politics in Haiti.* New York: St. Martin's Press, 1989.

Lanternari, Vittorio. *The Religions of the Oppressed: A Study of Modern Messianic Cults.* Translated by Lisa Sergio. London: MacGibbon and Kee, 1963.

Lawler, Lillian B. *The Dance in Ancient Greece.* Middletown, CT: Wesleyan University Press, 1964.

Le Bon, Gustave. *The Crowd: A Study of the Popular Mind.* Atlanta, GA: Cherokee, 1982.

Lefebvre, Henri. *Everyday Life in the Modern World.* Translated by Sacha Rabinovitch. New York: Harper Torchbooks, 1971.

Lehmann, Hartmut. "Ascetic Protestantism and Economic Rationalism: Max Weber Revisited After Two Generations." *Harvard Theological Review* 80, no. 3 (1987): 307–20.

Lever, Janet. *Soccer Madness: Brazil's Passion for the World's Most Popular Sport.* Prospect Heights, IL: Waveland Press, 1995.

Levine, Lawrence W. *Black Culture and Black Consciousness: Afro-American Folk Thought from Slavery to Freedom.* New York: Oxford University Press, 1977.

Lewis, I. M. *Ecstatic Religion: An Anthropological Study of Spirit Possession and Shamanism.* Harmondsworth, England: Penguin Books, 1971.

Lindholm, Charles. *Charisma.* London: Blackwell, 1990.

Lipsky, Richard. *How We Play the Game: Why Sports Dominate American Life.* Boston: Beacon, 1981.

Livy. *Rome and the Mediterranean*. Translated by Henry Bettenson. London: Penguin Books, 1976.

Lofland, John. "Crowd Joys." *Urban Life* 10, no. 4 (1982): 355–81.

Lonsdale, Steven. *Animals and the Origins of Dance*. New York: Thames and Hudson, 1981.

———. *Dance and Ritual Play in Greek Religion*. Baltimore: Johns Hopkins University Press, 1993.

Lovejoy, David S. *Religious Enthusiasm in the New World: Heresy to Revolution*. Cambridge, MA: Harvard University Press, 1985.

Lyons, Bridget Gellert. *Voices of Melancholy: Studies in Literary Treatments of Melancholy in Renaissance England*. London: Routledge, 1971.

MacAloon, John J., ed. *Rite, Drama, Festival, Spectacle: Rehearsals Toward a Theory of Cultural Performance*. Philadelphia: Institute for the Study of Human Issues, 1984.

MacDonald, A. J. *Trade Politics and Chistianity in Africa and the East*. New York: Negro Universities Press, 1969.

MacRobert, Iain. *The Black Roots and White Racism of Early Pentecostalism in the USA*. New York: St. Martin's Press, 1988.

Maffesoli, Michel. *The Shadow of Dionysus: A Contribution to the Sociology of the Orgy*. Translated by Cindy Linse and Mary Kristina Palmquist. Albany: SUNY Press, 1993.

Malcolmson, Robert W. *Popular Recreations in English Society, 1700–1850*. Cambridge: Cambridge University Press, 1973.

Malone, Jacqui. " 'Keep to the Rhythm and You'll Keep to Life': Meaning and Style in African American Vernacular Dance." In Caponi, pp. 222–38.

Martin, Linda, and Kerry Segrave. *Anti-Rock: The Opposition to Rock 'n' Roll*. New York: Da Capo Press, 1993.

Mazlish, Bruce. *The Revolutionary Ascetic: Evolution of a Political Type*. New York: Basic Books, 1976.

McKenzie, Peter. *The Christians: Their Beliefs and Practices*. Nashville: Abingdon Press, 1988.

McNally, Dennis. *A Long Strange Trip: The Inside History of the Grateful Dead*. New York: Broadway Books, 2002.

McNeill, William H. *Keeping Together in Time: Dance and Drill in Human History*. Cambridge, MA: Harvard University Press, 1995.

———. *The Pursuit of Power: Technology, Armed Force and Society Since A.D. 1000*. Chicago: University of Chicago Press, 1982.

Meeks, Wayne A. *The First Urban Christians: The Social World of the Apostle Paul*. New Haven, CT: Yale University Press, 1983.

Meltzoff, Andrew N., and Wolfgang Prinz, eds. *The Imitative Mind: Development, Evolution and Brain Bases.* Cambridge: Cambridge University Press, 2002.

Métraux, Alfred. *Haiti: Black Peasants and Their Religion.* Translated by Peter Lengyel. London: Harrap, 1960.

Michelet, Jules. *History of the French Revolution.* Translated by Charles Cocks. Chicago: University of Chicago Press, 1967.

Miller, James. *Flowers in the Dustbin: The Rise of Rock and Roll, 1947–1977.* New York: Simon and Schuster, 1999.

Mitzman, Arthur. *The Iron Cage: An Historical Interpretation of Max Weber.* New York: Knopf, 1970.

Momigliano, Arnaldo. *On Pagans, Jews, and Christians.* Hanover, NH: Wesleyan University Press, 1987.

Mooney, James. *The Ghost-Dance Religion and Wounded Knee.* Mineola, NY: Dover Reprints, 1973.

Moorehead, Alan. *The Fatal Impact: An Account of the Invasion of the South Pacific, 1767–1840.* New York: Harper and Row, 1966.

Morris, Desmond. *The Soccer Tribe.* London: Cape, 1981.

Mosse, George L. *Confronting the Nation: Jewish and Western Nationalism.* Hanover and London: Brandeis University Press, 1993.

———. *Masses and Man: Nationalist and Fascist Perceptions of Reality.* Detroit: Wayne State University Press, 1987.

Muchembled, Robert. *Popular Culture and Elite Culture in France, 1400–1750.* Translated by Lydia Cochrane. Baton Rouge and London: Louisiana State University Press, 1985.

Muir, Edward. *Ritual in Early Modern Europe.* Cambridge: Cambridge University Press, 1997.

Murphy, Joseph M. *Working the Spirit: Ceremonies of the African Diaspora.* Boston: Beacon Press, 1994.

Myerly, Scott Hughes. *British Military Spectacle: From the Napoleonic Wars Through the Crimea.* Cambridge, MA: Harvard University Press, 1996.

Nandy, Ashis. *The Intimate Self: Loss and Recovery of Self Under Colonialism.* Delhi: Oxford University Press, 1983.

Newberg, Andrew, Eugene D'Aquili, and Vince Rause. *Why God Won't Go Away: Brain Science and the Biology of Belief.* New York: Ballantine, 2001.

Newton, Peter M. "Samuel Johnson's Mental Breakdown and Recovery in Middle-Age: A Life Span Developmental Approach to Mental Illness and Its Cure." *International Review of Psycho-Analysis* 11, no. 1 (1984): 93–118.

Nietzsche, Friedrich. *The Birth of Tragedy and the Geneaology of Morals.* Translated by Francis Golffing. New York: Anchor Books, 1990.

Nijsten, Gerard. "The Duke and His Towns: The Power of Cermonies, Feasts, and Public Amusement in the Duchy of Guelders (East Netherlands) in the Fourteenth and Fifteenth Centuries." In Hanawalt and Reyerson, pp. 235–66.

Nye, Robert A. *The Origins of Crowd Psychology: Gustave LeBon and the Crisis of Mass Democracy in the Third Republic.* London: Sage, 1975.

Obbink, Dirk. "Dionysus Poured Out: Ancient and Modern Theories of Sacrifice and Cultural Formation." In Carpenter and Faraone, pp. 65–86.

Oesterley, W. O. E. *The Sacred Dance: A Study in Comparative Folklore.* Cambridge: Cambridge University Press, 1923.

Oesterreich, T. K. *Possession, Demoniacal and Other: Among Primitive Races, in Antiquity, the Middle Ages, and Modern Times.* Translated by D. Ibberson. New Hyde Park, NY: University Books, 1966.

Olmos, Margarite Fernández, and Lizabeth Paravisini-Gebert, eds. *Sacred Possessions: Vodou, Santeria, Obeah, and the Caribbean.* New Brunswick, NJ: Rutgers University Press, 1999.

Omari, Mikelle Smith. "Candomblé: A Socio-Political Examination of African Religion and Art in Brazil." In Blakely et al., pp. 135–59.

Oppenheim, Janet. *Shattered Nerves: Doctors, Patients, and Depression in Victorian England.* New York: Oxford University Press, 1991.

Orloff, Alexander. *Carnival: Myth and Cult.* Wörgl, Austria: Perlinger Verlag, 1981.

Otto, Walter F. *Dionysus: Myth and Cult.* Translated by Robert B. Palmer. Dallas, TX: Spring, 1981.

Ozouf, Mona. *Festivals and the French Revolution.* Translated by Alan Sheridan. Cambridge, MA: Harvard University Press, 1988.

Parker, Geoffrey. *The Military Revolution: Military Innovation and the Rise of the West, 1500–1800.* Cambridge: Cambridge University Press, 1989.

Parker, Noel. *Portrayals of Revolution: Images, Debates and Patterns of Thought on the French Revolution.* Carbondale: Southern Illinois University Press, 1990.

Patai, Raphael. *The Hebrew Goddess.* Detroit: Wayne State University Press, 1990.

Peukert, Detlev J. K. *Inside Nazi Germany: Conformity, Opposition, and Racism in Everyday Life.* Translated by Richard Deveson. New Haven, CT: Yale University Press, 1987.

Pierson, William D. "African-American Festive Style." In Caponi, pp. 417–34.

Plass, Paul. *The Game of Death in Ancient Rome: Arena Sport and Political Suicide.* Madison: University of Wisconsin Press, 1995.

Platvoet, Jan G. "Rattray's Request: Spirit Possession Among the Bono of West Africa." In Harvey, pp. 80–96.

Pope, Steven W. "Negotiating the 'Folk Highway' of the Nation: Sport, Public Culture and American Identity, 1870–1940." *Journal of Social History* (Winter 1993): 327–40.

Portefaix, Lillian. "Religio-ecological Aspects of Ancient Greek Religion from the Point of View of Woman: A Tentative Approach." *Temenos* 21 (1985): 144–51.

Porter, Roy. *Mind-Forg'd Manacles: A History of Madness in England from the Restoration to the Regency.* Cambridge, MA: Harvard University Press, 1987.

Pratt, Ray. *Rhythm and Resistance: Explorations of the Political Uses of Popular Music.* New York: Praeger, 1990.

Price, Robert M. "Christianity, Diaspora Judaism, and Roman Crisis." *Review of Rabbinic Judaism* 5, no. 3 (2000): 316–31.

Putnam, Robert D. *Bowling Alone: The Collapse and Revival of American Community.* New York: Simon and Schuster, 2000.

Raboteau, Albert J. *Slave Religion: The "Invisible Insitution" in the Antebellum South.* New York: Oxford University Press, 1978.

Rader, Benjamin G. *American Sports: From the Age of Folk Games to the Age of Televised Sports.* 2nd ed. Englewood Cliffs, NJ: Prentice Hall, 1990.

Rogers, Cornwell B. *The Spirit of Revolution.* New York: Greenwood Press, 1949.

Rogers, Nicholas. *Halloween: From Pagan Ritual to Party Night.* New York: Oxford University Press, 2002.

Roper, Lyndal. *Oedipus and the Devil: Witchcraft, Sexuality and Religion in Early Modern Europe.* London and New York: Routledge, 1994.

Ross, Robert, ed. *Racism and Colonialism.* Leiden: Nifhoff, 1982.

Roth, Marty. *Drunk the Night Before: An Anatomy of Intoxication.* Minneapolis: University of Minnesota Press, 2005.

Rouget, Gilbert. *Music and Trance: A Theory of the Relations Between Music and Possession.* Translated by Brunhilde Biebuyck. Chicago: University of Chicago Press, 1985.

Rubin, Julius H. *Religious Melancholy and Protestant Experience in America.* New York: Oxford University Press, 1994.

Rubin, Miri. *Corpus Christi: The Eucharist in Late Medieval Culture*. Cambridge: Cambridge University Press, 1991.

Rudé, George. *The Crowd in the French Revolution*. Oxford: Oxford University Press, 1959.

Ruiz, Teofilo F. "Elite and Popular Culture in Late Fifteenth-Century Castilian Festivals." In Hanawalt and Reyerson, pp. 296–318.

Sachs, Curt. *The World of the Dance*. New York: Norton, 1937.

Samarin, William J. *Tongues of Men and Angels*. New York: Macmillan, 1972.

Sánchez, Magdalena S. *The Empress, the Queen, and the Nun: Woman and Power at the Court of Philip III of Spain*. Baltimore: Johns Hopkins University Press, 1998.

Sass, Louis A. *Madness and Modernism: Sanity in the Light of Modern Art, Literature, and Thought*. New York: Basic Books, 1992.

Sawyer, Deborah F. *Women and Religion in the First Christian Centuries*. London and New York: Routledge, 1996.

Schnapp, Jeffrey T. *Staging Fascism: 18BL and the Theater of the Masses for the Masses*. Stanford: Stanford University Press, 1996.

Scott, James C. *Domination and the Arts of Resistance: Hidden Transcripts*. New Haven, CT: Yale University Press, 1990.

Scribner, Bob. "Reformation, Carnival and the World Turned Upside Down." *Social History* 3, no. 3 (1978): 303–29.

Sennett, Richard. *The Fall of Public Man*. New York: Norton, 1992.

Shirer, William L. *Berlin Diary: The Journal of a Foreign Correspondent, 1934–1941*. New York: Knopf, 1941.

Simpson, George Eaton. *Black Religions in the New World*. New York: Columbia University Press, 1978.

Small, Christopher. "Africans, Europeans and the Making of Music." In Caponi, pp. 110–34.

Smith, A. W. "Some Folklore Elements in Movements of Social Protest." *Folklore* 77 (1967): 241–52.

Smith, Morton. *Jesus the Magician: Charlatan or Son of God?* Berkeley, CA: Seastone, 1998.

———. *Studies in the Cult of Yahweh*. Vol. 1, *Studies in Historical Method, Ancient Israel, Ancient Judaism*. Edited by Shaye Cohen, J.D. Leiden: Brill, 1996.

Solomon, Andrew. *The Noonday Demon: An Atlas of Depression*. New York: Touchstone Books, 2002.

Spencer, Elizabeth Glovka. "Policing Popular Amusements in German

Cities: The Case of Prussia's Rhine Province, 1815–1914." *Journal of Urban History* 16, no. 4 (1990): 366–85.

Stallybrass, Peter, and Allon White. *The Politics and Poetics of Transgression.* Ithaca, NY: Cornell University Press, 1986.

Stoler, Ann Laura. *Race and the Education of Desire: Foucault's History of Sexuality and the Colonial Order of Things.* Durham, NC: Duke University Press, 1995.

Street, Brian V. *The Savage in Literature: Representations of "Primitive" Society in English Fiction, 1858–1920.* London and Boston: Routledge, 1975.

Styron, William. *Darkness Visible: A Memoir of Madness.* New York: Vintage Books, 1990.

Suryani, Luh Ketut, and Gordon D. Jensen. *Trance and Possession in Bali: A Window on Western Multiple Personality Possession Disorder and Suicide.* Kuala Lumpur: Oxford University Press, 1993.

Taiwo, Olu. "Music, Art and Movement Among the Yoruba." In *Indigenous Religions: A Companion,* ed. Graham Harvey, pp. 173–89. London and New York: Cassell, 2000.

Thompson, E. P. *Customs in Common: Studies in Traditional Popular Culture.* New York: New Press, 1993.

———. "Patrician Society, Plebeian Culture." *Journal of Social History* 7, no. 4 (1974): 382–405.

Thorsley, Peter. "The Wild Man's Revenge." In *The Wild Man Within: An Image in Western Thought from the Renaissance to Romanticism,* ed. Edward Dudley and Maximillian E. Novak, pp. 281–308. Pittsburgh: University of Pittsburgh Press, 1972.

Toland, John. *Adolf Hitler.* New York: Anchor Books, 1992.

Trilling, Lionel. *Sincerity and Authenticity.* Cambridge, MA: Harvard University Press, 1973.

Tripp, David. "The Image of the Body in the Protestant Reformation." In *Religion and the Body,* ed. Sarah Coakley, pp. 131–51. Cambridge: Cambridge University Press, 1997.

Trossbach, Werner. " 'Klee-Skrupel': Melancholie und Ökonomie in der Deutschen Spätaufklärung." *Aufklärung* 8, no. 1 (1994): 91–120.

Tuan, Yi-Fu. *Segmented Worlds and Self: Group Life and Individual Consciousness.* Minneapolis: University of Minnesota Press, 1982.

Turner, Ralph H., and Lewis M. Killian. *Collective Behavior.* 4th ed. Englewood Cliffs, NJ: Prentice Hall, 1993.

Turner, Victor. "*Carnaval* in Rio: Dionysian Drama in an Industrializing

Society." In *The Celebration of Society: Perspectives on Contemporary Cultural Performance*, ed. Frank Manning, pp. 103–24. Bowling Green, OH: Bowling Green University Popular Press, 1983.

———, ed. *Celebration: Studies in Festivities and Ritual*. Washington, DC: Smithsonian Institution Press, 1982.

———. *The Ritual Process: Structure and Anti-Structure*. Ithaca, NY: Cornell University Press, 1966.

Twycross, Meg, ed. *Festive Drama: Papers from the Sixth Triennial Colloquium of the International Society for the Study of Medieval Theatre, Lancaster, 13–19 July, 1989*. Brewer, 1996.

Underdown, David. *Rebel, Riot, and Rebellion: Popular Politics and Culture in England, 1603–1660*. Oxford: Clarendon Press, 1985.

Van de Velde, T. H. *Ideal Marriage: Its Physiology and Technique*. New York: Random House, 1961.

Vasil'ev, Aleksei Mikhailovich. *The History of Saudi Arabia*. London: Saqi Books, 1998.

Vellacott, Philip. Introduction to *The Bacchae and Other Plays*, by Euripides, translated by Philip Vellacott. London and New York: Penguin Books, 1954.

Vincent, Ted. *The Rise and Fall of American Sport: Mudville's Revenge*. Lincoln: University of Nebraska Press, 1981.

Voeks, Robert A. *Sacred Leaves of Candomblé: African Magic, Medicine, and Religion in Brazil*. Austin: University of Texas Press, 1997.

Wagner, Ann. *Adversaries of Dance: From the Puritans to the Present*. Urbana and Chicago: University of Illinois Press, 1997.

Walker, Williston. *A History of the Christian Church*. New York: Scribner's, 1959.

Walzer, Michael. *The Revolution of the Saints: A Study in the Origins of Radical Politics*. Cambridge, MA: Harvard University Press, 1965.

Wann, Daniel L., Merrill J. Melnick, Gordon W. Russell, and Dale G. Pease. *Sport Fans: The Psychology and Social Impact of Spectators*. New York and London: Routledge, 2001.

Ward, Kevin. "Africa." In *A World History of Christianity*, ed. Adrian Hastings, pp. 192–233. Grand Rapids, MI: Eerdmans, 1999.

Weber, Max. *The Protestant Ethic and the Spirit of Capitalism*. London and New York: Routledge, 1992.

———. *The Religion of China: Confucianism and Taoism*. Translated by Hans H. Gerth. New York: Free Press, 1951.

———. *The Sociology of Religion*. Boston: Beacon Press, 1991.

Weidkuhn, Peter. "Carnival in Basle: Playing History in Reverse." *Cultures* 3, no. 1 (1976): 29–53.

Weinstein, Fred, and Gerald M. Platt. *The Wish to Be Free: Society, Psyche and Value Change*. Berkeley: University of California Press, 1969.

Wiggins, David K., ed. *Sport in America: From Wicked Amusement to National Obsession*. Champaign, IL: Human Kinetics, 1995.

Wilken, Robert L. *The Christians as the Romans Saw Them*. New Haven: Yale University Press, 1984.

Williams, Roger L. *The French Revolution of 1870–1871*. New York: Norton, 1969.

Wilmore, Gayraud S. *Black Religion and Black Radicalism*. Garden City, NY: Doubleday, 1972.

Wilson, Bryan R. *The Noble Savages: The Primitive Origins of Charisma and Its Contemporary Survival*. Berkeley: University of California Press, 1975.

Wolpert, Lewis. *Malignant Sadness: The Anatomy of Depression*. New York: Free Press, 1999.

Wulff, David M. *Psychology of Religion*. New York: Wiley, 1991.

Zolberg, Aristide R. "Moments of Madness." *Politics and Society* 2, no. 2 (1972): 183–208.

ACKNOWLEDGMENTS

I can't possibly thank all the people who helped with this book, for the simple reason that a hurricane destroyed my original list of people to acknowledge, along with many precious books and files. So, with apologies to anyone omitted, I thank Matthew Bartowiak, Lalitha Chandrasekher, Alison Pugh, Hank Sims, and Mitchell Verter for their enthusiastic research assistance. Heather Blurton and Lauriallen Reitzammer also made valuable contributions.

A number of scholars and journalists graciously responded to my diverse and urgent questions, including Peter Brown, Peter Brooks, Reginald Butler, Michael Cook, E. J. Gorn, Allen Guttman, Edward Hagen, Arlie Hochschild, Riva Hocherman, Ann Killian, Marcel Kinsbourne, Simon Kuper, Peter Manuel, Jack Santino, James Scott, Laura Slatkin, Ellen Schattschneider, Wolfgang Schivelbusch, Katherine Stern, Ann Stolar, Michael Taussig, and Daniel Wann. I am especially indebted to Elizabeth Thompson for background on Arabian history and her translations from the Arabic.

Among the people who were kind enough to comment on drafts of chapters are Diane Alexander, Darren Cushman Wood, Ben Ehrenreich, Edward Hagen, and William H. McNeill. The latter's book *Keeping Together in Time* had helped convince me that the subject was worth pursuing in the first place.

Janet McIntosh's role in this project is impossible to categorize or express sufficient gratitude for. She began, while still a graduate student, as my research assistant, though *teacher* would be a better word, since her job was to send me stacks of readings that we would then discuss. There is very little in this book that she did not have something to say about, and I hope some of her brilliance and knowledge shines through.

At Metropolitan Books, my longtime editor Sara Bershtel brought her usual vast erudition and razor-sharp logic to the task. I am also grateful to my copy editor, Vicki Haire, whose diligent fact-checking has no doubt saved me from much embarrassment. Finally, I thank all the people in the printing industry who are responsible for turning a manuscript into an actual book.

INDEX

ABOUT THE AUTHOR

BARBARA EHRENREICH is the author of fourteen books, including the *New York Times* bestsellers *Nickel and Dimed* and *Bait and Switch*. A frequent contributor to *Harper's* and *The Progressive*, she has been a columnist at the *New York Times* and *Time* magazine.

She can be reached at www.barbaraehrenreich.com.